MW00961796

On Significant Components
of Spiritual Care

On Significant Components of Spiritual Care

Luis Elier Rodriguez, DMin, BCC, ACPE Educator, et al.

Edited by Tom Lehman

Houston Methodist
Spiritual Care and Values Integration

Cover photo by Cindy Lever.
Cover design by Dulce Lilian Gonzalez.

DEDICATION

To all *Anam Cara* (soul friends),
Helpful and insightful chaplains,
Spiritual mentors in life,
and
Personal sojourners in the time of spiritual care.

i

ACKNOWLEDGMENTS

I HAVE BEEN FORTUNATE to meet and relate in the field of spiritual care with the writers of this book. I would like to express my appreciation to each of the writers for understanding the value of this project and taking the time to participate in writing this book.

I would like to thank Dr. Charles Millikan, Vice President for Spiritual Care and Values Integration at Houston Methodist, for his support of this project, including by a grant application to the Houston Methodist Foundation that made the publication of this book possible.

I appreciate the role Tom Lehman played as the manuscript editor and editorial consultant and our mentor regarding editing and book art. Dulce Lilian Gonzalez designed the book cover. Robert Goodson was kind enough to review my chapters and provide valuable feedback. I would like to acknowledge Timothy Madison, Regina Allen, Trevor Burt, Robert Kidd, and Dian Kidd for their contribution to the final review of the book. I also acknowledge and appreciate the good work of Krissia Tellez and Anita Zapata, who assisted with the formatting and administrative aspects of this book.

Finally, I express gratitude to the Divine for helping us find the transcendent as we practice spiritual care.

Dr. Luis Elier Rodriguez

CONTENTS

iv

INTRODUCTION

T HIS IS A VERY PERSONAL BOOK because it contains parts of the pilgrimages of the writers in the field of spiritual care. This book addresses a variety of topics in ways that can offer suggestions for teaching. It identifies key issues and contains significant ideas to remember and integrate into one's practice of spiritual care. These can be used in classes on spiritual care, in PowerPoint presentations, for spiritual leadership formation, and as lessons for communities and personal learning.

This book is for spiritual clinical educators, spiritual leaders, Clinical Pastoral Education students, certified chaplains, students who are at the beginning of their careers of helping others, spiritual counselors, people with careers related to spiritual care and human services, and people in related professions. This book can be used as part of a spiritual caregiver's training curriculum, in spiritual retreats, seminary coursework, theological schools, and in Clinical Pastoral Education centers. Each chapter of this book is an opportunity to learn more about the topic at hand and to follow up on learning with new creative ideas and the integration of new paradigms.

In this book we have two chapters (1-2) that help us explore ourselves with the emphasis on reflecting upon our

1

pains, needs, and biases. These chapters are also related to self-understanding and the implications for our spiritual care practice. Spiritual caregivers are challenged to examine their motivations for considering a career in chaplaincy or one of the helping professions. Chapter 3 challenges us to reflect on the importance of reframing a future story. It's about providing guidance for the patient to reconstruct a future story during disrupted circumstances and events. Chapter 4 is about listening skills as a pivotal instrument of our spiritual care practice. It's the art of trying to imagine putting ourselves in our patients' shoes and to provide empathy and compassion.

Chapter 5 is a brief dancing journey through different spiritual care assessment models, reflecting on how we can use them in our provision of spiritual care. We also encourage spiritual caregivers to establish their own spiritual care assessments according to their patient's needs.

Chapter 6 on developing effective leadership, attempts to challenge new generations of chaplains by providing practical highlights to integrate into our leadership. In chapter 7, we see a reflection of and a model for facing institutional crises in a system. This model was effectively used in our Houston Methodist CPE program when we encountered accreditation challenges in 2013-14. In chapter 8 we have a very interesting topic of living in between. As Facundo Cabral, a singer from Argentina, states, "I am not from here, I am not from there." It is the tension that we have in our daily life: dealing with and being in two dimensions. Chapter 9 relates to cultural competence and prayer as a symbol of diversity and inclusivity. Chapter 10 addresses developing cultural competence through immersion.

Chapters 11 is related to the trauma of spiritual abuse and the implication of harm to the soul. This theme is very pertinent for spiritual caregivers. The chapter highlights ways this topic affects patients and identifies strategies to deal with this painfully traumatic dynamic.

Another topic of this book is the LGBTQ+ community, how to provide good spiritual care and how to learn more from this population that is increasingly more present in our society and professional life (chapter 12). In the next chapter we have a reflection of how human trafficking involves the use of force, fraud, or coercion to obtain some type of labor or commercial benefits (chapter 13). This topic is very pertinent because traffickers use force, fraud, or coercion to lure their victims and force them into labor or commercial sexual exploitation. As caregivers we need to recognize the signs of human trafficking in our patient population.

In the chapter on pastoral care to people dealing with chronic diseases we have a reflection regarding two groups of patients, those dealing with end-stage renal disease, or with brain injuries and severe brain damage (chapter 14). The chapter on the duality of professional obligations is an important challenge for our CPE students and chaplains in the hospital setting (chapter 15). The ethical aspect is a very important element in any healthcare system, hospital, or anywhere spiritual care is provided.

Chapter 16 is written by an attorney who is a minister in the United Methodist Church, on integrating the legal aspects of our spiritual care. The last chapter (17) is about COVID-19 and the implications of the pandemic for spiritual care. The baseline of this chapter is that humanity has been dealing with this pandemic like a global and spiritual crisis, which offers an opportunity for reflection on a new normal and an opportunity for new action.

I hope that this book will be a good friend to the readers and will help us in our lives and our spiritual care practice.

Dr. Luis Elier Rodriguez

REFLECTION AND PRACTICE
OF SPIRITUAL CARE

1

THE PAINS OF LIFE AND OUR ATTRACTION TO THE HELPING WORK WE DECIDED TO PERFORM

Luis Elier Rodriguez
Manager, System Clinical Pastoral Education,
Houston Methodist

WHEN I WAS 15 YEARS OLD, I attended a drive-in movie with several of my friends. We usually went on Wednesdays and met up with our girlfriends and other friends. That night, we had a great time telling jokes and discussing the two movies we had seen. When I left the cinema, I was with my best friends, Carlos Torres and Lee Tormes. We got out of the car outside the cinema and waited for other friends to come and join us. After a little chat, we got into our Volkswagen again. As an act of friendship, I let Lee sit in the front seat because I thought it might make him seem more important to a girl to whom he was attracted. I thought seeing him in the front seat would be a good show of status. I sat in the back seat with that understanding.

Then, while passing another car, we were challenged to a car race. Carlos was a good driver so we began to race the other car. The next thing we knew, our car had crashed into a light pole. I was totally disoriented. As I came back to myself inside the car, my life flashed before my mind's eye with great detail as though I was watching a movie. Someone took me out of the car, and I realized Carlos and Lee were dead. I knelt down and began to pray, even though at the time I did not know I was praying. Since then I have felt the very deep pain of guilt, and it has accompanied me throughout my life journey.

I believe that our pains are related to the work we do, especially if we decided to go into a helping profession. In my case, the pain of losing my two best friends and feeling the accompanying guilt resulted in my choice to become an Association for Clinical Pastoral Education (ACPE) educator, trying to help others in their losses, struggles, feelings, and related dilemmas. This experience of deep pain resulted in my desire to help others, although perhaps I am also helping myself to carry my own suffering. When I help another person, it is a way to alleviate my own sorrow and atone for my own guilt. In other words, it is no coincidence that I opted to become a Clinical Pastoral Educator and to serve as a chaplain and spiritual health caregiver.

Sometimes my life experience and suffering are directly related to my daily work as a chaplain and educator. Many spiritual caregivers become altruistic out of personal knowledge of what pain is or from an experience of very significant loss that is accompanied by deep feelings. When one's intentions and motivations are to help others, it is sometimes a way to combat one's own pain. It is also a creative process arising from our empathy towards others. It is a process whereby I de-emphasize myself to try to understand another person's world through the lens of my own pain. Our own pain can help us discover what our own needs are. It is healthy to discover the spiritual and emotional world of others and of our own as well.

In this chapter I will focus on an exploration of our relationship to pain and our own needs. I recognize that this is only one approach to the subject because neuroscience tries to understand these personal dynamics physiologically, but in this case I will focus on the pains we carry and our emotional needs.

As a Clinical Pastoral Educator I have had to ask myself the following questions, which I sometimes share with my CPE students. I encourage them, if they can, to recreate a painful event, visualizing the scene, characters, feelings, thoughts, and thereby learning a lesson.

1. If you can, recreate one of your greatest sufferings in life and reflect on the impact it has had on your ministerial choices.
2. How does that event impact your emotional and affective world?
3. How does that event impact your spirituality?
4. How does that event impact your desire to help others?
5. How does that event lead you to be more sensitive or empathetic?
6. How is that event directly or indirectly related to your ministerial calling or spiritual journey?
7. Is there still something you need to examine relating to the effect or impact of that event?
8. How does your call confront this matter?
9. How do you interpret the relationship of that pain and call to your spiritual care work?

I am aware that, as an educator, I must provide a safe environment for my students to carry out a reflection of this nature, so they can better understand how our pains are related to our choices. These reflections do not only have to be about pains. They can also be about moments of celebration or a high point in our life. But in this case, I will only talk about how a "nadir experience" or the worst moment in our life impacts our calling.[1] In my case the pain of loss resulted in my desire to make something positive out of that death, even though such a thing is impossible. These experiences can become motivations for caregivers and those motivations are reflected in our lives. I will identify some of them, using Corey and Corey to demonstrate the importance of paying attention to our needs and feelings, to understand each of them, and to challenge ourselves to find creative ways to deal with our needs.[2] I also added others (6-14) I considered especially significant:

1. *The need to make an impact*: You want to have a significant influence on the lives of those you serve. You need to know that you are making a positive difference in someone's daily life and existence. Although you recognize that you will not be able to change everyone, you derive satisfaction from empowering individuals. The challenge is when patients are not interested in changing or do not want your help. This may upset or frustrate you. The danger is when you are attempting to help dependent people, because they are going to try to find meaning in their life through your life.

2. *The need to return a favor*: You desire to emulate someone who was special in your life, like a teacher, pastor, deacon, priest, grandmother, uncle, father, or mother. In my case it was the need to pay Lee back because of his death and my feelings of guilt.

3. *The need to care for others*: Maybe you have been a caregiver for a long time. Were you the one in your family who attended to the problems and concerns of other family members? Do your friends find it easy to talk to you? Something like 25 percent of the people who want to care for others have been a "rescuer" in alcoholic

families. They need to care for others because they needed to stabilize their family. The challenge is to learn to ask for help, because you can easily become burnt out both personally and professionally.

4. *The need for self-help*: You have had some problems and issues and sometimes you see your patients' problems in yourself. Maybe you have some unfinished business, and you feel an attraction or attachment to people who are dealing with that same situation. For example, a female who works with women who are victims of partner abuse may try to work out her own unfinished business and conflicts by giving advice, and pushing these women to make decisions they are not yet ready to make. Because she has unfinished business, she may show hostility toward a controlling husband.

5. *The need to be needed*: Many of us entered the profession because we like to be needed and to have people depend on us.[3] The majority of caregivers have the need to be needed. They need appreciation for the hope they have given. It is good to be needed, but you need to be careful to not promote dependency. Many patients are not going to express appreciation for your ministry. You must deal with your own disappointment when you don't receive appreciation for your efforts.

6. *The need for power*: Some patients will put you on a pedestal, and you may like that position too much. Be careful with that dynamic because we can over-direct patients instead of helping them explore their own spiritual resources. In addition, we can make them dependent on us instead of promoting their autonomy. The temptation is to try to manipulate our patients to meet our own needs. The need to give is also a need to

feel powerful and to be on a pedestal when giving. It is true that it can be an altruistic expression, but it can also be an expression of feeling that others depend on you.

7. *The need to provide answers*: You have the need to provide advice and to provide "right answers." Caregivers with that need feel uncomfortable if they have friends or patients who come to them with a problem and they are not able to give them concrete advice. Maybe others need to be listened to and cared for, rather than to be told what they should do. The challenge is to resist the tendency to coach or provide advice through your answers. In spiritual care it is healthy to accept our limitations and accept that sometimes we don't have the answers. For example: Why do people suffer? We don't have answers to that question. Sometimes it is better to allow moments of uncomfortable silence than to fill the air with superficial answers. I think it is particularly important to listen, rather than to answer, as a meaningful expression of our humanity. We can also confront our patients with the opportunity to find their own answers to help in their own spiritual growth.

8. *The need to control*: Related to the need to provide others with advice and answers is the need to control others. Sometimes we need to know what others are thinking, feeling, and doing. When people are angry, upset, sad, or irritated, do you sometimes tell them that they should not feel that way, and do your best to change their state of mind? Do you at times have a strong need to change the way people who are close to you behave, even if what they are doing does not directly affect you?

9. *The need to take away a patient's pain*: This is when the other person's pain fills us with inner pain or makes us

feel uncomfortable, helpless, or inadequate. This is related to taking a shortcut in spiritual care and trying to take away the pain of the other. Instead of observing it and returning it, we try to remove it from the path of spiritual conversation.

10. *The need to be perfect*: This is when we try to hide our vulnerability, but the problem is that others will find out. The best option to deal with this need is to see our imperfections as opportunities for growth and for improving our interpersonal skills for ministry.[4] This need may reflect our need to get things right and that is good. At the same time it can also reflect our insecurities and our often unreachable or unrealistically high expectations of ourselves. This need may also reflect a resistance to accepting our own vulnerability to our shadows and dark places. The challenge is to offer your greatest gift—yourself, with your strengths and limitations.

11. *The need to be relevant*: Some in their childhood and adolescence were ignored and placed in the background. This can create a high sense of insecurity and feeling sidelined. That's why you can see some adults trying to preach instead of listening or trying to impress with their messages or intelligence, attempting to be relevant. This can be translated into caregivers who are quick to offer advice on what patients should do, how to do it, and why to do it, instead of promoting the patient's responsibility for their own spiritual growth. Therefore it is necessary that periodically the caregiver reflect on what their needs are, and on what it means to be a good caregiver.

12. *The need to be super spiritual*: This need is related to the need to be accepted and not rejected. A supposed high spirituality can guarantee acceptance and a certain status of superiority, or the person may be looking for a pedestal. The problem with this need is that it can be accompanied by a feeling of superiority to others by creating a hierarchy of spirituality.

13. *The need for intimacy*: This need has to do with an experienced existential loneliness where there is a lack of intimacy. This need is quite common in married persons or in families where people do not feel valued or accepted by their spouse or in the context of their family. The following thoughts may be related to this aspect: "Divorce is okay. Ending a relationship is fine. Starting from scratch is fine. Moving on is fine. Say no, it's okay. Being alone is fine. What's not right is staying in a place where you're not happy or feeling valued." When this need is present in caregivers, they may fulfill this need by being around patients who provide conversational intimacy. It's very easy to use our patients to receive emotional support and company in our existential loneliness. I suspect our awareness of this need is an ongoing process because loneliness never truly goes away throughout our human existence.

14. *The need for healing from a damaging faith community*: Spirituality and religiosity can be very therapeutic and positive, but at the same time they can be very dysfunctional and hurtful. This is present, for example, in the rejection of the LGBTQ+ community or in the rejection of someone's leadership by following policies focused on power differential, personalities, gender, ability, race, or ideological issues. Sometimes rigid

14

structures can create a sense that healthy elements are missing or that an authoritarian leadership style is being imposed on the group. The better choice is to participate in communities with healthy elements like open dialogue and different levels of participation—communities that develop public and private spaces and focus on values, with elements that combine familiarity and excitement and create a rhythm for the community.[5] I recognize that this is an issue that must be explored and studied more rigorously, especially as more people identify as being more spiritual than religious.

Focusing on the needs mentioned above can help us be more aware of our needs and reduce their negative impact on our spiritual care. It is also helpful to reflect on whether we are providing care for our patients or for ourselves. I think our old baggage has a significant influence on our provision of spiritual care. Throughout our life our needs will impact the way we provide spiritual care and our style of helping. The important thing is to be aware of these needs and to be creative in keeping them from negatively impacting our ministry.[6] The concept of bracketing challenges us as caregivers to manage our personal values and needs so that they do not contaminate our spiritual care. I recognize that most spiritual conflicts are not open to conscious control because they have been repressed and remain in the realm of the unconscious.[7] One question to ask after each visit is whether I took care of the patient, or was I just taking care of myself by fulfilling my needs. I also think we can use this needs list in our peer review or in our intentional consultation as a tool to identify our progress or awareness in working with them. This can be a process of moving through different stages of awareness:

1. *Unconsciousness and defensiveness of being*: In this stage, we do not realize our needs and they guide us in our pastoral interventions. This can be very dangerous as it can lead to an overflowing pseudo-empathy. If we are not aware of our needs, they will express themselves and will almost always work to benefit the caregiver, not the patient. I typically ask my students why they want to be chaplains, educators, or pastors. At first, they typically express altruistic attributes, but superficially, without going into expressing the needs that come from their pain and their shadow side. In this stage, there is high defensiveness and a feeling of self-sufficiency and "standing on your own two feet." This means you are your own person. At this stage, there is a high tendency to disconnect from self and others.[8] The tendency is to resist any focus on oneself and being unwilling to explore motivations, feelings, passions, or a sense of meaning. The problem here is the inability to see what we are doing in our ministry and the possible damage that might result.

2. *Some awareness and reflection, but at an unexamined level*: Here there is a breakthrough in consciousness, but it is not very deep. At this stage, we express and identify needs, but remain unwilling to discuss or reflect on them. It is like not accepting our own breath. It is like seeing our needs in a ballroom but not allowing ourselves to dance with them as a part of our lives. At this stage we can talk about others' needs, but we are not aware of or willing to talk about our own needs. This is difficult for people who are perfectionists or who possess a feeling of invulnerability. It is also difficult at times for people who have been injured to be able to accept and talk

about their wounds, because they are not sure if they can represent their pain and suffering to others. I believe our first goal is to help facilitate a ventilation of feelings, especially feelings of anger, sadness, and inadequacy. By refusing to address our own needs, we spiritual caregivers can become isolated, rather than taking responsibility to reflect on and deal with our needs in a creative way. We can transfer our needs to our patients, which can be detrimental to patient care.

3. *Accepting our needs and transforming them into a creative way to provide spiritual care*: This is the stage where dialogue opens and we present our needs, even to our peers. Consulting with others can be very productive. Therefore, I recommend having regular consultations with therapists or peers where we can ask if they are aware of some of our needs. I recommend periodically creating verbatim transcripts of spiritual care encounters and discussing how our lives are reflected in our spiritual interventions. This requires a strong desire to continue learning and flexibility in the face of discouragement.

   At this stage, dialogue and feedback are received as something to be welcomed, and one tries to integrate new paradigms and practices into spiritual interventions. The more we accept the needs in our life, the more effective and conscious we can be, but this also works in reverse, because the more unaware we are of our needs, the further away we will be from being effective spiritual care practitioners. It is a parallel maturity process, that is, the extent to which we are connected to ourselves is the same extent to which we are connected to others. Being unaware of our needs can make us aggressive, selfish, and even disconnected from others. This can even have an impact on sexual assaults. This is another topic that needs to be addressed with more time and attention.

Each of these stages can be interwoven and it is not easy to differentiate between them. Constant consultation can help us identify unexplored areas of our needs, any unawareness can result in providing poor spiritual care. After reflecting on our pains and needs it is good to ask ourselves: What do I need to eliminate or be careful in using as part of my spiritual care? What do I want to keep the same? What needs improvement? What should I incorporate into my spiritual care?

I believe we can set out some guidelines to help us deal with our needs and become aware of our needs or uncomfortable feelings. These can be useful in our spiritual care interventions:

1. Determine how your life story is present in your spiritual care interventions.
2. Determine whether the spiritual issue in question makes you connect with your own spiritual pilgrimage and any pain, grief, crisis, or unfinished business in your life.
3. Be aware if the patient doesn't want to talk to you or presents feelings of rejection toward you.
4. Accept your own limitations in providing spiritual care. Don't try to look for miracles where there's no chance of achieving miracles or healing.[9]
5. Provide your patient with a safe environment to explore their own spiritual resources and choose the right ones to be activated.

6. Accept that your patient may have a different spiritual perception than your own, including traditions and faith practices. This contextual consideration will be important in your approach to spiritual care, by giving your patient the opportunity to make the final decision on any conflict, crisis, grief, loss, or learning opportunity.

7. Become a facilitator of creative ideas to face any situation of spiritual distress, suffering, pain, or celebration in your patient's life, but remember that the spotlight is on the patient, not on you. As Gill Austern said about the midwife image in spiritual care, "You don't deliver the baby, you simply catch it."[10]

8. Provide open-ended questions, without predetermined answers.[11] Our challenge is to help our patients create their own spiritual meaning and purpose in life.

9. If you perceive an energy of discomfort, ask yourself, "Where is that energy coming from?"

10. It is healthy to ask what the patient means to you: mother, aunt, relative, friend, or any character that comes to your mind and relates to your patient. Try to check yourself for feelings of comfort or discomfort.

11. Double-check to see whether you are ignoring any comments, ideas, focus, conditions, or feelings for your patients or family members that may be invisible for you. This is related with selective attention, inattentional blindness, or biases.[12]

12. Educate yourself about your patient's background because all too often biases, prejudices, blind spots, and overreactions occur because of ignorance about cultural context.

13. Give your patient the space to receive information, process it, and create a spiritual outcome. Don't try to force it on your patient but be flexible and respect your patient's story. Don't mix your haste with your patient's reality.

In conclusion, our pains can impact those of us in the helping professions. Our pain can influence our style of helping. That is why it is important to ask our reason for being spiritual caregivers. It is also important to examine our needs and check to see if they are present in our provision of spiritual care and to analyze our degree of awareness of them. In this way, we can create principles that can help us be more effective in our spiritual care.

---

1 Dan P. McAdams, *The Stories We Lived: Personal Myths and the Making of the Self* (New York: The Guilford Press, 1993), 258-259.

2 Marianne Schneider and Gerald Corey, *Becoming a Helper*, 6th ed. (Pacific Grove: Brook/Cole, 2007), 4-8.

3 Jeffrey A. Kottler, *On Being a Therapist*, 5th ed. (Oxford University Press, 2017), 132.

4 Edward P. Wimberly, *Recalling Our Own Stories: Spiritual Renewal for Religious Caregivers* (Jossey Boss, 1997), 8-11.

5 Etienne Wenger, Richard A. McDermott, and William Snyder, *Cultivating Communities of Practice* (Boston: Harvard Business School Press, 2002), 49-64.

6 Judith V. Jordan, *The Complexity of Connection* (New York: Guilford Press, 2004), 56-59.

7 Gerald Corey, *Theory and Practice of Counseling and Psychotherapy*, 10th ed. (Boston: Cengage, 2017), 43.

8 Jordan, 56-59.

9 Kottler, 133.

10 Brita L. Gill Austern, "Pedagogy Under the Influence of Feminism and Womanism," in *Feminist & Womanist Pastoral Theology*, ed. Bonnie J.

Miller-McLemore and Brita L. Gill Austern (Nashville: Abingdon Press, 1999), 150.

11 Kottler, 133.

12 Howard J. Ross, *Everyday Bias: Identifying and Navigating Unconscious Judgments in Our Daily Lives* (London: Rowman and Littlefield), 42.

2

UNCONSCIOUS BIASES AS PART OF OUR LIFE PACKAGE

Luis Elier Rodriguez
Manager, System Clinical Pastoral Education,
Houston Methodist

IAS IS A PREJUDICE in favor of or against a thing or group compared with another. Usually it is considered unfair. When we impose our judgments about a specific person on the whole group or community this individual belongs to, then we have a bias. It is important to understand that biases can be innate or learned. According to Howard Ross, our unconscious beliefs and biases impact the way we perceive others, and our unconscious beliefs also impact how we view ourselves.[1] The reality is that all humans have biases, and as spiritual caregivers we cannot avoid them. Biases contain prejudices of thoughts and feelings, including stereotypes, generalizations, and attitudes against others. It is important to be transparent and acknowledge our biases, because spiritual caregivers who claim not to have biases are demonstrating a profound distance from a healthy spiritual self-awareness and self-consciousness. I suspect that the proclamation of the spiritual belief that "biases are bad" or that "good people and/or spiritual people are not biased" causes spiritual caregivers to deny this dimension of our spiritual life. My intention in this chapter is not to deny this aspect of our spiritual existence nor to avoid its reality. At the end of this chapter, we have some significant steps to deal with our biases instead of denying their unavoidable reality.

It is important to know that biases can co-occur and may need to be considered together. Another factor to be aware of is that biases are present in spiritual care. Therefore, it is important to review our humanity and mention and identify biases in our lives, and pay attention to their influence on our spiritual care practice.

The following section lists some basic biases that must be reviewed with an open mind. We must openly listen to others who point out the biases they observe in us. This process can create defensiveness, but it is also an excellent opportunity to demonstrate that biases will not direct us in our provision of spiritual care, as we can have control over them or mitigate their effect. I think it is important to talk openly and vulnerably about this issue.

Here are some of the most common biases:

1. *Selective attention or inattentive blindness*: This accounts for why certain diversity-related behaviors, cultural identity, and religious identity might be obvious to some people and completely invisible to others.[2] That is why in my Clinical Pastoral Education groups I am careful to make sure that female voices are heard and to check with the group to make sure they have received the same attention as when someone in the dominant group speaks (i.e. white, male, heterosexual, Christian). Sometimes I ask who has the most power in the group

and who is heard the most. In my general experience, students who are more listened to are white and male.

Also, for this reason, I like to use the model of cultural identity with an assertion of cultural empathy. In this way I facilitate the conversation to minimize selective attention as a high bias in the cultural dimension, using Charles Ridley, Debra Mollen, and Shannon Kelly's model of counseling as well as Charles Ridley and Sharranya Udipi's model of cultural empathy represented in four pivotal assertions:[3]

- Cultural identity can be learned. We agree that the capacity to develop empathy is innate, but the skills involved in cultural empathy are learned. The challenge is to increase our awareness of times when others are invisible to us.
- Cultural empathy is multidimensional. It has cognitive, affective, perceptual, apperceptual, somatic, and communicative dimensions. The challenge is to accept and be aware of different styles of relatedness.
- Cultural empathy is an interpersonal process and a way of relating with other people.
- Cultural empathy conveys an attitude of concern. Unless spiritual caregivers show an attitude of genuine concern about the welfare of their patients, they are unlikely to deal creatively with selective attention.

One question we can ask ourselves is: Is something invisible in my work as a spiritual caregiver? What did I pay more attention to in my spiritual dialogue? What possible important dimensions have I been missing?

Exercise: Discuss one example of a time when you felt invisible to others and you had to express your dissatisfaction? How did you call for empathy towards yourself? Discuss one event when others were invisible in your conversation and you became aware of your bias of invisibility? How did you promote your own empathy?

2. *Diagnosis bias*: This is the tendency to assess people, ideas, or things based on our previously held opinions. It is about our thoughts towards other people and how we see and/or label people. It is when we presuppose things about others and relate to others based on our assumptions and labels.[4] However, we must remember that 50 percent of our assumptions are wrong. That is why we must be aware of our initial assumptions, especially when we first meet our patients.

For example, on his first day, one of my Anglo students met with an African-American patient at the hospital. He assumed discussing the NBA would be a good way to establish rapport with this patient. He began talking to the patient about his impressions of Michael Jordan compared to Lebron James. After a while, the African American patient said, "Thank you for talking to me about basketball, but I'm an engineer and I don't follow or know much about basketball." This example shows us that our assumptions guide us on how we relate to our patients and that we may be wrong. This example also helps us to understand that we can make diagnoses based on something that is not intellectual, professional, or relevant.

Another example was when one of the students developed the assumption that his female patient had

25

little education or low self-esteem because she did not look him in the eye. In the end, he realized that this woman came from a culture where eye contact with a man who is not one's husband is not practiced. Her culture emphasized listening with ears rather than the belief that eye contact demonstrates active listening.

Exercise: Discuss these two examples and give your own example related to the tendency to make diagnoses where we sometimes devalue others.

3. *Pattern recognition*: This is the tendency to sort and identify information based on prior experience, characters, or habits.[5] It is the tendency to see situations, people, and objects as being the same as other things we have seen previously.[6] In this, transference is extremely important. I recommend using Virginia Satir's exercise where I tell participants to look at the person sitting next to them and ask if they remind them of someone. The person sitting next to you might remind you of a criminal, teacher, uncle, parent, another patient, or any other character in your life experience.

Exercise: It's important to ask the following questions during our visits: Why is it important to wonder who this patient reminds me of? What memory do they bring to me and what feeling does my previous experience present in my relationship with my patient? I think this motivates us to explore more transference and counter-transference dynamics.

4. *Value attribution*: This is the inclination to imbue a person or thing with certain qualities based on initial perceived values.[7] This is the bias to instantly value people, without even realizing we are doing so. For example, when Bob Kidd did his Clinical Pastoral

Education residency, he was surprised when a student from the island of San Andrés of Colombia was talking about Nietzsche, Tillich, Kafka, and other philosophers and educators.[8] Bob was surprised because for the first time he was before a CPE teammate who looked black, was Hispanic, bilingual, and had a lot more knowledge than Bob about philosophical issues. Bob had to evaluate his value attribution of Hispanic people and of his peer who, to his eyes, appeared to be black.

5. *Confirmation bias*: According to Kendra Cherry, confirmation bias is a type of cognitive bias that involves favoring information that confirms your previously existing beliefs or biases.[9]

   For example, a Christian student believed Muslim persons were radical and violent. In several interpersonal relationship sessions (IPR), we had this bias came out in the group when he referred to Muslims as second-rate believers and spoke about a supposed contradiction between what was preached in the Muslim community and what was actually done. He learned this from his experience as a soldier in Afghanistan in the US Army. He did this without knowing the background of his new Muslim CPE peer or his peer's interpretation of non-violence. The ex-soldier had to examine and confirm his existing opinion of the Muslims and develop critical thought in the face of his biases and seek different interpretations because of his new experience of having a CPE Muslim peer. This kind of educational experience is not always easy. In CPE, it becomes more bearable because there is a group that offers feedback and an educator who facilitates reflection. Another aspect is that CPE emphasizes listening to people with different opinions and this allows students to be open to the possibility of new paradigms. Therefore, it is always a challenge when a student of spiritual care closes their eyes to seeing other points of view.

That's why I agree with Kendra Cherry when she mentions that confirmation biases impact how we gather information, and in addition they also influence how we interpret and recall information.[10] During the CPE unit, I could see how the ex-soldier struggled with his bias against Muslims and how to use his new understanding in CPE with his Muslim CPE peer by re-examining the following trends:

- Only paying attention to information that confirms your beliefs about issues such as gun control and global warming
- Only following people on social media who share your viewpoints
- Choosing news sources that present stories that support your views
- Refusing to listen to the opposing side
- Not considering all of the facts in a logical and rational manner

6. *Socioeconomic bias*: This is believing that the lack of money or formal education indicates a lack of intelligence, and also assuming you can identify a person's education and intelligence level on meeting or seeing them for the first time. As spiritual caregivers, we have to take into consideration that the material conditions in which people grow up and live have a lasting impact on their

personal and social identities and that this influences both the way they think and feel about their social environment and key aspects of their social behavior.[11] For this reason, instead of quickly passing judgment on other's social and economic priorities and environment, we have to display spiritual sensitivity, including cultural and social empathy and compassion. This is expressed in the quote of an unknown author, "You have to walk in my shoes across several moons to start understanding me." Spiritual sensitivity is very important. One of the ironies of modern Western societies, with their emphasis on meritocratic values that promote the notion that people can achieve what they want if they have enough talent and are prepared to work hard enough, is that the divisions between social classes are becoming wider, not narrower. This irony often reinforces a predisposition we have for looking at things through the lens of a certain paradigm; we have these prejudices and sometimes they are in contradiction with the values of a spiritual caregiver. The book *Bridges Out of Poverty: Strategies for Professionals and Communities* identifies the effects of living in poverty rather than in a middle-class environment.[12] The following table is an adaptation using this book, with a general characterization of two social classes, recognizing my own biases and perhaps incorrect assumptions in communicating their potential differences. I am aware that whenever biases and assumptions become widespread, one runs the risk of passing judgment and having the wrong assumptions:[13]

Low-income (Poverty)	Middle Class
To help one another to survive	To achieve goals and security
Focus on day-to-day survival	Strong future orientation
Pessimism about future	Optimism drives planning
Destiny determined by fate	Feeling of being in control of own destiny
Life is full of bad luck	You make your own luck
Education is not a realistic option	Education is a realistic option
Never enough money, use for little pleasures	Money is something to manage
Money barely covers daily needs	Budget for present and future
Feeling of being looked down on	Defend own class position
No health insurance or government coverage	Private health insurance
Expect low respect from staff	Expect respect from staff
Success feels almost unattainable	Belief in meritocracy, everybody can succeed if they work hard
Feel powerless against government	Believe they can influence government

After becoming familiar with this list, try to improve and gain awareness of the impact of an individual's socioeconomic environment and reflect on your own biases related to status and class. Also, be aware of the influence of socioeconomic classes from generation to generation, and how they impact motivational forces, understandings of power, and how your patients relate with medical staff and with you as a caregiver. In addition, we must be reminded that generational poverty and situational poverty are different. Generational poverty is defined as being in poverty for two generations or longer.[14] Situational poverty lasts for a shorter time and is caused by circumstance (e.g., death, illness, divorce, etc.) [15]

7. *Linguistic and accent biases*: Apparently, accent bias occurs because people evaluate others based not only on how they look (appearance) but also on how they sound (speech).[16] Accent "refers to *pronunciation* differences."[17] According to Megumi Hosoda, another way of defining accent is to say that those in power are perceived as speaking "normal, unaccented English" and any speech that differs is called an accent.[18] The reality, however, is that everyone speaks with an accent. Those in the minority who are perceived as sounding different are discriminated against. Accent bias can be conscious, but more often it is unconscious. According to several researchers, it takes us less than thirty seconds to linguistically profile a speaker and make quick decisions on their ethnic origin, socioeconomic class, and their backgrounds. Apparently, we are more likely to be biased against speakers who have accents different from our own, as we unconsciously identify certain accents as being markers for undesirable characteristics. According to Dr. Pragya Agarwal, we form a hierarchical view of accents ranked by societal and cultural acceptability,

31

assigning to them values such as pleasantness and prestige as well as intelligence. For this reason, speaking English with an accent usually invokes a foreigner stereotype and can trigger discrimination. All the inconveniences, discomfort, and discrimination in navigating daily life can be stressful and eventually lead to stress and feelings of frustration, sadness, anxiety, and a sense of insecurity which will increase levels of psychological distress or acculturative stress. This dynamic can trigger depression in many Latinos, Asians, and persons from other minorities experiencing social vulnerability.[19] It is very detrimental to receive unfair treatment, residential isolation, and to be stereotyped as a perpetual foreigner, experiencing daily language discrimination. The following list describing potential biases against nonstandard English speakers vs. fluent English speakers reveals the impact of this bias and prejudice:

Nonstandard English	Standard English
Is not a very smart person	Is very smart
Lower intelligence	Higher intelligence
Intellectually inferior	Intellectually superior
Disadvantaged accent	Advantaged language
Slow learner	Quick learner
Poor educational performance	Good educational performance
Nothing significant to contribute	Significant things to contribute
Related to learning difficulties	No learning difficulties
Less academically capable	More academically capable

This dynamic has sharpened during COVID-19. For example, according to Brigham and Women's Hospital in Boston, it appeared to be killing more Black and brown patients than whites.[20] Apparently, for Latino patients, there was an additional warning sign— language. Patients who didn't speak much, if any, English had a 35 percent greater chance of death. Clinicians who couldn't communicate clearly with patients in the hospital's COVID units noticed it was affecting outcomes. "We had an inkling that language was going to be an issue early on," says Dr. Karthik Sivashanker, Brigham's then-medical director for quality, safety, and equity. "We were getting safety reports saying language is a problem."[21] Sivashanker dove into the records, isolating and layering the characteristics of each of the patients who died. He investigated their race, age, gender, and whether or not they spoke English.

After reading the list of Nonstandard English and Standard English biases, take time to reflect on how you evaluate others based on their looks (appearance) and also on how they sound (speech) and how those aspects impact your spiritual care

8. *Organizational bias*: This occurs when an organization promotes a normative belief among its members. We must be reminded that often different organizations have assumptions and ways of interpreting things that the given organization has invented, discovered, or developed in learning to adapt to its internal and external influences.[22] Unconscious organizational patterns or norms of behavior exert an enormous influence over organizational decisions, choices, and behaviors.

Identifying organizational culture can be an opportunity to celebrate inclusiveness or to evaluate patterns that foster a deliberate status quo that can promote homogeneity and exclusivism where some people may feel inferior or discriminated against in the organizational culture.

Therefore, it is important to check whether the organization promotes women, minorities, persons with disabilities, and employees with different accents and if the organization's leadership values inclusivity and equity. It is important to check whether there is diversity or not in the positions of managers, directors, and vice presidents. Sometimes there can be a contradiction between the diversity being promoted and the absence of diversity in organizational leadership.[23]

In summary, as spiritual caregivers, we have some significant steps to take to address these biases:

1. Try to walk in your patient's shoes for few moons (empathy).
2. Try to identify your biases as they apply to diversity, inclusion, equity, ethnicity, race, gender, class, religion, language, and sexual orientation.
3. Try to invite people into your home from different cultural heritages, economic levels, sexual orientations, and ethnicities to gain awareness of your potential biases related to the particular group.
4. Be motivated to be fair.
5. Be reflective about yourself and the implications of your spiritual care to different patient populations.

6. Be open to reflect on how oppression, racism, prejudice, discrimination, and stereotyping affect your patients and your spiritual care practice.

7. Try to obtain information about the ethnicity and background of the patient to whom you will be offering spiritual care.

8. Try to identify some of your biases and reflect on the impact of the way you think, feel, and provide spiritual care.

9. Try to identify biases that could inhibit or adversely affect your ability to work effectively with people different from yourself.

10. With what group do you feel uncomfortable in ways that cause you to act differently in your spiritual care? What kind of patients do you feel uncomfortable with?

11. Try to reflect on the implications of language discrimination biases and how it impacts your patients and your spiritual care.

12. What steps would you like to take to confront or challenge your biases?

13. Try to reflect on the Association of Spiritual Care's mission: to positively affect people's lives by nurturing connections to the sacred through experiential education and spiritual care.

14. Try to identify some biases involving social, racial, and religious ideas that were created to legitimatize prejudices and possibly discrimination.

15. Try to learn if your patient talks about fair treatment and respect.

16. Try to reflect on the following values of the Association of Clinical Pastoral Education and their implications for dealing with your biases and your spiritual care:

- Diversity and inclusion—demonstrated through cultural humility, attentiveness, and collegiality.
- Integrity—demonstrated through trust, respect, and excellence.
- Curiosity—demonstrated through listening, experiential models, innovation, and creativity.
- Process—demonstrated through action/reflection, listening, experiential and relational models.
- Service—demonstrated through compassion, authenticity, and growth.

The Association of Clinical Pastoral Education is emphasizing the following resources that are good tools for promoting cultural diversity and confronting biases against certain cultures and religions:[24]

1. Professional development opportunities for staff to gain training in cultural and religious diversity and racial equity.
2. Professional development opportunities that are designed for students to gain training in cultural and religious diversity and racial equity.
3. Non-discrimination policies.
4. Examples of learning activities and evaluation strategies demonstrating the development and integration of intercultural competence.
5. Examples of how student support services are culturally responsive in serving the needs of your students.
6. A presentation on how the CPE center creates a relational learning environment that models affirmation and respect for diversity and difference and fosters mutual trust, respect, openness, challenge, conflict, and confrontation.

I am glad that Houston Methodist Hospital has its I CARE values that create a helpful philosophical and practical resource to deal with our daily biases. The I CARE values are:

Integrity—"We are honest and ethical in all we say and do."

Compassion—"We embrace the whole person and respond to emotional, ethical and spiritual concerns as well as physical needs."

Accountability—"We hold ourselves accountable for our actions."

Respect—"We treat every individual as a person of worth, dignity, and value."

Excellence—"We strive to be the best at what we do and a model for others to emulate."

In short, I believe that identifying our biases helps us to be more aware and effective in our spiritual care. It also helps us guide our biases instead of being guided by them in our spiritual care. At times this requires a process of learning and detachment from our beliefs and assumptions. I suspect this will be an ongoing, lifelong process.

———————————————

1 Howard J. Ross, "Exploring Unconscious Bias," *CDO Insights*, 2:5.

2 Howard J. Ross, *Everyday Bias: Identifying and Navigating Unconscious Judgments in Our Daily Lives* (New York: Rowman and Littlefield, 2014), 42-43.

3 See more information in Charles Ridley, Debra Mollen, and Shannon Kelly, "Counseling Competence: Application and Implications of a Model," *The Counseling Psychologist*, 39, no. 6 (August 2011): 865-886.

4 Ross, *Everyday Bias*, 45-46.

5 Ibid., 46-49.

6 Ibid., 47.

7 Ibid., 49-50.

8 I used this example with the permission of Robert Kidd.

9 Kendra Cherry, "An Unbiased View of Cognitive Bias and How to Think Critically," *Verywell Mind*, July 8, 2020.

10 Cherry, "An Unbiased View. "

11 Antony S. R. Manstead, "The Psychology of Social Class: How Socioeconomic Status Impacts Thought, Feelings, and Behaviour," *British Journal of Social Psychology*, 57, no. 2 (2018): 267-291.

12 Ruby K. Payne, Philip E. DeVol., Terrie Dreussi Smith, *Bridges Out of Poverty: Strategies for Professionals and Communities* (Highlands, TX: Aha! Process, 2006), 39-49.

13 Ibid., 49-63.

14 Ibid., 7.

15 Ibid., 7.

16 William Y. Chin, "Linguistic Profiling in Education: How Accent Bias Denies Equal Education Opportunity to Students of Color," 12 *Scholar* 355 (2009-2010). Available at SSRN: https://ssrn.com/abstract=2987351.

17 In this section on accent biases, I am hugely grateful for the contribution of the presentation "El idioma dolor y esperanza: Language Grief and Hope," by ACPE Latinx Community of Practice presented in the ACPE 2021 conference. Special thanks to Bicri Hernandez, ACPE Certified Educator, for helping me to reflect on this topic and for sharing some of her materials.

18 Lucas Torres, "Predicting Levels of Latino Depression: Acculturation, Acculturative Stress, and Coping," *Cultural Diversity & Ethnic Minority Psychology*, 16, no. 2 (2010): 256-63.

19 Ibid., 20.

20 https://www.wbur.org/news/2021/01/29/mass-general-brigham-covid-community-intervention.

21 https://www.wbur.org/npr/989928262/the-pandemic-imperiled-non-english-speakers-in-a-hospital.

22 See more information in "Proven Strategies for Addressing Unconscious Bias in the Workplace," *CDO Insights*, 2, issue 5.

23 See more information about the racism dynamic in *White Fragility* by Robin Diangelo.

24 Association of Clinical Pastoral Education, 2021 *Manual.*

3

THE SIGNIFICANCE OF REFRAMING A
FUTURE STORY

Rev. David Wethington, MA, BCC
Chaplain at Shepherd Center, Atlanta, Georgia

Bad news often comes when it is least expected. A person might be unprepared, unaware, or unable to process the news he or she has been given. Life is moving along at a decent pace and then the unforeseen happens. Life is turned upside down. Future hopes and dreams are put on pause for the moment, or possibly forever. The person thinks to himself or herself, "Now what?" A future story has been altered and disrupted by the present circumstances. Time seems to stand still. The person ponders what life will be like going forward. Then, in walks the spiritual caregiver. The person looks up, in despair, longing for someone to help. The spiritual caregiver actively and empathetically listens to the person's story, in search of clues that might assist them as they think of how to help this person.

The spiritual caregiver listens to the person's story and asks questions of the care recipient, which helps the care recipient to reflect on the changes that are now apparent in the present circumstances. This reflection allows the care recipient to identify internal strengths and personal resources that may assist with the reconstruction of a future story. Through the guidance of the spiritual caregiver, the person begins to reconstruct a future story in the midst of a disrupted future story with strengths and resources that have been self-identified. The visit concludes and the care recipient expresses a feeling of decreased anxiety, compared to when the spiritual caregiver came to visit. The present circumstances are still challenging for the care recipient, but a new perspective has been uncovered from his or her own resources, which appears feasible. A new future story has begun to be constructed.

Various tools are available to the spiritual caregiver that can be applied when a future story has been disrupted. One of the tools that assists in the reconstruction process is the reframing of a future story. A future story is interrupted by the circumstances of life and the outlook moving forward does not look favorable from the care recipient's initial perspective. The spiritual caregiver looks at all the aspects of a person's future and guides them towards a different perspective with the resources available to that person. In this instance, the care recipient's story has been reframed into something different than it was before the spiritual caregiver began interacting with the care recipient. Spiritual caregivers have a unique and significant role in guiding care recipients in the reframing of a disrupted future story that can provide a different perspective, which leads to a future story of hope.

An Altered Future Story

An altered future story is something that spiritual caregivers encounter on a regular basis. Unexpected circumstances change the course and direction of where a person plans and believes life is going. This happened to me in November 2012. I was

41

young and healthy. My wife and I had just discussed starting our family. I had a career in the engineering profession ahead of me that I looked forward to. I had worked in the engineering profession for over ten years and I had transitioned into engineering management. My future story was full of hope. Life was going very well.

Stress was part of the new engineering management role and I began to experience dizziness. Initially, I shrugged it off as if it were related to the new stress. However, my primary care doctor referred me to an ear, nose, and throat doctor, who advised that I get an MRI, just in case. I had an MRI and a subsequent appointment was set up with a neurosurgeon to review the results. At the appointment, the words from my neurosurgeon could not have been clearer. The neurosurgeon told me I had a brain tumor about the size of a baseball at its widest point. The tumor was large and it was in a critical location. My brainstem had become the shape of the letter "C" and the tumor was growing close to my carotid artery. The neurosurgeon indicated that this tumor needed to come out as soon as possible. My future story began to change.

I had successful brain surgery the week after Thanksgiving. The majority of the tumor was removed. Some of the tumor was left in place at the discretion of neurosurgeon because of the residual tumor's proximity to the brain stem. I spent a few days in the hospital ICU and the next few days in a regular hospital room. Soon, I was transferred to an inpatient rehabilitation hospital where I began comprehensive neuro-medical rehabilitation to relearn how to walk, speak clearly, feed myself, and function with the changes in my post-surgery life. Additionally, I had an evaluation by a neuropsychologist to address my cognitive functioning. I was discouraged by all of the physical changes in my life, but nothing prepared me for the news I received from the neuropsychologist. This news was life changing.

About a day after the evaluation, the neuropsychologist delivered upsetting news to me. The neuropsychologist informed me that I was cognitively impaired. He indicated that it would take a significant amount of time and therapy for me to return to the cognitive functionality I had as an engineer. The news was delivered to me in a matter-of-fact way, not in a compassionate manner. I could not cognitively or emotionally process what I learned in that moment. In an attempt to make this news clearer, the neuropsychologist made suggestions of what types of jobs I might be able to return to one day. None of these suggestions involved engineering and none of them brought me any hope. Hearing this news was devastating. It became clear to me that someone who was cognitively impaired would not return to a career in engineering. I felt I no longer had a future in engineering or even a purpose in the moment. What was I going to do? I could not walk and I could not return to my profession. My future story was altered, disrupted, and changed. I knew my physical disabilities might improve with therapy, but the news did not sound promising with regard to my cognitive abilities. I felt all my future hopes and dreams were gone forever. I was in a place where I could not see past the present moment.

I received a visit from the hospital chaplain several days after I had found out this devastating news about my cognitive impairment. I remember that my first thought was that the chaplain was going to remind me of hopeful biblical passages, in light of the state of devastation that I was in. I knew many of these passages and, honestly, they did not provide much comfort to me in the moment. I did feel God's presence in a way I had never felt it before, but I still felt something was missing. I trusted in God's plans for me, but I could not see past the information I had just learned about my cognitive impairment. I was not sure what help the chaplain could provide for me, except maybe to pray for me.

Instead, the chaplain helped me and guided me in a way I had not imagined. The chaplain completely surpassed my expectations. The chaplain was fully present with me in my moment of devastation and he did not try to solve my concerns. The chaplain actively and empathetically listened to me. The chaplain understood that my faith was important to me and that helping others was a significant part of who I was. Additionally, the chaplain pointed out some observations he had made regarding me as a patient. The chaplain highlighted that he had seen me visiting with and encouraging fellow patients. He indicated that I was functioning as a chaplain to the other patients, while I myself was a patient. The chaplain guided me to a new perspective, which was one where I was helping my fellow patients. The chaplain guided me towards reframing my current situation into something that gave me hope and a purpose. This reframing did not solve the bigger issue of cognitive impairment. However, the chaplain helped guide me to a place of hope, which allowed me to find purpose when I felt I had lost my purpose. I felt comfortable with the different perspective the chaplain had guided me towards, even though I did not understand how I would return to the functionality I had prior to my surgery. Regardless of my thoughts, I now had a new future story and a purpose that was attainable in the present moment.

The Role of the Spiritual Caregiver

The spiritual caregiver is invited into the sacred space of the care recipient's story. The disruption of a future story in a person's life brings about changes that were not anticipated. Future plans and expectations shift in ways that can be both positive and negative. Often, the recipient of the disrupted future story cannot see past their present circumstances. When I was a patient, I could not see past my time in the hospital. The spiritual caregiver's role is one that helps guide a person in their current circumstance towards a new future story that offers a different perspective. The spiritual caregiver enters at a point in a person's story, which allows the person to share the challenges and opportunities that have arisen as a result of the changes in their future story. In *Professional Spiritual & Pastoral Care*, Robert A. Kidd states, "An effective listener stays attuned to the present."[1] The hospital chaplain entered a point in my disrupted future story and was attuned to the present moment. Thus, the chaplain guided me towards a perspective that was understandable and attainable in the present moment. There are various assessments, methodologies, techniques, and interventions that a spiritual caregiver has available to assist in this process. Guiding a person towards reframing a future story may provide that person with hope and a new perspective.

The spiritual caregiver guides the care recipient, but allows that person to direct the conversation towards a new perspective. This is the art of reframing. In *Basic Types of Pastoral Care & Counseling*, Howard Clinebell states, "Reframing means looking at issues through more effective lenses or seeing them from clearer perspectives."[2] The spiritual caregiver is able to see a perspective by listening to the care recipient's story and circumstances. The spiritual caregiver does not impose personal views on the situation. Rather, the spiritual caregiver listens to the person, notices non-verbal cues, and makes other observations that guide the care recipient towards a deeper understanding of himself or herself in the midst of the disrupted future story. The spiritual caregiver is present in the moment as the story is shared, in order to highlight aspects that might allow the care recipient to reconstruct a future story and develop a clearer perspective. Thus, the care recipient develops his or her own new future story with the help of the spiritual caregiver. This new future story enables the care recipient to become aware of the skills, resources, and hope that are available in the midst of their changed circumstances.

Reframing guides the care recipient towards a different perspective. Reframing does not necessarily provide a solution to the challenges in the present circumstances. Reframing guides the care recipient towards a new trajectory that previously might not have seemed attainable. For example, life changing news can cause one to think that future goals are now unattainable. Reframing helps one to think of future goals that are attainable in light of the change in circumstances. A future story is still attainable, but it may not be what the care recipient had originally anticipated. The spiritual caregiver guides the care recipient towards seeing a future story that is attainable with his or her own capabilities and resources.

Reframing a Challenging Future Story

It is important to remember that the reframing of an altered future story may not address all of a person's concerns. In the example of my future story, there were future hopes and dreams that were not addressed at the time. I had built a successful career in engineering and I was working my way through engineering management. My wife and I had hopes of starting a family. This was part of my future story and it would be challenging to resume that future story in light of my circumstances. In that moment, I was a patient in a wheel chair and I was cognitively impaired. The chaplain listened to all these concerns. I wanted my future hopes to still come to fruition and my biomedical challenges to resolve themselves through therapy. However, in the moment I felt I had lost all purpose. None of these future hopes would be attainable if I remained in a state of despair.

An altered future story can become a dysfunctional future story. In the book *Hope in Pastoral Care and Counseling,* Andrew D. Lester highlights the differences between functional future stories and dysfunctional future stories. Lester notes that a dysfunctional future story is one "that cannot fulfill the purpose of future stories, to provide reasons to keep on moving into the future with hope."[3] This was the state I was in regarding my future story. In contrast, Lester states, "Functional future stories are those projections of our core narrative that open up life and invite us into an exciting, meaningful tomorrow."[4] These functional future stories motivate and provide hope for the person, helping them look forward to what may be in store in the future. Functional future stories bring a person out of dysfunction.

This is exactly what a chaplain did for me during my stay at the inpatient rehabilitation hospital. I felt my future story in engineering was not possible, given the prognosis regarding cognitive impairment I had received from my doctor. I had begun to lose hope in spite of my faith. My future story prior to brain surgery was to go back to a career in engineering, to provide for my family. My dysfunctional future story after brain surgery was that I no longer had a purpose in life. The chaplain helped to reframe my dysfunctional future story into a functional future story that gave me hope and a purpose, given my present circumstances. This future story guided me out of a place of despair, so I could make progress in the other areas of my neuro-medical rehabilitation therapy.

Reframing is just one of the tools spiritual caregivers have available as part of the deconstruction process with regards to dysfunctional future stories. It can be a very powerful tool. In the art of reframing, the spiritual caregiver listens to the care recipient's story to learn what is shaping a future story and also what might be helpful in guiding the care recipient towards a reframed future story. As Lester states, "Some of the projected content is based on actual data from the history of that person and/or from what is happening in that actual person's present situation."[5] Thus, a person is projecting what a future story may look like based on his or her understanding of their circumstances. The spiritual caregiver begins to understand the care recipient's story. The spiritual caregiver ask questions that are informed by the person's story, questions that may guide the care recipient towards a different perspective and a reframed future story.

The spiritual caregiver guides the patient towards a new perspective of their future story in light of their present circumstances. Often, the present circumstances involve a crisis, which adds to the care recipient's inability to understand a functional future story. This crisis then leads to a dysfunctional future story. A spiritual caregiver helps the care recipient to see past the crisis and guides him or her to an open-ended story. Therefore, the care recipient's perception of his or her dysfunctional future story begins to be deconstructed with the assistance of the spiritual caregiver. The spiritual caregiver takes into account all the information that has been learned about the care recipient's past and present realities. This understanding assists in the reframing and reconstruction of a new future story.

My future story of despair was deconstructed and then reconstructed into something that I could find purpose in.

Through the spiritual care provided by the hospital chaplain I was able to understand that I still had a purpose. I wanted to get well during my hospital stay so I could resume my future hopes and dreams. I understood that recovering might not allow my pre-brain surgery future story to come to fruition. However, through the reconstruction of my future story, I was able to understand that there was something in store for me in the midst of suffering. The reframing of my future story allowed me to see a new perspective with respect to my life that was independent of how well I recovered from my neuro-medical rehabilitation. A spiritual caregiver has the opportunity to enter into a place of concern or despair and provide guidance to the care recipient. In my example, the chaplain guided me to a place of self-understanding and self-awareness that gave me a feasible future story of hope while I was still a patient. Specifically, the chaplain took time to get to know my story, my concerns, and my desires. The chaplain was aware that I wanted to walk again and function at a cognitive level that would allow me to return to engineering. Rather than guide me towards constructing a future story that led to a solution to all of my concerns, the chaplain helped me to construct a future story of present hope that was specific to me.

Reframing a Story Without Imposition

A spiritual caregiver must be careful to not impose or project his or her own beliefs on the care recipient. A reframed story is constructed through the thoughts and beliefs of the care recipient. Robert A. Kidd states, "Effective listeners stay as objective as possible during conversations."[6] A spiritual caregiver has beliefs, opinions, and experiences with others, which may not match those of the care recipient. For example, in my story the hospital chaplain learned through our conversation that I was deeply connected to my faith in God. Additionally, the chaplain had observed my interactions with others. Guiding me towards a personal self-awareness that I was functioning as an encouragement to others was a reframed future story that was specific to me. The chaplain did not impose his Christian beliefs on me. Nor did the chaplain project his experiences with other patients on me. Additionally, I was functioning in a way that may have provided assistance to the chaplain. Therefore, the chaplain could have easily projected his beliefs, opinions, and experiences on me. Rather, the chaplain understood my faith background and guided me to a place of understanding that I was functioning like a chaplain to the other patients. This reframed story was my own future story and not someone else's future story.

My reframed future story was something I came to on my own. Specifically, the fact that the chaplain guided me to this self-understanding was more impactful because it allowed me to truly internalize that this was indeed a future story where I could find hope and purpose in the moment. The other important piece to note is that my future story was not someone else's future story. This reframed story was something I could appreciate and identify with based on what the chaplain learned about me. I could now see that I had a purpose, which allowed me to function appropriately with respect to all my other neuro-medical rehabilitation therapies.

Reframing a Future Story Brings Hope

Reframing a future story connects the care recipient to a place of hope and brings forth healing. In my example, the hospital chaplain guided me out of a place of despair and into a place of hope that allowed me to heal during my inpatient hospital stay. I was unsure how my physical recovery was going to turn out, but

I had hope that was connected to an open-ended future. Andrew D. Lester explains in *Hope in Pastoral Care and Counseling*, "How a person thinks and feels toward the not-yet is crucial to physical, emotional, and spiritual health."[7] This thought is important to the holistic understanding of how a spiritual caregiver can work with a person to reframe a situation, which contributes towards overall health. As a patient, I participated in all of my neuro-medical rehabilitation because of the motivation and hope of an open-ended future. The hospital chaplain guided me to a place of hope which encouraged my participation in healing therapies, which led to my physical recovery. I willingly interacted with others, which addressed my emotional needs. My perspective and future story were reframed early during my inpatient stay, which motivated me to function to the best of my abilities throughout my recovery.

Spiritual caregivers bring a theological perspective to the person they visit, in addition to helping that person focus on hope. The spiritual caregiver blends his or her understanding of theology with the hopes and dreams of the care recipient. Again, the spiritual caregiver does not impose his or her beliefs on the care recipient, but the spiritual caregiver's theological understanding undergirds the visit. A person might explain future hopes and dreams to a spiritual caregiver. If appropriate, the spiritual caregiver may be able to help the care recipient connect his or her hopes with a theological understanding of the present situation. Lester states, "Used theologically, the word hope describes a person's trusting anticipation of the future based on an understanding of a God who is trustworthy and who calls us into an open-ended future."[8] A person's present circumstance is connected to a future story that is greater than the moment. God is still active in the midst of the disrupted future story, but the care recipient might not be able to accept this or understand this.

The process of guiding a person towards hope does not necessarily involve a theological conversation. A hopeful and reframed future story can be conveyed in spiritual caregiving by understanding a person's past experiences and their present circumstances, in order to connect a person to their own understanding of hope. Simply listening to a person telling their story can provide clues the spiritual caregiver can use to guide the visit and subsequent conversations towards a place of hope about their current situation. Allowing a person to focus on their hopes for the present may ultimately bring them to an understanding of future hope. In the example of my story, I was able to focus on the present hope of having a purpose in encouraging other hospital patients. This allowed me to look forward towards personal open-ended goals that were connected to a greater story of infinite hope.

Hope is essential during a time of crisis. Hope gives a person something to focus on during the pain and suffering of their present circumstances. Lester states, "In any crisis or facing any tragedy, those with hope more easily wait for the present to pass because they trust the future."[9] This statement really resonates with me as I reflect on my time as a patient. The pain and suffering of that moment, being told that I was cognitively impaired, were devastating. The hospital chaplain guided me towards the reframing of this devastating situation, which allowed me to find hope and purpose. I trusted in the promises of God and this helped the waiting period for recovery to be more bearable. This enabled me to come to a place of peace during my stay as a patient.

I come from a Christian faith tradition. The future open-ended story of Christian eschatological hope connected well with the reframed story the hospital chaplain guided me towards. I looked forward to the day when I would no longer be in a wheel chair and I would no longer be cognitively impaired. However neither the hospital chaplain nor the doctors could give me an indication of if or when that might occur. I was suffering in the middle of my disrupted future story. The reframed future story gave me purpose in the moment and it connected to the future open-ended story of eschatological hope. The book of Revelation is widely debated by biblical scholars with respect to its exegesis. However it is clear that there will be a future return of Christ and that one day there will be no more tears and no more pain (Rev. 21:4 NIV 2011). Eschatology is all about hope. Therefore, helping a person to connect their future hopes to the greater eschatological story of hope is important. A present hope connects to a future open-ended hope. Present hope provides purpose and motivation so that future hopes become a reality.

A New Future Story

Today, I have recovered well with respect to where I was as a patient. I am able to walk without the use of a wheel chair. My speech is clear and articulate. My cognitive functioning has returned to my pre-surgery level and I was able to go back to the engineering profession. My wife and I are proud parents of a daughter. I completed a master's degree in seminary and became a Board Certified Chaplain with the Association of Professional Chaplains. I now serve as a chaplain at Shepherd Center on the brain injury unit where I was once a patient. Most people who encounter me are not able identify any disabilities. However, I still face challenges such as permanent deafness in my right ear and double vision. I do not dwell on these challenges because of the future hope that I have in Christ.

Jesus says, "But seek first his kingdom and his righteousness, and all these things will be given to you as well. Therefore, do not worry about tomorrow, for tomorrow will worry about itself. Each day has enough trouble of its own." (Matthew 6:33-34 NIV). These verses are in the forefront of my mind as I offer spiritual care as a hospital chaplain today. Additionally, I am motivated by a new future story that began when I was a patient in the hospital. The possibilities a spiritual caregiver has to assist a care recipient in reframing a disrupted future story are endless.

———————————

1 Robert A. Kidd, "Foundational Listening and Responding Skills," in *Professional Spiritual & Pastoral Care: A Practical Clergy and Chaplain's Handbook*, ed. Stephen B. Roberts (Woodstock, Vermont: Skylight Paths Publishing, 2016), 93. Original work published in 2012.

2 Howard Clinebell, *Basic Types of Pastoral Care & Counseling* (Nashville: Abingdon Press, 2011), 133. Original work published in 1966.

3 Andrew D. Lester, *Hope in Pastoral Care and Counseling* (Louisville: Westminster John Knox Press, 1995), 125.

4 Ibid.

5 Ibid., 128.

6 Kidd, "Foundational Listening," 94.

7 Lester, *Hope in Pastoral Care,* 59.

8 Ibid., 62.

9 Ibid., 68.

4

LISTENING SKILLS: WHY AND HOW CHAPLAINS LISTEN,
AND IMPLICATIONS FOR SPIRITUAL ASSESSMENT

Robert Goodson
Former Intern and Resident at Houston Methodist Hospital
and 2nd Year Resident at Baylor St. Luke's Hospital

*"We have to listen to understand in the same way
we want to be understood."* — Brené Brown[1]

Laying the Foundation: Why Do We Listen?

"I DON'T WANT YOU TO DO ANYTHING about it, I just want you to listen." Not to reinforce a gender stereotype, but I would venture to say that most married men have heard this statement from their spouses. This is largely due to the way most of us have been trained to listen. We learn these tendencies in our families of origin, our social contexts, sometimes even in our profession. Most often, we find ourselves listening not to understand what the other person is trying to communicate but merely to reply. We are listening with only half an ear, while our response has already begun to form and percolate in our minds. This is not truly listening. While it is important to keep the conversation moving and flowing, it should not be to the detriment of our conversation partner. In the context of chaplaincy and pastoral caregiving, if we cannot stop and truly listen to the person, we are not doing our job right. Sometimes a free-flowing conversation is exactly what is needed and can be healing to the patient. At other times, there is a need for sacred silence. This is the time to take a moment and gather one's thoughts and to pause so that both parties can process their own thoughts and emotions.

Even the best chaplains and pastoral caregivers can be distracted. When that happens, however, there is normally an opportunity to come back to the present moment, to apologize if necessary, and to more fully engage with the patient. I remember being very distracted during one of my first pastoral visitations at a small rural church I served in East Texas. One of the wonderful ladies of the church was driving me around to meet with members who were homebound. One was an elderly woman who lived very close to the church, Ms. Dolly.[2] We entered her home and I introduced myself to her and her caregiver, Nancy. We talked, both asking questions about the other. She wanted to get to know her new pastor, and I wanted to get to know her as well. During the conversation, I looked over and saw Nancy, perched on an old kitchen chair, pumping some sort of gun. Having grown up in the suburbs, this was something very much out of the ordinary for me. After admitting my distraction, and inquiring what Nancy was doing, I learned that she was trying to dissuade the squirrels that were getting onto Dolly's bird feeder by shooting little pellets at them. After getting this piece of information, I could return my attention more fully to Dolly and we moved forward with the visit. Hopefully none of your visits as a chaplain will involve any sort of firearm, but I mention this just to show how anyone can get distracted during a visit. The point is to bring one's focus back to the present and the patient. I find it quite like the work of mediation. The point is not that you will eliminate all thoughts from your mind. You are going to think about things, but you can acknowledge the thought and let it float away, like a leaf in the breeze. The important thing is to keep your mind and your self focused on the person in front of you.

Another important aspect is to listen openly. This is also referred to as listening with your heart, or with your third ear. We all have personal histories, social contexts, and theological beliefs that may or may not line up with those of the patient. Our job in providing spiritual care to our patients is to be open and present to them. When you open the door to the patient's room, you may have very little information about them. You may have a cursory sense drawn from their medical record and vital statistics, but we cannot know anything about their lived experience until we hear it from their mouths. As Anton Boison, the founder of Clinical Pastoral Education, put it, each person is their own living human document.[3] Their past, present, and hopes for the future; their attitudes and beliefs about God, illness, and hope; as well as God's providence, mercy, and grace, are all there. They are all contained in that living human document which you can peruse, if you are willing to ask the questions and if they are willing to share their thoughts and feelings with you. Perhaps I can make this a bit clearer with an analogy. While printed documents are normally fixed and unchanging, a person is not the same yesterday as they are today. They have been changed, even if ever so slightly, because of the experiences they have had, the people they have met, or maybe because a book or article they read changed their perspective on a certain issue. None of us can go through life without changing or evolving, so why would it be any different for our patients?

It is not our job to plot that trajectory for the patient and certainly not to alter it with our thoughts or opinions, but rather to be open and present to the person, just as they are in that moment. Illness has an interesting way of slowing us down and giving us space. It can call on us to reassess our present state and ways of thinking, and can be an impetus for profound change. A time of illness or hospitalization can be a liminal or "in-between" space and time. You may encounter patients who are in this liminal moment, and the best thing you can do is to help them marshal their inner resources. We can listen and support them in their effort to get where they want to go without imposing ourselves on the experience. One of the great and difficult things about this work is that, in distinction from what we may have experienced in prior pastoral or parish work, it is not our job to give our patients the answers. It is our job to ask the right questions so that they can discover those answers in themselves.

One tool that I find particularly useful in maintaining openness is unconditional positive regard (UPR). Unconditional positive regard is a concept put forth by psychologist Carl Rogers. He defines it as "Caring for the client, but not in a possessive way or in such a way as simply to satisfy the therapist's own needs ... It means caring for the client as a separate person, with permission to have his own feelings, his own experiences."[4] The American Psychological Association defines it as "An attitude of caring, acceptance, and prizing that others express toward an individual irrespective of his or her behavior and without regard to the others' personal standards."[5] In other words, it means caring for the person regardless of your personal opinions on their ideas or behavior.

You will be called upon to provide pastoral care to people you do not like personally, but that does not make them undeserving of your care, concern, and compassion. Theologically speaking, my basis for using UPR is that every patient is made in the image and likeness of God. In the creation narrative in Genesis it reads, "So God created humankind in his image, in the image of God he created them; male and female he created them."[6] Every person reflects the image of God and possesses God's original intention for goodness inside of them, regardless of their actions or our perceptions. As spiritual care providers, we are called to support all people, not just the ones who agree with us.

This extends to persons of different faiths. A colleague once told me about a Wiccan patient for whom he provided care. My colleague did not necessarily approve of this person's faith, but he wanted to support them where they were. One thing he did was to raise the window, to let the sunshine into the room so that the person would be more connected to the earth, an important aspect of their faith. It meant a lot to the patient that the chaplain showed respect for their faith, even though the chaplain did not share the patient's beliefs.

Another important aspect of a chaplain's job is empathetic listening. This is a skill that undergirds everything we do as spiritual care providers and chaplains. Dr. Steven Covey, author of the perennial favorite leadership book, *The 7 Habits of Highly Effective People,* speaks about the importance of empathy and empathetic listening. He highlights an important difference between empathy and sympathy. Empathy "gets inside another person's frame of reference. You look out through it, you see the world as they see the world, you understand their paradigm, you understand how they feel."[7]

This is in distinction to sympathy which is, in Covey's words, "a form of agreement, a form of judgment."[8] People need more to be understood than to have someone simply agree with them. Empathy empowers the other person to express their feelings, their needs, to engage their spiritual, emotional, and intellectual resources. Through this engagement with their own inner resources, they can create for themselves a plan of action and they can begin to move in a new direction, whatever that may look like. Sympathy can be disarming yet suffocating. It surrounds the object of sympathy in a metaphorical cocoon, rather than engaging them regarding the reality of the situation. There is nothing wrong with sympathy or being a sympathetic person, but in a spiritual care conversation, sympathy can stunt any possible growth or change before it has even begun.

According to Covey, listening occurs on five levels. The first level, which can barely be regarded as listening is ignoring.[9] In other words, the speaker's words are "going in one ear and out the other." The second level is pretend listening, which consists of nods, gestures, maybe even small words of encouragement, but the listener is not actually present to the speaker.[10] The third level is selective listening, where we listen to only certain parts of the conversation.[11] Dr. Covey uses the example of listening to a preschool child who is constantly chattering away.[12] The fourth level is attentive listening, where the listener is attentive and focused, expending energy in listening to the speaker's words.[13] This differs from empathetic listening in that one is listening from their own point of reference, their own autobiography, as Covey refers to it.[14] They are not placing themselves in the shoes of the speaker. The last level is empathetic listening. In empathetic listening, you are seeking to truly understand the other person. You are paying attention, not only with your ears, but your eyes are attuned to the body language of the speaker, and your heart, your "third ear," is actively engaged as well. You're listening, as Covey says, "for feeling, for meaning, [...] for behavior. You use your right brain as well as your left. You sense, you intuit, you feel."[15]

Covey provides a great summary of the importance of empathetic listening by saying,

> Empathic listening is so powerful because it gives you accurate data to work with. Instead of projecting your own autobiography and assuming thoughts, feelings, motives, and interpretation, you're dealing with the reality inside another person's head and heart. You're listening to understand. You're focused on receiving the deep communication of another human soul.[16]

I must take issue with the late Dr. Covey in one part of his analysis of empathetic listening. In his discussion, he denigrates the role of active and reflective listening in conversation. While he may have a valid point for the business or organizational structures of his experience, active/reflective listening is the bedrock of pastoral caregiving. He argues that when one does this, they listen "with an intent to reply, to control, to manipulate."[17] In the context of pastoral care, he could not be further from the truth. Active and reflective listening is done by a chaplain so that we can confirm or alter our initial assessment. For example, after a significant piece of the conversation, asking a patient, "So, I hear you saying that you are [angry, concerned, afraid, etc.]" You are making sure that your assessments are accurate, and that what you are seeing, hearing, and intuiting matches what is going on inside the patient. I agree that it is not a skill that you want to overuse, for an entire conversation of questions would feel more like an interrogation instead of a caring, pastoral conversation.

Another important aspect of listening in a pastoral conversation is trusting one's intuition. For those in the Christian tradition, I would call it listening to the leading of the Holy Spirit. Some of us are more naturally intuitive than others. Like so many other skills, intuition can be developed with time, attention, and practice. Intuition sounds like a rather nebulous term at first, but it is a skill we use all the time in our personal and professional lives. For example, when we hear that slight change in our partner's voice that indicates annoyance or good humor, or we hear something slightly off in the voice of a good friend over the telephone, or notice the sag of our colleague's shoulders indicating that something is weighing on them. These are all examples of how we naturally use our intuition.

This is because we are naturally wired for intuition. Our eyes receive the data of the world around us. Our eyes even manage to fill in blanks of which we might not even be aware. The information then goes to the brain for interpretation and categorization. The data we receive is interpreted in a myriad of ways through the different parts of the brain. Here, I am drawing on the work of Andrew Lester, professor of Pastoral Care at Brite Divinity School, who is drawing on the work of Dr. Joseph LeDoux, a professor of neuroscience at New York University and the author of several popular books on the brain. He speaks about the rational or "thinking brain" represented by the prefrontal cortex, and the emotional brain, represented by the amygdala and limbic system.[18] There is also evidence of a circuit constituted by the prefrontal cortex and the hippocampus, which is where our episodic memory is stored.[19] Of course, the interactions between these two systems or circuits are far too complex to be covered in this short chapter.

In essence, we see things, interpret them, and have emotional reactions to them within milliseconds, for example, when we react emotionally and physically to a particularly sad scene in a film or when we feel the joy of seeing relatives after a long absence. All of this is to say that our bodies are incredible, as Scripture says, we are "wonderfully made" and our brains are designed to give us these intuitive "hits" and/or "nudges" in our conversations with patients so that we can be the best possible pastoral caregivers.[20]

Theologically speaking, these intuitive hits and nudges can be guided and/or supplemented by the work of the Holy Spirit. It reminds me of a story about the prophet Elijah. Elijah is fleeing from pursuers sent by King Ahab and Queen Jezebel.[21] He flees into the wilderness and asks God to take his life, lest the forces of the royal couple take it from him. An angel of the Lord, a representation of God's presence, provides food and drink for Elijah. Elijah then travels to Mount Horeb, a particularly important place in the Judeo-Christian tradition, for it is where Moses received the Ten Commandments. Elijah is spending the night in a cave, and he hears God speaking to him, asking, "What are you doing here, Elijah?" Elijah answers, in essence, "I have done what you have asked and yet, here I am alone and pursued by those who wish to kill me!" Elijah hears God tell him to go outside because the Lord is about to pass by. This is how it is described (emphasis mine), "Now there was a great wind, so strong that it was splitting mountains and breaking rocks in pieces before the Lord, but the Lord was not in the wind; and after the wind an earthquake, but the Lord was not in the earthquake; and after the earthquake a fire, but the Lord was not in the fire; and after the fire *a sound of sheer silence.*" This sound of sheer silence is alternatively translated as a gentle whisper or my favorite, a still, small voice. God was not in the great fire, the great wind, or in the earthquake, but in a still, small voice, a gentle whisper, or the sound of sheer silence. That still, small voice and that gentle whisper continue to speak to us today.

My intuition is by no means perfect. I once visited a young woman. Ms. B. was a teacher who was concerned with the amount of time that she was having to take off work to diagnose and treat a persistent medical issue. These absences from work greatly disturbed her and made her concerned for her job, though it was clear that she loved and took pride in her work. We talked about her job, her life, and her faith journey. Towards the middle of the conversation I heard that voice say, "Put your burdens in my hands." I heard it clearly in my heart and soul, but I shook it off. As we continued the conversation, I heard the same thing a few minutes later. Again, I shook it off, thinking, "This woman is going to think I'm nuts." Finally, as our conversation was beginning to meander to its conclusion, I said, "What would it be like for you, if you put these concerns and worries in God's hands?" She said that she had really needed to hear something like that, and I could tell in her expression, posture, and manner that she was much more relaxed. We prayed and I asked that God provide a clear diagnosis and treatment, and that God would lift these burdens from her so she could concentrate on getting better and going back to her students. That was the first time I trusted myself in a real way, when I listened to that still, small voice, that intuitive hit, and it made a profound impact on the visit. No one is perfect at this, but God has given you these wonderful and beautiful gifts of hearing, listening, interpreting, and intuiting so that you can be a blessing to your patients and provide the best pastoral care possible.

How We Listen: Practical Skills in Caring Conversations

In the practice of pastoral care and chaplaincy, listening is a whole-body experience. It happens not only through what we hear, but also what we see. One thing we should do when we enter a room is to observe what is present and who is present with the patient. Does the patient have flowers or balloons sent from friends or family? Do they have personal items in the room with them, pictures, books or magazines, even a Bible? These objects that we observe may not only serve as jumping-off points to begin a conversation with the patient, but may also help the chaplain establish a rapport with them. This rapport will help the chaplain be as successful as possible in their provision of care. For example, on a certain visit, I established rapport with a patient by noticing the book she was reading, a book by a popular mystery and thriller author I also happen to enjoy. Through this connection, we went on to talk about her health journey, her important relationships, and the meaning religion and spirituality held in her life. Of course, it is possible I could have established rapport with the patient another way, but even the simplest of observations may lead to important intuitions and nudges from the Holy.

As we all do, I approach listening from my own experiences and social location. I am an introvert in a very extroverted profession. I have known many wonderful and talented extroverted chaplains and can see how both introverts and extroverts have both blessings and challenges when it comes to listening in a clinical situation. As a Christian, I am reminded of the admonition from the Epistle of James to "be quick to listen and slow to speak," but this places certain limitations on your provision of care.[22] In some situations, especially situations of crisis (codes, deaths, perinatal losses), speaking is necessary.

One must inject oneself into the situation in a caring but solid manner. It is impossible to have a ministry of presence if no one is even aware of your presence! However, more extroverted chaplains may tend to speak too much, which can sometimes result in the chaplain inserting their proverbial foot in their mouth. Thus, we cannot be so circumspect that we have no impact or so gregarious that we end up doing more harm than good in the situation. I believe, however, that there is a powerful and necessary middle road. For introverts, it behooves us to take hold of our pastoral authority and to use it more powerfully and intentionally to engage with the persons in our care. For extroverts, it is a call to use that wonderful gift of gregariousness with more precision and focus.

After one has observed the situation into which they are entering, several useful skills can be used throughout the pastoral conversation. In this effort, I lean on the work of Rev. Robert Kidd, System Director for Spiritual Care and Values Integration at Houston Methodist Hospital. These skills are useful in continuing the conversation and encouraging the patient to express their feelings, needs, and concerns. For the chaplain, the skills help to make sure that they are accurately hearing what is being communicated by the patient, and not making unhelpful or even harmful assumptions.

One of the simplest and most intuitive of these skills is what Kidd refers to as minimal encouragement, or "tell me more." These can include head nods, hand gestures to continue, and small utterances like "mm-hmm," "I see," or "tell me more about that."[23] This is something most of us do naturally in everyday conversation, but being aware of it can help encourage the patient to continue without shining the conversational spotlight back onto the chaplain. This skill, if not overused, demonstrates to the patient that the chaplain is present and interested in what they are saying to him/her. The chaplain can help light the conversational fuse with the use of open-ended questions. An open-ended question is one that cannot be answered with a simple "yes" or "no" response.[24] The overuse of Yes/No questions can turn a pastoral encounter into a perceived interrogation or inquisition of the patient by the chaplain. Conversely, questions such as "How does that make you feel?," "How has your faith been a support to you in this time?," or "What kind of support are you receiving from family or friends since you've been here?" are questions that invite the patient to look inside themselves and to express thoughts or feelings they might not even know they had until they were asked.

A skill that allows the chaplain to check their own understanding of the conversation is the use of paraphrasing: taking a sustained part of the conversation and sharing it with the patient as the chaplain understands it.[25] For example, a patient expresses through a protracted narrative that they have been having a difficult time relating to their sister since they have been ill. The chaplain could respond, "What I'm hearing is that you are having difficulty communicating with your sister since this diagnosis. Are there other family members who would be a better support for you?" This allows the patient to either affirm the chaplain's reading of the conversation ("Yeah, this diagnosis has been really tough on our relationship, maybe my brother would be more helpful.") or to correct the chaplain's misunderstanding ("Even though it's a strain, my sister is still my best helper. I can always count on her!").

One of the most useful skills is that of reflecting, or naming the feeling in the room.[26] For example, the patient expresses to you multiple times or in different ways throughout the pastoral conversation that they are not feeling heard by the nursing staff.

The chaplain may offer a statement like, "I'm hearing that you are frustrated with the nursing staff on the unit," or more specifically, "I'm hearing that you are not feeling very listened to by the staff today." This communicates to the patient and/or family that their feelings are heard and honored by the chaplain. Sometimes, it is more helpful to be more general in naming the feeling than being overly specific, and the patient will correct you if you are off in your analysis of the situation.

Another useful skill is what Rev. Kidd refers to as hovering: approaching an important topic of conversation and keeping the focus there.[27] It is especially useful in situations of grief and loss or emotionally charged subjects.[28] For example, when supporting a grieving family during a death, it might be useful for them to share memories of their loved one. The chaplain can say something like, "It is obvious from seeing all of you that Mr. C. was deeply loved. Would any of you like to share some of your favorite memories of him?" The chaplain can help facilitate this sharing for the benefit of the family and to help them begin to process their loss. If one member begins to go too far afield, the chaplain can bring it back to the subject at hand in a caring and delicate way.

One hybrid skill that combines these conversational aspects with observations is calling attention to something.[29] An example might be when the chaplain observes something like a tear and brings attention to it to delve into the underlying emotion. This skill is most useful once a rapport has been established between the chaplain and patient, and may be off-putting in an initial visit. The chaplain can ask, "What is behind that tear?" or "You've mentioned your siblings and your husband, but not your brother, is there a reason for that?" This invites the patient to further explain and to ventilate their feelings on an important subject.

One last skill is that of summarizing. I have found it to be particularly useful at the end of a visit. It hits the high points of what has been discussed during the visit and opens possibilities for future conversations. One of the most effective uses I have found for it is in a closing prayer, if the patient is open to receiving it. In the prayer, you name the things that have been discussed. For example, if the patient has expressed distance with a certain family member and a desire to heal that rift, you could pray that God would bring healing to that relationship. This shows that you are engaged with the patient and that they have been deeply heard and their needs are respected.

Integration of Listening Skills in Spiritual Assessment

At this point, one might think, "Well, if I use these skills, then I have done my job!" These skills, however, are best used in the service of a spiritual assessment. This is where one uses both the art and science of chaplaincy to get the most out of an interaction with a patient. It is only through using these skills of reflecting, hovering, paraphrasing, calling attention to things, and summarizing that one can make a holistic and spiritual assessment of the patient's situation and put themselves in position to provide the best possible care. It is the use of open-ended questions and being present and attentive to the answers that follow that allows for a thorough spiritual assessment. In this analysis, I will be using three spiritual assessment models: 1) D.W. Donovan's 4 L's of looking, language, leads, and learnings; 2) Rev. Dr. Brent Peery's Outcome Oriented Chaplaincy assessment model, which evaluates the patient's needs, hopes, and resources spiritually, emotionally, relationally, and biomedically and; 3) George Fitchett's more comprehensive 7 x 7 model.[30]

Regarding the first model, Donovan's 4 Ls, one observes (looking) and listens (language) in the conversation for people, groups, or ideas that are very meaningful to the patient. The chaplain, using the above skills, helps the patient expound on those meaningful relationships or ideas. The leads are those flickers or intuitions a chaplain develops that help them go deeper with the patient. Lastly, from the conversation, what are the most important aspects (learnings) that need to be shared with the interdisciplinary care team to facilitate the patient's healing in all aspects of life?

As to the Rev. Dr. Peery's Outcome Oriented Chaplaincy model of assessment, your skills will serve you well in asking the best questions to obtain the answer you are seeking from the patient. Regarding the patient's spiritual needs, hopes, and resources, you can ask questions like, "How has your faith been a support to you since you've been in the hospital?" or "Have you received a call from your pastor/priest/rabbi/imam or a member of your community of faith?" These answers might also flow naturally throughout the conversation.

As to their emotional needs, hopes, and resources, one can observe physical signs or clues to the patient's emotional state, e.g., high blood pressure, agitation, or the patient's expression. You can gently call attention to what you observe and invite the patient to share their perspective. Observation can also be helpful in assessing the patient's relational needs, hopes, and resources, especially when family or friends are present. This is because they can share with the chaplain another person's perspective, but you also must be aware that they might have their own agenda that might color what they share with you. Through the conversation, you can pick out names that are mentioned often or not mentioned at all, which may be an invitation to dig deeper and to engage one's sacred intuition about where to go conversationally. The patient's biomedical needs might not be readily apparent, but as they do arise, they can be immensely helpful to the interdisciplinary care team so they can give the patient the best care possible.

George Fitchett's 7 x 7 model is much more comprehensive and looks at the patient from a social, psychological, and spiritual perspective over many dimensions. All the above skills will be needed to engage the patient on this level. The first dimension is medical, and how the patient's past and current diagnoses may impact their well-being and functioning.[31] The second dimension is psychological and asks if the patient has any psychological conditions and/or is undergoing any treatments that may impact his/her personality or general disposition.[32] The third dimension concerns the patient's family system and how the patient's current situation is influenced by current or past relationships in their family of origin.[33] The fourth dimension is the psychosocial dimension and concerns the patient's social context, especially any current or past crises that may impact that patient's life, both now and going forward.[34] The fifth is ethnic/cultural and asks if or how the patient's ethnicity and/or cultural values and traditions influence their spiritual identity.[35] The sixth is the social issues dimension, which asks if there are any societal issues or issues of social justice that might affect the patient's sense of well-being and overall functioning.[36]

Then, we move into the spiritual side of the assessment. The first spiritual dimension is beliefs and meaning, which asks how the patient finds meaning or purpose in their life.[37] The second dimension is vocation and consequences, which asks what are the duties, responsibilities, or obligations the patient feels they are called to fulfill.[38] The third dimension is experience and emotion, which asks if the patient has had any encounters with the demonic or the divine and how that interaction affected them and influenced their spirituality, and what is the predominant affect of the patient's spirituality.[39] The fourth spiritual dimension is courage and growth, which asks if the patient can engage spiritual challenges and doubts, which leads to growth and transformation.[40] The fifth dimension is ritual and practice, which inquires about what rituals and practices are most meaningful to the patient or best express their calling or vocation.[41] The sixth dimension is community and asks what groups of shared beliefs, meaning, rituals, and practices the patient belongs to and how these communities affect the patient's well-being.[42] The last dimension is authority and guidance, and asks in whom or in what does the patient find the authority for their beliefs, values, meaning, sense of vocation, rituals, and practices, especially in difficult times, and where does the patient turn for guidance, comfort, and hope.[43]

This model is much more in-depth but is also a natural outgrowth of the other models. By using one's listening skills when discussing issues of faith, one can pick up on many important pieces of the spiritual side of the assessment. In addition, a conversation about the patient's emotional, relational, and biomedical needs, hopes, and resources will inform the holistic arm of the assessment. Your listening skills and the compassion and empathy you bring to the pastoral conversation will guide you in asking the right questions in the right way so you can get the fullest picture of the patient in the limited time you have to care for each patient. The best way to hone these skills is to practice them. All these things, listening skills and assessment models, are tools in a chaplain's toolbox. Initially you might be floundering, looking for the right tool for the right moment. However, the more experience you gain and the more you practice these skills, the more they will become innate. They will become a part of you, and you will become, as my supervisor used to say, unconsciously competent. The most important thing you can do is to be open and to treat each patient as a unique individual created in the image of the Sacred. Open yourself to them and their unique story and use your tools and you will be an effective chaplain. I pray for God's blessing on you and your journey.

———————————————

1 Brené Brown, *Braving the Wilderness: The Quest for True Belonging and the Courage to Stand Alone* (New York, NY: Random House, 2019), 83.

2 All names have been changed in the interest of privacy.

3 Anton T. Boisen, *The Exploration of the Inner World: a Study of Mental Disorder and Religious Experience* (Chicago, IL: Willett, Clark, and Company, 1936). The term is coined in this work.

4 Carl Ransom Rogers, "The Necessary and Sufficient Conditions of Therapeutic Personality Change," *Journal of Consulting and Clinical Psychology*, 21: 1957: 95.

5 APA Dictionary of Psychology https://dictionary.apa.org/unconditional-positive-regard

6 Genesis 1:27 (NRSV).

7 Stephen R. Covey, *The 7 Habits of Highly Effective People* (New York, NY: Simon & Schuster, 2020), 278.

8 Ibid., 278.

9 Ibid., 278.

10 Ibid., 278.

11 Ibid., 278.

12 Ibid., 278.

13 Ibid., 278.

14 Ibid., 277.

15 Ibid., 278.

16 Ibid., 279.

17 Ibid., 278.

18 Andrew D. Lester, *The Angry Christian: A Theology for Care and Counseling* (Louisville, KY: Westminster John Knox Press, 2003), 78-79.

19 Ming Li, Cheng Long, and Li Yang, "Hippocampal-Prefrontal Circuit and Disrupted Functional Connectivity in Psychiatric and Neurodegenerative Disorders," *BioMed Research International 2015* (March 31, 2015): 1-10, https://doi.org/10.1155/2015/810548, 5-6.

20 Psalm 139:14 (NRSV).

21 1 Kings 19:1-12 (NRSV).

22 James 1:19 (NRSV).

23 Robert A. Kidd, "Foundational Listening and Responding Skills," in *Professional Spiritual & Pastoral Care*, ed. Stephen B. Roberts (Woodstock: Skylight Paths Publishers, 2012), 99.

24 Ibid., 97.

25 Ibid., 96.

26 Ibid., 95.

27 Ibid., 101.

28 Ibid., 101.

29 Ibid., 101.

30 D.W. Donovan, "Assessments," in *Professional Spiritual & Pastoral Care*, ed. Stephen B. Roberts (Woodstock: Skylight Paths Publishers, 2012), 47.; Rev. Dr. Brent Peery, "Outcome Oriented Chaplaincy: Intentional Caring," in *Professional Spiritual & Pastoral Care*, ed. Stephen B. Roberts (Woodstock: Skylight Paths Publishers, 2012); George Fitchett, *Assessing Spiritual Needs: A Guide for Caregivers* (Lima, OH: Academic Renewal Press, 2002), 42-50.

31 Fitchett, *Assessing Spiritual Needs*, 43.

32 Ibid., 43-44.

33 Ibid., 44.

34 Ibid., 44.

35 Ibid, 44.

36 Ibid., 44.

37 Ibid., 45.

38 Ibid., 46.

39 Ibid., 47.

40 Ibid., 48.

41 Ibid., 48-49.

42 Ibid., 49.

43 Ibid., 49-50.

5

DANCING WITH MODELS OF
SPIRITUAL ASSESSMENT

Luis Elier Rodriguez
Manager, System Clinical Pastoral Education,
Houston Methodist

IN RECENT YEARS, the process of making a spiritual assessment has proved to have incalculable value in medical/hospital, spiritual, and therapeutic contexts. Professional chaplains, spiritual counselors, and spiritual directors have differentiated themselves from other disciplines that contribute to a climate of effective and collaborative interdisciplinary care. Through this differentiation, spiritual assessment has been found to be a helpful process for patients, families, and staff from all different backgrounds and faiths. Also, more and more studies are revealing that the patient's spirituality is a significant resource in their recovery process. However, we must continue working to demonstrate this differentiation between the one or two questions asked when the patient is admitted to the hospital or when someone from the medical staff wants to explore a basic spiritual dimension of the patient and a more complex spiritual assessment performed by a specialist.[1] The following definition of spirituality helps us in this process of dealing with such a complex dimension of life and with the challenge of making an appropriate spiritual assessment: "Spirituality is the aspect of humanity that refers to the way individuals seek and express meaning and purpose and the way they experience their connectedness to the moment, to self, to others, to nature, and to the significant or sacred."[2]

According to Gowri Anandarajah, human beings are complex, with physical, mental, and spiritual aspects. Suffering can result from issues pertaining to any of these interrelated aspects. This means we must develop a good understanding of how to assess spirituality in our interventions as spiritual caregivers. To provide effective care surrounding this significant aspect of our shared humanity, it is necessary to establish differences between spiritual screenings, spiritual histories, and spiritual assessments. Below is a summary of each using the metaphor of dancing, like being a dancer on the dance floor using different models of steps according to the rhythm and circumstances of the dancers on the dance floor.

Dancing with Spiritual Screening

In spiritual screening, one or two questions are asked that are designed to elicit basic preferences and identify any obvious distress that warrants follow-up. This is often completed at admission or by lay ministers. In spiritual screening, triage-level care requires very little spiritual knowledge or expertise. For example, one question can be: "What is your faith tradition or your community of faith?"

Spiritual screening employs a few simple questions, which can be asked by any health care professional in the course of an overall screening. Often the questions are focused on identifying those who want to see a professional chaplain.

1. Is religion/spirituality important to you as you cope with your illness? (Yes/No)
2. (If Yes to #1) How much strength/comfort do you get from your religion/spirituality right now?
   A. All that I need,
   B. Somewhat less than I need,
   C. Much less than I need,
   D. None at all.

Answers C or D should trigger an automatic referral to chaplaincy.

The role of the professional chaplain in setting up the screening process is to educate the medical staff about why these questions are important and how to make referrals. All good screening questions are designed so that they can be administered by anyone on the team without any special training, and these questions fall into that category. In institutions with electronic medical records, it is often possible to program the system so the chaplain referral is made automatically and electronically as soon as the appropriate questions are answered in the screening tool.[3]

Dancing with Spiritual History

In this process, we collect the patient's basic spiritual or religious story. It can be completed by an MD, RN, or other healthcare professional. The traditional models of assessing the patient's spiritual history are known by the acronyms of FICA and HOPE.

FICA is a model developed by Christina Puchalski of the George Washington University Institute for Spirituality and Health. This model can be useful for doctors, nurses, social workers, and other medical personnel. The medical staff can use this model to refer their patients to chaplains or other spiritual resources at the hospital for follow-up, or to open doors for spiritual conversation with patients by identifying spiritual aspects of the patient and spiritual needs. It is not surprising that every day more clinicians find that inquiry into the spiritual beliefs of patients opens the door to conversations about many issues the patients may be experiencing concerning family, work, faith, depression, or anxiety. These models are short, easy, versatile, and focused. Let's start with FICA's four components:

The FICA Assessment [4]

F(aith)
- What is your faith or belief?
- Do you consider yourself spiritual or religious?
- What things do you believe in that give meaning to your life?

I(mportance)
- Is faith important in your life?
- What influence does it have on how you take care of yourself?
- How have your beliefs influenced your behavior during your illness?
- What role do your beliefs play in regaining your health?

C(ommunity)
- Are you part of a spiritual or religious community?
- Is this of support to you, and how?
- Is there a person or group of people you really love or who are really important to you?

A(ddress):
- How would you like me, your health care provider, to address these issues in your care?

Another model of spiritual history is the HOPE assessment developed by Gowri Anandarajah at the Brown University School of Medicine. She made this assessment with the understanding that the majority of the population in the United States believes in God, that physicians should consider their patients' spiritual needs, and that many patients believe that physicians should inquire about spiritual and religious beliefs more.[5] She developed this model with the understanding that spirituality is interrelated with three significant aspects of life, the cognitive, experiential, and behavioral aspects.

1. *Cognitive aspects* have to do with the way we make sense of the world around us. They include the big picture questions such as: "What is the nature of the universe?" "Is there a God?" "Why do bad things happen to good people?" "What happens after death?" "What beliefs and values are most important to me?"
2. *Experiential aspects* have to do with connection and inner resilience. They encompass questions such as: "Am I alone or am I connected to something bigger?" "Am I able to give and receive love?" "Do I feel an inner sense of peace and resilience?" "Can I find hope in this difficult situation?"
3. *Behavioral aspects* have to do with ways in which a person's spiritual beliefs and inner spiritual state affect his or her behavior and life choices.[6]

Here is the model she created, which I recommend as a basic model of how to obtain the spiritual history of others. Using this model can create a basic spiritual screening to know more about the patient's history regarding spirituality and can open the door for basic dialogue regarding spirituality.

The HOPE Assessment

H (spiritual resources)
- What are your sources of hope, meaning, and comfort?
- What do you hold onto during difficult times?

O (organized religion)
- Are you a part of a religious or spiritual community?

P (personal spirituality/practices)
- What aspects of your spirituality or spiritual practices do you find most helpful to yourself personally?

E (effects on care)
- Has being sick affected your ability to do the things that usually help your spirituality?

Dancing with Spiritual Assessments

Spiritual assessment is a detailed process of listening to, interpreting, and exploring spiritual needs and resources. This type of assessment is usually completed by a professional chaplain trained in CPE, CPE students, or spiritual professional counselors or psychotherapists.

It is extremely important to clarify that only some professional personnel traditionally trained in Clinical Pastoral Education can complete professional spiritual assessments, due to their complexity. The consequences of not being trained and relying only on a good motivation to provide spiritual care can include harming the patient emotionally and spiritually because there would be a high risk of not listening and imposing ideas without exploring the internal and external resources of the patient.

Hospital administrators need to know this because it is one of the fundamental differences between a lay minister or other healthcare professional, and a professional chaplain or Clinical Pastoral Education student. Basic spiritual care such as bringing presence, listening skills, and compassion to each encounter can be provided by physicians and volunteers. However more complex issues will require the expertise of well-trained spiritual care caregivers such as chaplains trained in Clinical Pastoral Education, especially assessing patients in a hospital setting.

This distinction is important because it can be very easy to fall into the trend of developing a volunteer program with the notion that they are offering spiritual care as if they were professional chaplains or spiritual counselors. This may give the false impression that chaplains or spiritual caregivers without proper training can be sufficient. Hospital administrators should be made aware that they must not fall into that trend.

Another aspect exacerbating this situation is that many chaplaincy programs offering certification or specialization are unaccredited or lack Clinical Pastoral Education units. In the United States and Canada, I always recommend that if the student is going to invest the time, money, and effort to get a chaplaincy degree, they should do so in an accredited institution, otherwise it would be a bad investment.

To summarize: providing spiritual care requires knowledge of the basic questions of spirituality and an understanding of how to collect data on a person's spiritual history, as well as skills in observing, listening, interpreting, and verifying what would be the best approach in terms of a spiritual intervention. It is extremely important that Clinical Pastoral Education programs, training of lay ministers, and theological seminary programs utilize more creativity here. Especially now—when training programs in hospitals are proliferating and it is expected that by 2050 more than one-quarter of North American citizens will not have any religious affiliation—it is crucial to be prepared to utilize spiritual care creatively and select models of spiritual interventions that are more relevant for each role, whether that of certified chaplain, professional healthcare provider, lay minister, or volunteer.

Later I want to share some spiritual assessment models. These methods are related to how we confront life with its celebrations and sufferings. Each of them has its strengths and weaknesses and the professional chaplain, spiritual caregiver, or CPE student must identify which is the most relevant and useful, depending on their context and circumstances, as well as the needs of patients and their family.

In the spiritual assessment model, we identify any related spiritually significant components, such as those Anandarajah identified (cognitive, experiential, and behavioral aspects), but we add details such as observation and analysis of areas such as psychological, sociological, theological, personal meaning, and spiritual aspects. Using multiple disciplines, we make our intervention a constellation of possibilities holding spiritual implications. For this reason, in the verbatim form or case report in CPE, we usually include the following aspects:[7]

1. *Psychological concerns*: What is the level of emotional awareness/expressivity? What are the major needs or conflicts (expressed and not expressed)? What is the level of insight and self-awareness? What is the person's self-image? Is what the patient tells you about himself/herself congruent with what you experienced? Where is the power/control in the patient's life (internal/external)? What part of themselves are they

not experiencing? Did they relate to you as a person of higher, lower, or equal status?

2. *Sociological concerns*: How does the patient relate to the hospital environment? How does the nursing and medical staff relate to the patient? Is there a supportive community surrounding the patient? What sort of environment will the patient be returning to?

3. *Theological concerns*: What are the central life issues for the patient? What is the patient's ultimate concern? What is the key concept this patient attempted to communicate to you? Who is God to this patient? How does this patient experience God? Did you witness/experience God's presence in the patient? Did you witness/experience any understanding of grace, providence, repentance, forgiveness, resurrection, reverence, hope, fellowship, etc. in the patient's life? If the patient were to preach a sermon, meditation, devotional, reflection, what would it look like? What is the meaning and significance of life (and illness) for this patient? Did the patient situation parallel any Biblical characters or themes?

4. *Spiritual assessment*: Provide a spiritual assessment of the patient and how this assessment was informed by your understanding of the patient's current hospital admission and all that it entails.

5. *Personal meaning*: What personal meaning did you derive from this visit? What connections did you make to your own faith/personal journey that informed your visit?

These questions make it easier for the spiritual care student in training to reflect on their action, reflection, and return to action with new paradigms and understandings of spiritual care.

It is very important to understand that in our spiritual interventions we must have comprehensive tools to strengthen our interventions, especially a desire to learn, to increase our flexibility, and to listen to others deeply. These questions also help us to use our knowledge related to human behavior and the behavioral sciences.

Below I will mention some models of spiritual assessment so we can select the most practical and prudent one depending on the type of interventions we are making. I will start with the model presented by Paul Pruyser, who despite being a therapist, helped us to find our identity as spiritual caregivers in an interdisciplinary atmosphere. His book, *The Minister as Diagnostician*, provides a good start on to how to do a spiritual assessment from a pastoral and spiritual perspective.

Dancing With Paul Pruyser's Spiritual Assessment Model

Pruyser was a pioneer regarding spiritual assessment models even though he was a psychotherapist. In his book, *The Minister as Diagnostician*, he recommends seven themes:

1. *Awareness of the Holy (and the unholy)*: What is sacred to this patient? Do they present themselves as one who is ultimately dependent on a power or mystery beyond themselves?
2. *Providence*: Does the patient perceive a divine purpose in their life? Do they believe that their world is ultimately benevolent or friendly? Do they possess or lack a sense of basic trust in the world?
3. *Faith*: Is the patient's attitude life-negating or life-affirming?

4. *Grace*: Can the patient accept kindness, generosity, and self-acceptance, or do they insist on the finality of their self-rejection?

5. *Repentance*: Does the patient have an awareness of themselves as an agent in the problem that they face? Do they shoulder the appropriate responsibility for their situation?

6. *Communion*: Does the patient feel like an actual participant in the groups with whom they interact (family, friends, fellow faith members)?

7. *Vocation*: Is the patient a cheerful participant in the scheme of creation such that they have a sense of purpose and dedication? Do they have a sense of personal competence and effectiveness? Do they experience passion in their life and ministry?

Pruyser presents the following questions to guide the chaplain's discussion with the patient to help determine specific needs for spiritual care:

1. Awareness of the Holy
   - What, if anything, is sacred, revered?
   - Any experiences of awe or bliss, when, in what situations?
   - Any sense of mystery, of anything transcendent?
   - Any sense of humility, awareness of own limitations?
   - Any idolatry, reverence displaced to improper symbols?
2. Providence
   - What is God's intention toward me?
   - What has God promised me?
   - Belief in cosmic benevolence?
   - Related to capacity for trust?

- The extent of hoping versus wishing?
3. Faith
    - Affirming versus negating stance in life?
    - Able to commit self, to engage?
4. Grace
    - Kindness, generosity, the beauty of giving and receiving?
    - No felt need for grace or gratefulness?
    - The desire for, versus resistance to, blessing?
5. Repentance (the process of change from crookedness to rectitude)
    - A sense of agency in one's own problems or one's response to them, versus being a victim, versus being too sorry for debatable sins?
    - Feelings of contrition, remorse, regret?
    - Willingness to do penance?
6. Communion
    - Feelings of kinship with the whole chain of being?
    - Feeling embedded or estranged, united or separated in the world, in relations with one's faith group, one's church?
7. Sense of vocation
    - Willingness to be a cheerful participant in creation?
    - Signs of zest, vigor, liveliness, dedication?
    - Aligned with divine benevolence or malevolence?
    - Humorous and inventive involvement in life versus grim and dogmatic?

The following is an example of how one of my students used Pruyser's guidelines in her intervention, in her own words:

Spiritual Assessment:

1. Patient demonstrates an awareness of the Holy. She speaks of praying, of having faith and belief.

2. Providence: For J., God is punishing and testing, and she doesn't feel like God hears her prayers. There's not a sense that she trusts God because she fears the possible outcomes of this illness.

3. Faith: J. expresses belief in God, but her faith does not seem to be empowering for her.

4. Grace or Gratefulness: J. is able to express gratitude for family and for friends and for the care she has received in the hospital. This is a strength for her and a possible avenue for spiritual healing and hope.

5. Repentance: While J. feels that she is being punished for something, her circular reasoning about the cause for testing or punishing is unclear. She says she feels guilty for not being able to be with her family. An exploration of the source of that guilt could be an avenue for repentance and forgiveness.

6. Communion: J is connected with family and friends, but her hospitalization leaves her isolated from them. I did not discern whether she was connected to an organized religious community.

7. Sense of vocation: J.'s primary purpose for herself appears to be involvement with and care for her family. She stated a desire to return to work, but that appeared to be for the financial support to care for her family rather than for the work itself. There does not appear to be a sense of connection to a greater purpose and how her care for her family connects with the rest of the world.

Brief Interpretation:

Patient is understandably self-focused, given the length and severity of her illness. Cultivating a sense of connection to the world beyond the hospital could help draw her out of the whirlpool that she seems to be drowning in.

The weakness of this model is that you have a perception in purely Christian terms. This makes the model less effective in making spiritual assessments of patients of other creeds and faiths. It can, however, be very useful for Christian patients.

Dancing with George Fitchett's 7 x 7 Spiritual Assessment Model

Another model of spiritual assessment is presented by George Fitchett in his book *Assessing Spiritual Needs*.[8] He called it the "7 by 7 Model for Spiritual Assessment," distributing significant components in two dimensions: the holistic and spiritual assessment. As the following information will illustrate, his model is a good contribution for chaplains to consider in their spiritual interactions. He explains in detail:

Holistic Assessment:

1. *Medical dimension*: What significant medical problems has the person had in the past? What problems do they have now? What treatment is the person receiving?
2. *Psychological dimension*: Are there any significant psychological problems? Are they being treated? If so, how?
3. *Family system dimension*: Are there at present, or have there been in the past, patterns within the person's relationships with other family members which have contributed to or perpetuated present problems?

4. *Psycho-social dimension*: What is the person's life history, including place of birth and childhood home, family of origin, education, and work history, and other important activities and relationships. What is the person's present living situation and what are the financial resources?

5. *Ethnic, racial, or cultural dimension*: What is the person's racial, ethnic, or cultural background? How does it contribute to the person's way of addressing any current concerns?

6. *Social issues dimension*: Are the person's present problems created by or compounded by larger social problems?

7. *Spiritual dimension*: How the person find meaning and relate with the Divinity?

Spiritual Dimension:

1. *Belief and meaning*: What beliefs does the person have that give meaning and purpose to their life? What major symbols reflect or express meaning for this person? What is the person's story? Is the person presently or have they in the past been affiliated with a formal system belief?

2. *Vocation and obligation*: What are the person's beliefs and sense of meaning or duty, vocation, calling, or moral obligation? Will any current problems cause conflict or compromise in their perception of their ability to fulfill these duties?

3. *Experience and emotion*: What direct contacts with the sacred, divine, or demonic has the person had? What emotions or moods are predominantly associated with these contacts and with the person's beliefs, meaning in life, and associated sense of vocation?

4. *Courage and growth*: Can the person let go of existing beliefs and symbols in order to allow new ones to emerge?

5. *Ritual and practice*: What are the rituals and practices associated with the person's beliefs and meaning in life? Will current problems, if any, cause a change in the rituals or practices they feel are required or in their ability to perform them?

6. *Community*: Is the person part of one or more formal or informal communities of shared belief, ritual, or practice? What is the style of the person's participation in these communities?

7. *Authority and guidance*: Where does the person find the authority for their beliefs, meaning in life, for their vocation, ritual, and practices?

All spiritual assessments have strengths and weaknesses. For example, the last two (Pruyser and Fitchett) tend to have a Christian undertone. Their language of grace, vocation, and authority can be seen as part of the Christian tradition. However, I think that simply providing our patients a way to externalize their emotional and spiritual issues and to identify opportunities for reflection and learning represents an excellent opportunity for effective intervention. As David Hodge notes, by having clients or patients relate an area of prominent strength, an altered, therapeutically beneficial construction of reality is fostered. In turn, this new perception enables patients to ameliorate problems, for example by giving patients a new inner vocabulary, which depicts them as capable individuals who have the resources and abilities to solve life's complex issues.[9]

Dancing with the Existential Model of Howard Clinebell

Howard Clinebell proposed nine spiritual needs in our spiritual interventions, that are as follows:[10]

1. The need to develop a viable philosophy of life, a belief system, and living symbols that give meaning to life.
2. The need to develop creative images and values to guide our life constructively.
3. The need to have a growing relationship with and commitment to a loving God that integrates and energizes our life.
4. The need to develop the high self or soul as the center of our whole being.
5. The need to regularly renew our basic trust, in order to maintain hope in the midst of the losses and tragedies of our life.
6. The need to discover ways to move from the alienation of guilt to the reconciliation of forgiveness.
7. The need to develop ways to undergird self-esteem and reduce alienation and narcissism with an awareness of being deeply valued by God.
8. The need to have regular moments of transcendence when one experiences the eternal in the midst of time.
9. The need to belong to a caring community that nurtures and sustains our spiritual journey.

These spiritual needs identified by Clinebell can help us when we have patients who are facing existential dilemmas, human developmental crises, existential conflicts, making decisions, seeking meaning for life, and facing vulnerability, suffering, and eventual death. This model is good for getting a better awareness of the existential situation the patient is living through, and for making plans to take concrete action on their existential dilemmas and problems and opportunities in life. Also it is useful for helping to identify and recognize their paradoxes, contradictions, fear of death, and tensions in their spiritual life. In other words, it can help increase insight into our patient's current spiritual condition and assist them in making decisions they consider right. I should add that it is important to make it easier for the patient to reflect on the social and cultural factors that may be influencing their existence, especially their cultural assumptions. This model may not be suitable when the patient is low on energy, has problems verbalizing, or has cognitive challenges.

From Clinebell's perspective, spirituality enhances personal growth in the following dimensions: mind, body, spirit, relationships with others, relationship with nature, work and play life, and relationships with organization and institutions.

Another contribution of Clinebell is that he describes pathogenic or unhealthy spirituality as growth-blocking, resulting from rigidity, idolatry, authoritarianism, and practices that are life-constricting or that deny reality.

Dancing with the Spiritual Narrative Approach Model

This is a model I like to introduce to my CPE students to increase their reflection.[11] It can be used as a map, guiding the spiritual caregiver and their humanity on a journey of spiritual meeting with the patient and his or her humanity, honoring both the humanity of the patient and the patient him or herself. The challenge is to hear the patient's story and determine how they see their life experience and their relationships.[12] This model represents a good opportunity to check how the other responds or wants to respond to their history. Sometimes, it could present a good opportunity for the patient to re-author their story or to reflect on a new paradigm or course of action.[13]

It is very significant to check how the history of the patient connects with the story of the helping caregiver and the importance of being aware of this dynamic. Let's see some significant components of this model using my own story:

1. *Your patient's story*: Giving people the opportunity to share their life story helps them in characterizing whatever opportunity or situation with which they are dealing. People can find their own feelings, images, metaphors, and spiritual resources. I believe that when problems or crises can be externalized, healing can take place. Let me use my own story with my son as an example of how to use this model.

   My Own Story and My Case as Your Patient

   Twenty-eight years ago, I went to the river on a holiday with my family and several friends. It was a day of relaxation, walks, and very enjoyable conversations. It was a relaxing and peaceful environment. When my second son came back, he couldn't walk. Some said he had to walk and challenged him to do it. I realized that something weird was going on and I took him on my shoulders and then put him on my back and started the journey back.

   After we got to the house, it was a while before he could walk again. In my mind, a lot of questions passed without being answered. I took him to several medical examinations, and finally the doctor called me to give me a final report. She diagnosed him with muscular dystrophy and said: "Luis, I took time out to be with you and walk with you in the middle of this news." My mind was clouded, and I didn't know where to go. I didn't know what to do or where to go on my walk. I saw people around me as cloudy without being able to distinguish them and everything became darkness in my soul. I cried many nights because I was going through moments of immense darkness of the soul.

I had to stop working because I couldn't see patients and give them spiritual care. Some people told me that maybe God was testing my faith or wanted to teach me. Inside I was very angry when I listened to such comments or pseudo-theologies. I remember when I got back to work, the hospital social worker was waiting for me and hugged me. She didn't say anything, she was silent. It was a speechless embrace, but it was of great emotional and spiritual sensitivity. It is a hug that I have not forgotten and I have valued it because it was an empathetic encounter and of great existential value.

Time has passed and when I pray, I turn to God and see God as having a handicap, as having limitations. This image helps me move forward in my pain at seeing my son, who increasingly loses his mobility and motor skills.

2. *Patient's feelings*: Your first challenge as a spiritual caregiver is to identify the feelings of your patient and to avoid trying to fix your patient's feelings. They are feelings and we don't have to pass judgment on them. I recommend identifying comfortable or uncomfortable feelings. My feelings as your patient, for example, were sadness, anger, fear, despair, and hope. This is the way your patient's story has affected their emotions. Also, you have to remind yourself that sometimes uncomfortable feelings contain elements of grief, anger, inadequacy, and helplessness. Uncomfortable feelings can be the way your patient makes meaning out of their existential crises and suffering and pain. Your role is to

legitimize your patient's feelings, to have unconditional acceptance, and to try to help them examine the unexamined in their life. As Kenneth I. Pargament said, "In the search of the sacred, people encounter the full range of emotions, positive and negative: peacefulness, gratitude, excitement, joy, awe, anger, sadness, fear, jealousy, and shame." These emotions often contain important clues about the patient's spiritual status. For example, sadness or anger can hint at sacred loss or violation; excitement and joy can point to sources of sacredness; peacefulness and calm can suggest powerful spiritual resources. Conversely, the absence of emotion often suggests spiritual disengagement.[14] We have to be reminded that for some people it is hard to express and honor emotions. It is likewise difficult to express our deepest wishes, values, and power, but especially our own emotions. Such a non-empathic response to our emotions invalidates ourselves and disavows our emotions.

3. *Spiritual caregiver's feelings*: Your challenge as a caregiver is to identify your own feelings associated with your patient's story. It is important to be aware of the powerful feelings and emotions toward your inner self and how they impact your interaction with the patient. Remember that the energy of uncomfortable feelings is not necessarily negative energy. As Miriam Greenspan says, "The energy is available to be used in some form— for good or ill." She also says energy is information. "The energy of uncomfortable feelings brings us information about the self and the world; about our past, present, or future. About our inner and outer worlds and the connections between them. The information we get

alerts us to be attentive to something important and guides us to transformational change."[15] For this reason, it is important to consider whether your encounter with your patient is a good opportunity to learn about youself and how your life story is present in your interaction with your patient.

4. *Spiritual caregiver's connection and resonance*: Your story as a caregiver and your connection/association/ identification with the story of your patient. This can be a direct expression of something that is highly valued by the spiritual caregiver or an expression of suffering or lament over the absence of something highly valued.[16] Sometimes these emotional resonances in the history of the chaplain's or counselor's life experiences reflect what the chaplain has accorded value to in his or her life history.

5. *Images*: What image or images of your patient hold your attention, for example, images of the Divine, the transcendent, and humanity? What images emerge in the spiritual conversation that describe your patient's spirituality? At times the images represent the identity that is evoked and the characterization of that which is accorded value. Do the images significantly shape my actions? Do they have a significant impact on how you deal with your patient's suffering, crisis, loss, or celebration? For example, in my case, my image of God as handicapped is not a traditional image of God and can create some theological challenges for the spiritual caregiver, but we need to remember that it has been a very meaningful image in my case.

6. *Energy*: This is about the Divine/Higher Power/ Transcendent energy present in your patient's story. The

following questions can help us to identify this important component. Where did you see the unique energy of the divine present in your patient's story? Do you identify a traditional or non-traditional way to see the divine/transcendent/higher power and humanity in your patient's story?

7. *Your patient's spiritual resources*: It is very important to verify the resources and spiritual needs of your patients. You are a facilitator of the activation of those resources to deal with any loss, violence, suffering, or celebration in life. Usually, two questions are important regarding spiritual resources. First, what specific spiritual resources does the patient use to confront life's challenges? Second, what kind of spiritual resources does the patient have available in the present to address life's current challenges or how does the patient want to cope with the present event using his/her spiritual resources?

I like to consider four different types of human and spiritual resources using this model and the implications for spiritual care:

1. *Intrapersonal spirituality (to self)*: Maturity, meaning, self-awareness, strength, wisdom, personal understanding of life; disposition to externalize spiritual conversation; use of imagination; ability to connect with humor and irony in life; ability to share the experience of sorrows, hopes, and dreams; finding ways to take action either individually or with others that are in accord with the person's values and beliefs; receiving and providing comfort to oneself; the ability to care for others and oneself. Each of these can be a pathway for spirituality that may engender positive outcomes.[17]

98

2. *Interpersonal spirituality (to others, relatedness)*: Relationships with others your patient trusts, that help them discern about their spiritual life. One question for the caregiver is whether your patient is a self-listener and if they can listen to the divine/transcendent/higher power? Does your patient have influential or significant people in their life and how have these people contributed to and impacted your patient's life, especially regarding values? How are these influential people impacting your patient in the present, and how might they in the future? Is your patient linking with others through song, music, prayer, photographs, images, drawings, through a sharing community, through art, and by sharing experiences of sorrows, hopes and dreams, and purposes? Another significant aspect is that our culture promotes individualism, not offering a sense of community, support, or spiritual and social connection. This represents a challenge and an opportunity for everybody to expand their concept of spiritual support and relatedness. This, together with materialism, can create an absence of support in your relationships.

3. *Supra-personal spirituality (beyond)*: Concerning spirituality, this is an excellent opportunity for the patient to reflect whether they need to do something different regarding self-awareness, strength, wisdom, spiritual peak experiences, and convictions of ultimate reality or ultimate importance; through spiritual practices such as fasting, chanting, or re-authoring life through gaining power, hopes and dreams; and by gaining new perspectives or modifying previous actions; by using spiritual practices to honor and remember people in case of grief, healing of memories, meaning and

reflection of what is important for your patient. Also, whether the person talks to the divine and dialogues with the higher power is important.[18]

4. *Implications for spiritual care (action):* We can ask how spiritual caregivers can provide spiritual care, considering the spiritual implications of our interaction. We can identify areas such as peace, forgiveness, reconciliation, unfinished business, attachment vs. separation, venting feelings, energy, hope, faith, communication, healthy vs. unhealthy spirituality, values concerns, self-esteem, tension, dimensions or opportunities for transformation or re-authoring the story, etc. ...

It is important to make sure the spiritual caregiver doesn't impose theological or spiritual understandings to which people do not relate. It is also important not to impose advice or solutions that are discordant with what the patient values in their spiritual life and with what the patient intends for their life. In the words of Carrie Doehring, this is an important component of trust, because the element of empowering is an essential ingredient for helping the patient feel safe.[19] Also, the helping spiritual professional can alleviate any apprehension by expressing genuine empathic and supportive responses and by honoring the patient's spiritual framework. Also, according to *The American Book of Living and Dying* by Groves and Klauser, spiritual pain is related to one of four timeless qualities that we need to hear with empathy and use to make a diagnosis: meaning, forgiveness, relatedness, and the pain of hopelessness.[20]

Another implication for spiritual care is to explore whether it is necessary to do spiritual reframing. This is always an opportunity for the patient to see whether their dilemmas, life events, or even childhood values can be reframed from the perspective of their adult life, with other lenses. This can help the patient acquire a new perception of their present experience or difficulty.

I recommend seeing the checklist of David Denborough, especially when doing spiritual narratives while responding to individuals, groups, and communities who have experienced trauma.[21]

In summary, dancing with spiritual interventions plays a significant role in getting an awareness of patients', families', and medical staff's spirituality and life's existential challenges. This chapter provides basic information to help identify some of the different types of spiritual interventions, from basic human dimensions to more complex interventions.

---

1 R. D. Fallot, "Spirituality and Religion in Recovery: Some Current Issues," *Psychiatric Rehabilitation Journal*, 2007; 30:261-270.

2 Christina M. Puchalski and Betty Ferrell, *Making Health Care Whole: Integrating Spirituality into Patient Care* (West Conshohocken, PA: Templeton Press, 2010).

3 See more information in "Model for Chaplaincy in Palliative Care," by Rev. George Handzo, BCC, CSSBB.

4 Puchalski, *Making Healthcare Whole*. Also, you can find more information in the article "The Role of Spirituality in Health Care," by Christina M. Puchalski in *Baylor University Medical Center Proceedings*, 14, no.4 (2001).

5 See more information in the article "Spirituality and Medicine Practice: Using the HOPE Questions as a Practical Tool for Spiritual Assessment," *American Family Physician*, 2001, January 1:63 (10 81-89).

6 G. Anandarajah, "Doing a Culturally Sensitive Spiritual Assessment: Recognizing Spiritual Themes and Using the HOPE Questions," *Virtual Mentor*, May 2005, 7, no. 5.

7 *Houston Methodist CPE Handbook*, 2021, 42-50.

8 George Fitchett, *Assessing Spiritual Needs: A Guide for Caregivers* (Lima, OH: Academic Renewal Press, 2002).

9 David R. Hodge, *Spiritual Assessment: A Handbook for Helping Professionals.* (Botsford, CT: North American Association of Christians in Social Work, 2003), 25-26.

10 See more information in his book *Basic Types of Pastoral Care Counseling.* Updated and revised, by Bridget Clare McKeever. Pages 65-82.

11 I heard about this model for the first time from Carlos Sánchez who is a ACPE Certified Educator at Memorial Hermann Hospital in Houston, Texas.

12 Martin Payne, *Narrative Therapy: An Introduction for Counselors* (London: Sage), 62 ff.

13 See more information in Michael White, *Maps of Narrative Practice* (New York: W.W. Norton, 2007), 81 ff.

14 Kenneth I. Pargament, *Spiritually Integrated Psychotherapy: Understanding and Addressing the Sacred* (New York: Guilford, 2011), 230.

15 Miriam Greenspan, *Healing Through the Dark Emotions* (Boston: Shamblala Boulders 2004), 86

16 Michael White, *Narrative Practice: Continuing the Conversations* (New York: W.W. Norton, 2011), 72-73.

17 Ibid.; Hodge, *Spiritual Assessment*, 41.

18 James L. Griffith and Mellissa Elliot Griffith, *Encountering the Sacred in Psychotherapy: How to Talk with People About Their Spiritual Lives* (New York: The Guilford Press, 2002), 115 ff.

19 Carrie Doehing, *The Practice of Pastoral Care: A Postmodern Approach* (Louisville, KY: Westminster John Knox Press), 18.

20 Richard Groves and Henriette Anne Klauser, *The American Book of Living and Dying: Lessons in Healing Spiritual Pain* (Berkeley: Celestial Arts, 2009), 84.

21 See more information in David Denborough, *Collective Narrative Practice*, (Adelaide: Dulwich Centre Publications, 2008), 132-133.

SPIRITUAL CARE LEADERSHIP

6

SIGNIFICANT POINTS IN
SPIRITUAL CARE LEADERSHIP

Robert Kidd, Mdiv, BCC
System Director of Spiritual Care and Values Integration,
Houston Methodist

O
UR PROFESSION IS IN THE MIDST of a leadership
challenge. Our professional organizations do a good
job of training and certifying clinical chaplains, but are
not particularly successful at shaping professional chaplain
leaders. Why is this? In my experience, certain types of clergy
tend to gravitate toward healthcare chaplaincy. For example,
professional chaplains are often on the edges of their faith
groups. Chaplains focus so much on "being vs. doing" that we
lag a bit in the active "doing" required for effective leadership.
Some of us struggle with authority issues, which can lead us to
be somewhat undemonstrative in leadership settings or on the
other extreme, notably contrarian. Many of us are not at home
with statistics and charts, and rely on anecdotal information to
demonstrate our effectiveness. We don't like confrontation and
often struggle with managing for performance when team

members need redirecting. We like to be liked. We are more prone to delve into what others want and think rather than claim what *we* want and what *we* think. We tend to be better at responding than initiating. We far too often wait for our executives rather than step forward to claim responsibility for initiatives. William Willimon has quoted Stanley Hauerwas referring to some clergy as simply "a quivering mass of availability."[1] Needless to say, all this does not bode well for chaplains when we look through our ranks for highly successful leaders. The objective reasons for this gap in leadership talent would be a very fruitful topic for future research.

Regardless of the reasons, our profession must focus much more energy on developing leaders. Spiritual care in healthcare settings is becoming increasingly challenging just now, demanding more expertise, exactitude, and facility with quality measures. Spiritual care in these settings puts chaplain leaders in increasing contact with executives who expect proficiency in interpersonal relationships, data gathering and interpretation, public speaking, project planning and execution, and strategic thinking. This is a step forward for our discipline, but it also puts new demands on those who aspire to spiritual care leadership. Whether leadership comes naturally or not, the good news is that we can learn leadership skills, hone them, and pass them on to others.

Different leaders have varying degrees of excellence in the following leadership imperatives, but in order to succeed, they must be at least passably proficient in them all. With this background, I posit ten leadership imperatives:

1. Set challenging personal goals.
2. Strategize effectively with your team.
3. Collaborate widely and constantly.

4. Listen carefully.
5. Engage your team energetically.
6. Communicate effectively with executives.
7. Be a coach.
8. Master public speaking.
9. Look your part.
10. Mind your manners.

This chapter is only an introduction to these ten imperatives. An amazing array of resources is available for each one. Seek these out by regularly reviewing business best-seller lists, conferring with leadership mentors, and attending continuing education events. You will find that as you explore resources for enhancing these skills, your exploration will yield still more resources. I hope you will make leadership skill development your life's work.

Set Challenging Personal Goals

Goal setting often separates the truly effective and successful from the rest. I am amazed at how many are filled with trepidation and shy away from professional goal setting and yet do it every day in other areas. I contend that personal goal setting can be begun in a pleasant way. Begin by thinking of what you want to be like or what you want to accomplish in your work life. Find a relaxed setting and begin by writing about what you want to do, or be, or accomplish. Describe how it will look or how you will benefit or how you will feel. Write out who will be involved. Whom or what will be impacted? How much will it cost? How long will it take? Simply spend some time writing about what you want to do or who you want to be, then consider your reflections from as many angles as possible. If you can, write this all in one brief sitting, then leave it alone for a day or two. Go back to it after a rest period and then begin refining it. Break down your desired accomplishments into steps. Again, don't stress over this or try to complete it all at once. Then let it rest again for a few days. Once this is accomplished, enlist a trusted colleague to help you talk through the necessary actions to make your aspirations real. Invite them to vet these personal goals and temper them—and challenge you to aim higher. Work with your colleague to put some initial timelines in place. Then, again, let it rest for a few more days. Then go back and do a reality check. The SMART goal format is available digitally and will help you sharpen your goals into meaningful statements that will actually guide your goal activities going forward.

Set strong goals. I find that team members are often prone to set dull and unchallenging goals so they do not risk missing the mark and suffering failure. Of course, it is unhelpful to set goals that are not based in reality, but at the same time, refuse to settle for low, easy goals. Think of what you really, truly want to accomplish and why. Make a practice of talking about your goals with others. Talking about them and writing them down has a remarkable way of making goals into realities. Develop the discipline of reviewing your goals often with your direct report. Your direct report can help you shape and sharpen these goals to make them more useful to you and the organization. Also, this is a great point of connection between you and your direct report, significantly deepening your relationships and helping your direct report know about your heart-felt aspirations. Let them support you in this. It's important to hold yourself accountable for accomplishing your goals rather than waiting for others to hold you accountable. Since they are your personal goals for yourself, own them for yourself.

Set comprehensive personal goals. As stated earlier, goal setting is what often separates the ordinary from the truly excellent. Consider setting goals in a wide variety of categories such as Community Involvement, Family Relationships, Finances, Personal Development, Philanthropy, Physical Health, Professional Growth, and Spiritual Development. Write out your goals as declarative, present tense sentences. Here are some examples:

Professional Growth:
- I mentor three professional chaplains at all times.
- I write one article by invitation each year for a professional management journal.

Spiritual Development:
- I go on a personal solitary spiritual retreat twice a year.
- I am a certified spiritual director.

Strategize Effectively With Your Team

I think strategizing has gotten a bad reputation among professional chaplains, who see it as a dry, soul-shredding, overly calculating exercise that robs their ministry of vitality. I suggest that strategizing can be rewarding, relationship-building, and a key to guiding your department toward sustained institutional impact. To begin any strategic plan, it's important to involve your direct report executives. Engage your executive in dialogue about what visions they have for your organization—not just your department. There is more about executive engagement later in this chapter under the heading "Communicate Effectively with Executives."

While you are engaging your executive in dialogue about the work of your department, begin involving your entire workgroup in strategic planning. Remember, you cannot complete your strategic plan alone. Begin in the same fashion as when formulating personal goals. Invite your team to talk with you about their collective vision for your department in five years. Think of all the things you would like to accomplish together and the resources at your disposal. Discuss the things your institution needs from your department. Engage in dialogue about how your team can most powerfully impact your organization. Set challenging, aspirational goals for yourselves. Even if you fail to meet them all, you will still have challenged yourself and your team. Then, as with your personal goals, let this list of aspirations rest for a while.

A short time later, lead your team back to review your strategic plan draft. What is still resonating and seems on target? Check for themes and similarities in your list. Consolidate where needed. After you have done this, conduct a straw poll to reveal your team's top four or five highest leverage activities or accomplishments. Then, resume your dialogue with your direct report executives. Sustain this back and forth dialogue between you, your staff, and your executive leadership until you have crafted a strategic plan that everyone is committed to.

At this point, you are ready to set time lines and assign accountability for various aspects of the plan. As the leader, be wary of taking responsibility for too many things yourself. Accountability and commitment mean personal investment. Let your team have the satisfaction of owning various parts of your strategic plan. Then, set up regular check-ins to assess your strategic plan's progress.

Collaborate Widely and Constantly

There is a saying, "If you want to go fast, go alone. If you want to go far, go together." The bigger and more challenging your goals, the more critical it is that you have partners working with you. This is just common sense: you will not be able to do the lofty things you envision without help. This means collaborating widely, vigorously, and constantly. Seek partners everywhere. You do not know when your relational network will be useful to you, nor when you will be able to help someone else. Collaborate with people throughout your organizational structure. Have coffee with other organizational leaders. Stop eating lunch at your desk every day and at least occasionally enjoy meals with people outside your immediate departmental sphere. Sooner or later, your networking will pay off in big ways. Make a practice of asking others for consultation about upcoming decisions. Freely own your knowledge gaps. There is no shame in this since no one knows everything about every aspect of their day-to-day decisions. Sometimes, lower stakes decisions make particularly good collaborating opportunities, enabling others to get to know you under low stress circumstances, and paving the way for higher stakes collaboration later. When others ask for your input (and they will) provide it candidly, and be sure to help them feel good about asking for consultation. Never, ever leave others feeling diminished because they asked for your input.

Listen Carefully

In healthcare organizations filled with experts who charge high fees for their expertise, listening is more often talked about than actually done. As mentioned above, as a leader, people will surely come to you with their concerns and problems. You likely will feel pressured to deliver expert, sage advice. While the pressure of these expectations is often real, your best shot at actually delivering the expected wise advice is to listen carefully first. Remember your clinical training! Many times—an astounding number of times—what people truly want is simply to be heard. Our upbringing has frequently enculturated us to spend conversational time planning our responses rather than deeply focusing on what others are saying to us in the moment. Good listening skills are critically important because they provide you with information to make helpful and effective responses. Good listening skills help you ask productive questions and give your conversational partners space to express themselves fully. Good listening skills slow you down and help you avoid snap judgments. Good listening skills help you peel through the layers of issues that underlie many of the thorny problems that will be presented to you. Good listening habits engender strong, trusting, healing, transformational relationships. They are the foundation of high-quality leadership outcomes. Excellent listening skills lead people to seek you out because of how they feel when they interact with you. Marshall B. Rosenberg has written a superb book about this, *Nonviolent Communication: A Language of Life.*[2] This book carefully details how to listen accurately and respond in ways that lead to stronger relationships and maximally effective leadership.

Engage Your Team Energetically

Collaborating, as we discussed above, is a fundamental leadership approach which you should apply in broad strokes all over your organization. In contrast, however, engaging team members focuses on involving them in matters that directly impact their daily professional lives. It is likely that you spend more time with your work group than you do with most of your family members. Because of this, it is critical to strengthen your relationship to them continually and invest them in your shared vision. Communicate with them constantly to that end. Find out what is important to *them*. Ask *their* opinions. Pay attention to *their* agendas. Find out what *they* want to accomplish. Rather than be the organizational fixer, cultivate the habit of discovering where action is needed, determining who has interest and skill in handling the issue at hand, and then delegating responsibility to those team members. At that point, be sure to establish progress markers and step back without losing touch with progress. People generally don't like to feel "managed." In his book, *Leaders Eat Last*, Simon Sinek asserts that employees who have more control tend to feel more empowered and less anxious. The greater the autonomy your team members experience, the more engaged they will feel in their work, the more pride they will take in times of success, and the more responsibility they are likely to share when times are tough.[3] This common concept is also borne out in scholarly research.[4] To promote a culture of engagement, spend time every month one-on-one with each of your team members, finding out what is important to them, what their aspirations are, and what enriches their work experience. Find out about their joys and sorrows. Know the names of their family members and pets. Know what hurts them and what makes them happy. In your one-on-one meetings, stay positive. Focus on what can be done, conveying your belief that solutions can be found and that challenges are opportunities for growth and innovation. A caveat: this consistent positivity does not mean you turn a blind eye to issues that need addressing or fail to correct unacceptable behavior. Redirecting such situations is part of your leadership responsibility and neglecting to do this will be noted unfavorably by your team members. When circumstances call for team member redirection or correction, Ken Blanchard's classic, *The One Minute Manager*, is a good place to start.[5] He provides extensive guidance on redirecting team members. With that exception, however, your one-on-one meetings should chiefly be spent on positive, "can do" issues. Quint Studer has an excellent guide sheet for these one-on-one meetings in in his book, *Hardwiring for Excellence*.[6] Finally, this one-on-one time with your team members is not optional. If you are not spending one-on-one time with each of your team leaders, you are not leading well. Trust me on this. Always, always, always communicate that you have time for your team members. They will return the favor.

Communicate Effectively With Executives

Communicating with executives is tricky since each one is different. Some are approachable and informal. Others are all business and want bullet points, outlines, and crisp action plans. You will need to find out what works with your executive. To learn more about how your executive processes information and communicates, it is often a good idea to talk to others who are in your executive's inner circle. Ask what informational formats resonate most with your executive. Befriend their administrative support staff and ask them. Be assured, if they are long-tenured, they know! Since your executive relationships are so varied, I will offer a few general guidelines that have wide application.

First, try to speak the same language as your executive at least part of the time. For instance, it's a good idea to read the organizational reports your executive reads in order to familiarize yourself with your organization's jargon, acronyms, statistical data, and overall business issues. In your executive conversations, as opportunity arises, discuss these topics to demonstrate that you are mindful of these concerns and are seeking to offer assistance. Be creative and find ways for the spiritual care department to address these organizational needs. Most likely, your executive will be happy and somewhat surprised that you, a clergy person, are interested in the business aspect of the organization.

Second, when communicating with your executive in writing, be brief. Executives are infamous for their short attention spans and unfortunately, many new leaders get anxious and wordy. Understandably, they want to present their needs thoroughly, but they often fail to edit. When drafting written executive communication, you might start by creating a free-flowing, stream-of-consciousness document that lays out all the things you want to say. Then, ruthlessly edit your document so that essential information is presented quickly and clearly. If needed at all, offer detail later in the document. Where possible, reduce narrative passages to bullet points. If your executive wants more information, it will be requested. If you have time, have your written document reviewed by a trusted team member, checking for concision, thoroughness, and logic.

Third, when in dialogue with your executive, be clear about your desired outcome. Is the interaction for relationship-building? Then less agenda is required. Is the dialogue to gain permission or support for a specific action? If so, have your bulleted data points at hand. Do you simply want to gain executive consultation about an action you are contemplating? In this case, have your pros and cons at your fingertips. Whatever your desired outcome, it is generally helpful for your executive to know this up front.

Fourth, seek to overcome executive intimidation if executive-level interactions are challenging for you. Remember that executives are just like you with likes and dislikes, strengths and weaknesses. Take the risk and put yourself in situations where you interact with them. Speak to them in hallways, seek them out and greet them at gatherings, ask thoughtful, honest questions during meetings. While this is anxiety-producing for many of us, using an amicable, collegial approach with the executive team opens many doors for broader organizational influence and greater opportunities for spiritual leadership.

Finally, always remember that you are a spiritual support for your executive. My spiritual director once told me, "Bob, now that you are at a new level of leadership, do not allow yourself to become mostly an administrator. If you fail to hang on to your primary identity as a minister, you will have neglected your calling as a pastor." That set me back on my heels, but I have never forgotten it. It is vitally important to remember your role as a spiritual support for your executive staff. Truly, this is possibly the most important and highest-leverage part of your job. Do not end meetings with your executive without first discovering something that is making them happy or sad right now. Find out how their families are. If you can, find out what things are keeping them up at night. Find out what they are reading. Find out what inspires them. Use your clinical training to ask good, open-ended questions and use your good empathetic, reflective listening skills.

And pray for your executives. I have found it very fruitful to send periodic emails to our CEOs and vice presidents, assuring them of my prayers. On a rotating schedule, about every four to five months, each of our hospital system CEOs and vice presidents gets an email from me on Monday morning that says something like, *Claire: In the coming week, please know that you will be in my prayers. I plan to pray that you will feel God's strength empowering you, God's peace stabilizing you, and God's love reassuring you when plans don't go your way. If there are other needs you'd like to share with me— confidentially, of course—just let me know. You are one of God's good gifts to our hospital system. Thanks for your partnership and for letting God work through you.* Then, on the following Monday, I close the loop by sending another email that says *Claire: It was a pleasure to pray for you this past week. I hope you felt God's encouragement, comfort and strength. It's a privilege to be on this team with you.*

I have lost count of the responses I have gotten from executives who say how timely their email was and how much it sustained them. Think about it: almost no one ever sends your executives an email that simply offers them personal support. Instead, people continually ask your executives for help, guidance, money, and time. Your email will stand out as a point of refreshment and nurturance in their (sometimes) desert of wants and needs. Such interactions with your executives constitute spiritual care at a new level.

Be a Coach

Any effective leader will tell you that coaching others is not only your responsibility as a leader, but is also an excellent way to keep yourself in top leadership form. Because it is a broad term in frequent usage, it's helpful to clarify what coaching means in this leadership development context. The *Harvard Business Review* states that coaching is usually about developing the capability of high-potential team members. Coaching is not personal therapy. Instead, coaching is a way to develop and sharpen leadership skills, offer an objective sounding board to the person being coached, or to help the person avoid unnecessary roadblocks and organizational potholes.[7] Some coaching opportunities are single occasions, but the best ones are relationships that evolve and bloom over time. These are the priceless relationships that change careers and deepen professional ties.

While coaching is a natural part of leadership, starting and maintaining a coaching relationship takes care and sometimes diplomacy. Begin by making sure that objectives are clear and that outcomes are agreed upon. Once these are in place, it's often helpful to begin by focusing on some type of objective data brought by the person being coached, such as a personality or leadership assessment or a recent performance review.

Coaching offers yet another prime opportunity to use your hard-won listening skills. Use reflective and empathetic responses often in your coaching conversations. Watch the other person's body language. Pay particular attention to indications of increased engagement and excitement as well as signs of defensiveness or resistance. Be gentle and respond with empathy, acknowledging and accepting the other's feelings. Remember not to take on their problems. Offer feedback, ideas, and suggestions, but ensure that the person being coached understands that they ultimately are responsible for making changes. Again, it's important to stay positive and hopeful. Find ways to offer affirmation often. When making suggestions, it is a good idea to do this in a tentative way using open-ended questions, such as "What do you think would happen if you approached it this way…?" Or perhaps, "How would it work if you tried this…?" Provide concrete assistance by offering to review future work, or steer them toward books, seminars, or other resources which may also be helpful. Continue to affirm their openness to coaching or their continual striving for excellence. If the other person is open to it, follow up regularly or encourage them to arrange periodic follow-up meetings. Finally, when you hear positive things about the person you are coaching, pass on the good word. Remember, part of your responsibility as a leader is to celebrate your colleagues' successes. Their success is your success.

Master Public Speaking

Like so many other topics in this chapter, this section on public speaking could comprise an entire book by itself. The longer I have worked as a chaplain leader, the more critical this skill seems to be. It is no accident that one of the most common fears professionals have is public speaking. It's a hard truth, but if you are fearful of public speaking now, it will probably take considerable practice to overcome. Nonetheless, this particular skill will pay extraordinarily high dividends for you. Although it is a scary discipline, sustained practice will help allay your fears, so begin now seeking opportunities to get in front of an audience. If possible, start with short presentations like speaker introductions, departmental spiritual reflections, or prayers before meetings.

Keeping your audience engaged is key. It can often be anxiety-reducing to start your presentation by involving your listeners somehow. Ask for a response, request a show of hands—anything that gets them physically or mentally invested in your topic. Do this early and repeat it periodically in your presentation. To help create engaging presentations, continually be on the hunt for vivid illustrations on topics relevant to your organization. Examples are everywhere, so read voraciously and stay attuned to the current popular culture. Learn to communicate with your whole body. Add visual interest to your presentations by using meaningful gestures at appropriate times, regularly adjusting your body posture, and changing speaking locations in the room. Use your full vocal range and alter the pace of your speech to underscore major points. Also, beware of making your presentation notes do double duty as your PowerPoint slides. This tactic will *guarantee* a quick and merciful death for your presentation. If you use visual aids at all, edit the verbiage ruthlessly. Pictures are better. Though most people vigorously resist this, it is incomparably helpful to video record yourself during public speaking opportunities. Enlist a trusted friend who is a good speaker to view the video with you and offer feedback. Together, be alert for distracting unconscious habits such as "um" or "ah." Watch for superfluous movements such a fidgeting, pointless pacing, or static postures. If video review is not possible, then ask a friend to watch your presentation "live" and give you candid feedback. While this is admittedly terrifying, look at it this way: Your audience is hearing and seeing the same thing. Would you rather remain unaware of how you appear? Be brave and get feedback.

Look Your Part

It is well known that others quickly make long-standing assessments about us during the first few seconds of contact. Because of that, your personal appearance makes a daily difference in your leadership credibility. When you look good—and know it—you walk with greater purpose, your posture improves, and your overall sense of confidence is bolstered.

There is far too much about personal appearance to discuss in this one chapter, so I will stick to the basics. First, do everything in your power to stay in good physical shape. This is not merely an aesthetic issue. You are a steward of the body God has given you. Don't abuse it by overfeeding and under-exercising it. You will shorten your life, your career, and will make a poor first impression to boot. This often takes steely commitment and tremendous self-discipline but it is worth it in every regard. Second, personal hygiene matters more than you know, and when this becomes a problem, you are often the very last to know. Be vigilant. This particularly includes oral cleanliness and hair care. Third, be attuned to your organization's culture in matters of clothing. Basically, if you have choices about what you wear to work, dress like those one level above you. Dress for where you want to be rather than where you are organizationally. In more formal settings, appropriate clothing is a significant financial outlay and can't usually be obtained at a fell swoop. No matter what the clothing expectations in your organization, build a good wardrobe over the years. Invest particularly in foundational pieces that will get a lot of wear. You can economize on less often used accent items. Talk to trusted colleagues or family members who regularly look good. Ask where they purchase their clothes and, if possible, get them to go shopping with you. Find a style that suits you and stick with it. This may take experimentation, but that can be the fun part. You'll find a look that fits your personality. Pay attention to colors and patterns that flatter your body type and skin color. Especially notice what you are wearing when people compliment your appearance. Maintain your clothing well. Discard or repair items as needed, paying special attention to areas on your clothes that get hard wear such as cuffs, elbows and knees.

A special word is needed about footwear. It is incredible how often otherwise well-dressed people neglect their shoes. Buy good ones. In the long run, they wear longer and look better. A good pair of shoes can be resoled many times before the leather wears out. Men and women: if your shoes are designed to take a shine, they should shine. Polish your shoes often and don't forget the heels and edges of the soles. In general, for professional wear, shoes should match or at least coordinate with your belt or other accessories. The formality of the shoes should match the formality of the rest of the outfit. Remember it is not important to look *different* every day, but it is critically important that you look *good* every day. You never know who you will meet or what setting you may be in before the day is over.

Mind Your Manners

The etiquette maven, Emily Post, said it best: "Manners are a sensitive awareness of the feelings of others. If you have that awareness, you have good manners, no matter what fork you use." Etiquette is a matter of thinking of others and using common sense. Yes, there are some arcane etiquette rules that are mostly designed to intimidate and show who's "in" and who is not, but those are not matters for treatment here. Instead, since etiquette is intensely culturally conditioned, I merely encourage you to learn some basics for the culture you are in. What is appropriate in one culture may be wildly inappropriate in another. In this section, I am only speaking of our general culture in the United States—and even that is an amazingly diverse subset!

Business meals can be filled with etiquette landmines so we will begin here. Learn where items are located on standard table settings. Place your napkin in your lap immediately upon sitting down and when finished, loosely fold your napkin to the left of your plate. Wait to begin eating until everyone else at your table has been served or until the host invites you to begin. When appropriate, pass food to others at the table rather than only serving yourself. Be polite to the wait staff. When finished eating, place your utensils diagonally at the four o'clock position on the plate rim.

Here are a few additional etiquette pointers for common professional situations. If you get to a door first, open it for those after you. This applies to men and women equally. Pay attention to those with mobility needs and offer to assist without getting in their way. Learn to introduce yourself to others clearly and briefly. Learn to listen for others' names when they are introduced to you. If conversational partners do not know one another, introduce them and if possible, help them find some point of commonality. If you are seated, stand up when introduced to a new person. Look others in the eye when talking to them. When invited to a social function, reply promptly, stating whether or not you will attend, using the

RSVP instructions given on the invitation. When invited to a private social function, send a note of gratitude within the next few days after the event—no later than one week. Send notes of acknowledgement for gifts or special recognitions. Handwritten notes are best and are often cherished, but other media can work well, too. Be present with those you are with; put phones and electronic devices away during social events unless absolutely necessary. In summary, be a student of etiquette. When you are unsure, ask advice from others, or research the answer on reliable etiquette websites.

Summary

Leadership is a complex and nebulous issue that evolves and develops over time. Paying attention to the topics in this chapter—and the many other facets of leadership—will help you grow as a professional, increase your sense of personal confidence, and will inspire others around you. Each topic in this chapter has received detailed treatment in other publications and I encourage you to explore the ones that most engage your interest, or which hold the most relevance for your personal growth. Leadership development is a life's work and is worth all the effort it entails.

---

1 William Willimon, *Pastor: The Theology and Practice of Ordained Ministry* (Nashville: Abingdon, 2002), 60.

2 Marshall B. Rosenberg, *Nonviolent Communication: A Language of Life* (PuddleDancer Press, 2003).

3 Simon Sinek, *Leaders Eat Last: Why Some Teams Pull Together and Some Don't* (New York: Penguin Books, 2014).

4 J.D. Cohrs, A.D. Abele, D.E. Dette, "Integrating Situational and Dispositional Determinants of Job Satisfaction: Findings From Three Samples of Professionals," *Journal of Psychology*, (July 2006), 363-96.

5 Ken Blanchard, Spencer Johnson, *The One Minute Manager* (HarperCollins Publishers; 2003).

6 Quint Studer, *Hardwiring Excellence* (Studer Group 2003).

7 Diane Coutu, Carol Kauffman, "What Can Coaches Do for You?," *Harvard Business Review*, (January 2009).

7

SYSTEMS THINKING AS A RESOURCE
FOR CAREGIVERS

James H. Furr, PhD
President and Professor of Church and Culture Emeritus,
Houston Graduate School of Theology

WHETHER THE FOCUS is a family, organization, or community, virtually everyone acknowledges that human systems are complex, interconnected, and changing, even as they routinely attempt to over-simplify complicated relationships and spotlight isolated snapshots of reality instead of ever-evolving stories.[1] Caregivers and the leaders of their organizations are deeply affected by the way they understand group dynamics and should make the stewardship of human systems a high priority.[2]

"Systems thinking [is] a way of thinking about, and a language for describing and understanding, the forces and interrelationships that shape the behavior of systems."[3] The primary objective of this brief chapter is to introduce some concepts, principles, and tools that can nurture the practice of systems thinking and ultimately enhance the quality of spiritual care.[4]

Principles of a Systems Perspective

Human social behavior tends to demonstrate fairly predictable patterns that may be described as principles or laws. Principles focus attention on the holistic nature of systems rather than a reductionistic concentration on their parts.[5] The following eight principles address organizational life from a systems perspective.

1. *Organizations are living systems:* The organic nature of social systems may seem obvious but organizations are often viewed more like machines than relational networks. Attention to units, functions, and outputs may displace concern for relational vitality, cultural trends, and a shared vision for life together. This legacy of the Industrial Age reflects how popular mental models often view people as the parts or "human resources" of production systems rather than rich relationships negotiated for common purposes. While organizational charts may accurately reflect key responsibilities, groups form identities as much as they identify functions.

   The unique culture of every organization also helps explain why attempts to replicate the programs of other groups or to make personnel changes are not automatically successful. Organizations are predisposed to repel external intrusions just like human bodies naturally reject organ transplants.

   Questions for reflection and dialog: In what ways do perceptions of our organization reflect the image of an inanimate machine rather than a living system? How can we better honor vibrant covenantal relationships at the core of the organization?

2. *Organizations get what they really want:* Organizations reflect the patterned behavior of the individuals who comprise them and are called a system's *structure*. These familiar and comfortable processes reinforce group norms, values, beliefs, and practices. So revered are these ways of life, they must be learned by newcomers, and participants experience sanctions for noncompliance. *This is who we are and how we do things around here.* Groups develop narratives about their stated purpose and histories. Stories of celebration describe goals that have been accomplished. Stories of lament provide rationales that reaffirm the stated purpose *and* explain why the organization does not fully achieve that purpose year after year.

In response to unmet goals, groups commonly insist they *really* want different outcomes even when behavior is rigidly repeated and change is carefully avoided. To claim to value what is not actively pursued is to express a *velleity* (slight desire) rather than a value. When different outcomes are *genuinely* desired, changes are made. Actions always speak louder than words.

Questions for reflection and dialog: How do our stories of celebration affirm a sense of purpose and progress? What stated values are technically velleities because we choose not to act on them? How do stories of lament rationalize patterns of behavior that need to be more honestly acknowledged and realistically addressed?

3. *The past is always present:* Humans learn to adapt to real or imagined contexts. Reality is constantly assessed through the mental, emotional, and relational lens developed over a lifetime. These perceptions and

expectations create patterns that guide values and lifestyles passed from generation to generation. They endure in shared cultures even when the people in those systems change.

A common response to an undesirable experience is to say "The past is past so let's move on." This sentiment can be useful insofar as it helps avoid fruitless reactivity to chronic anxiety. The problem is pretending those influences are no longer making a difference when they really are. In those instances, individuals may need to go back to resolve a matter in order to move ahead. The opposite dilemma can also occur. Many organizations beyond their developmental prime become obsessed with the *good old days* and try to replicate activities from the past. In those cases, a group needs to become truly present and deal with the circumstances at hand.

Questions for reflection and dialog: To what past trauma does the group continue to react in ways that are not justified by the current conditions? What achievements of the past now distract leaders from more realistic emphases on today's challenges and opportunities?

4. *Systems are systems of systems*: In order for a system to operate, groups of people within them comprise interactive and interdependent subsystems. The effectiveness of a system is highly affected by the degree to which those individuals and subgroups are culturally aligned with the larger system. The study of living systems reveals the fascinating phenomena of *fractals* in which organisms are comprised of increasingly complex layers of simple structures that constitute their essential

design and adaptive capacities.[6] For organizations, these fractals or basic designs may be expressed as core competencies, habits, or practices. Systems should also demonstrate a good balance between the diversity required for complex tasks and the unity required to discern and support shared purposes.

Questions for reflection and dialog: In what ways does our organization experience strength from the cultural alignment of its subsystems? In what ways do any of those subgroups need to interact more harmoniously to support the larger purpose of the organization? In what ways do any of those subsystems need to encourage other parts of the system to live up to stated purposes?

5. *Every change changes everything*: Because every facet of a system is connected, a change in any part affects every other part to some degree. The effects may be difficult to see due to the subtle and nuanced quality of the impact and because the consequences may require long periods of time to emerge. Peter Senge's related law of systems asserts that "Cause and effect are not closely related in time and space."[7] Still, few leadership impulses are more powerful than the desires to predict and control. While not denying some reasonably straightforward causal relationships among organizational variables, leaders make a perilous conjecture if they assume every course of action or its consequences are obvious.

Leaders, then, essentially have two options. The first is to create unrealistic and artificial fables that overstate knowledge and control. The second is to embrace personal and organizational learning with humility and collaboration. Diagnostic tools specifically designed with systemic assumptions and processes can assist leaders to fulfill these intentions.

Questions for reflection and dialog: In what ways does our organization unduly presume to control and predict its life and context? How can the group exhibit reasonable levels of confidence in its actions while cultivating the art of learning?

6. *"Solving" a problem can make things worse*: Leadership is popularly conceived as fixing problems as efficiently as possible. The assumption is that new answers are needed for familiar and "obvious" questions. A key premise of systems thinking and generative learning is that creative analysis and adaptive initiatives often require new questions and models of evaluation.[8]

Leaders are understandably attracted to interventions that are the most familiar, comfortable, and cost effective (by whatever measure of investment one chooses). Almost inevitably, interventions tend to be shallow and reactive insofar as they are propelled by ease, the fearful avoidance of risk, and popular appeal. In the short run, the consequences of ineffective actions may be denied or disguised by creating artificial scapegoats, by deferring a response until a later time, or by moving the problem within the system. Often as not, these tactics simply perpetuate or even exacerbate problems.

Questions for reflection and dialog: What undesirable patterns or reoccurring problems routinely challenge our group or organization? If these concerns are symptomatic aspects of deeper issues, are the underlying issues recognized? If so, is the group willing and able to address them? Why or why not?

7. *Feedback tells the tales:* Feedback tracks observable change in system-related phenomena. In systems dynamics, feedback is observed as change in *behavior over time* and is conveyed when system variables spiral in desirable or undesirable directions. Those reinforcing loops are commonly offset by other factors that effectively slow or balance those forces.[9] Leaders can monitor feedback to interpret systemic patterns and to gauge the results of intentional change efforts.

   Questions for reflection and dialog: To what feedback does the organization tend to listen, ignore, or distort? Why? What trends are evident or subtle? How can the organization become better at monitoring, interpreting, and using meaningful feedback?

8. *The right leverage makes a difference:* Despite the acknowledged challenges, the language, insights, and actions consistent with systems thinking can be acquired. Wise interventions may be less obvious, dramatic, or immediate than one imagines. Their effectiveness grows from the capacity to engage complexity, be ruthlessly honest and realistic, risk imaginative change, and display patience.

   Questions for reflection and dialog: What are the most constructive practices of the group that engender vitality, hope, and energy? What are the most destructive practices of the group that drain vitality, hope and energy? What new habits will be encouraged? How will we think and act from a systems perspective more consistently?

The next section of the chapter describes practices that support such initiatives. They represent some of the essential disciplines related to systems thinking.

Tools for Systems Thinkers

Several tools or techniques are available to help facilitate a systems approach to learning and leadership. The Ladder of Inference portrays the typical and often misleading ways mental processes move from observation to action. Johari's Window highlights the powerful benefits of self-disclosure and feedback. Tools like Five Whys and Bridge Diagrams help identify a broader range of factors that affect organizations at deeper levels of influence. Causal Loop Diagrams enable groups to tell the stories of shared endeavors and envision new designs for action. Systems archetypes describe common organizational patterns that can yield powerful insights.

Ladder of Inference:

The Ladder of Inference was designed by organizational scholar Chris Argyris to underscore the defensive mechanisms that thwart interpersonal and leadership effectiveness in organizations.[10] The model presented here reflects a slight adaptation of Rick Ross's expanded version.[11] The model illuminates the limited capacity of the human brain to process overwhelming amounts of information and the problematic consequences of data selectivity, generalization, and interpretation.

As depicted in Figure 1, (beginning from the bottom) humans unavoidably select from the full range of available data to which they are exposed. To the selected data, they add meanings upon which assumptions and conclusions are based. Increasing levels of abstraction form as beliefs are adopted, which, in turn, guide actions. A powerful phenomenon occurs in the form of a *reflective loop*. Not only do actions reinforce the beliefs that shaped them, but actions and beliefs narrow the field of observed data and experience in the future. Most of the process occurs at a subconscious level so the lack of awareness of the progression resists examination and modification. This erosive and self-deceiving process produces four commonly held convictions.

1. Our beliefs are *the* truth.
2. The truth is obvious.
3. Our beliefs are based on real data.
4. The data we select are the real data.[12]

In addition to individuals, groups use collective processes of inference so that shared perceptions repel new information and explanation. Individuals experience pressure to conform to acceptable group beliefs and routines.

Figure 1: The Ladder of Inference

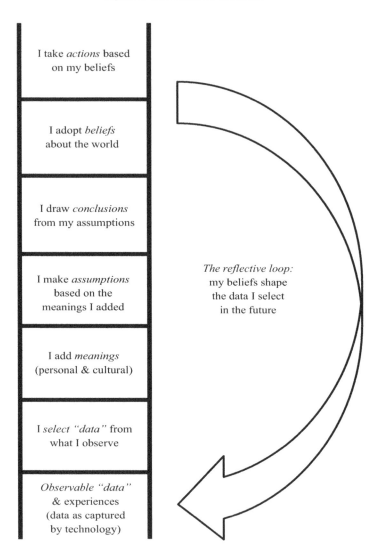

I take *actions* based
on my beliefs

I adopt *beliefs*
about the world

I draw *conclusions*
from my assumptions

I make *assumptions*
based on the
meanings I added

The reflective loop:
my beliefs shape
the data I select
in the future

I add *meanings*
(personal & cultural)

I *select "data"* from
what I observe

Observable "data"
& experiences
(data as captured
by technology)

Johari's Window:

Joseph Luft and Harry Ingham developed a framework called Johari's Window that portrays the significance of self-awareness and social interaction. The model identifies four possible quadrants of experience. A *public* realm exists in which individuals know themselves and others also know about them. A *blind* arena exists to the degree that individuals do not know themselves in ways that others are aware of. A *private* zone is so labelled when individuals know things about themselves they do not share with others. When both individuals and others lack awareness, the convergence is called the *unknown* area. As sketched in Figure 2, two processes enhance and expand the desirable public or open area. *Feedback* from others makes it possible for individuals to learn characteristics about themselves that others know but they do not. In popular language, this helps caregivers reduce their "blind spots." Likewise, when individuals practice self-disclosure that enlightens others, the public area of awareness grows in ways that increase the vitality of individuals and the groups of which they are a part.

Figure 2: Johari's Window

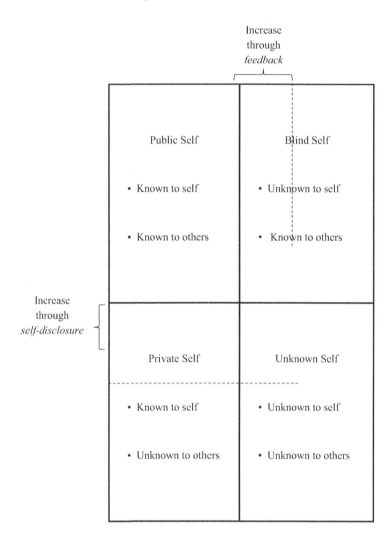

Increase
through
feedback

Public Self

• Known to self

• Known to others

Blind Self

• Unknown to self

• Known to others

Increase
through
self-disclosure

Private Self

• Known to self

• Unknown to others

Unknown Self

• Unknown to self

• Unknown to others

Five Whys:

Five Whys is a technique that helps individuals and groups consider a wide range of factors perceived to influence an issue of concern. Variables are also examined at deeper systemic levels of impact than most superficial, reactive analysis. To use this technique, identify a pressing concern and write the issue on a board or large piece of paper. Then draw lines to three to five words or phrases that contribute to the issue (typically expanding the diagram from left to right). Continue to extend the network of notes by adding several possible factors for *every* variable identified.[13] Several benefits quickly become obvious in most instances.

1. Simplistic cause-and-effect explanations may be replaced by more realistically complex considerations.
2. After adding several *layers* of factors, attention will often crystalize around critical stimuli that are *deeper* in the system, which means their influence may be easily overlooked or underestimated.
3. The graphic arrangement itself is likely to illustrate the impact of variables in several plausible directions.
4. Rather than propagate quick fixes, the technique often generates additional questions and inspires creativity toward more effective responses.
5. The quality of dialog in a group process may promote constructive disclosure and feedback about participants' assumptions, conclusions, beliefs, and actions.
6. When a group works together to articulate its story, participants generally are better able to develop a shared response.

A variation of Five Whys is called a Bridge Diagram in which the issue of concern is placed in the middle of a drawing surface. Key factors perceived to influence the presenting issue are arrayed to the left and key factors that are perceived to be influenced by the central issue are arrayed to the right.

A spirit of the exploration and dialog is critically important. Many leaders and organizations feel compelled to blame specific individuals (scapegoats) for perceived shortcoming even though everyone in a system contributes to the way things are and therefore shares responsibility for the overall outcomes. Better understanding is generated when the participants practice curiosity, creativity, and collaboration rather than rigidity, defensiveness, and criticism. Ideally, the technique kindles a journey of discovery for strengthening the organization and supporting the participants.

Sketching a Story:

The Five Whys and Bridge Diagram exercises help to identify key factors that influence the life of an organization. The ultimate objective is to arrange those variables to tell an organization's story and to discern opportunities for desired change. Inevitably, certain behaviors will be increasing, decreasing, or generally holding steady. A causal loop diagram (CLD) is a way to depict the flow of influence between key factors or variables that describe significant patterns in the organization's life. With basic instruction and a little practice, groups can learn to diagram their narratives in helpful ways. Many resources are available to make causal loop diagrams accessible and useful.[14]

Imagine a scenario in which a hospital chaplain is learning new competencies from participation in a Clinical Pastoral Education (CPE) program which contributes to her increased capacity for caregiving and learning. Aware of that increased capacity, the chaplain's Certified Educator is more confident in her capabilities and increases her workload. Initially, the chaplain simply works harder and longer hours but eventually fatigue and resentment contribute to less effective care and even burnout.

A causal loop diagram of the story can summarize how the selected factors or variables are increasing, decreasing, or resisting movement. Ultimately, the factors are best described in terms that don't state the current direction of their trends or behavior over time. When a factor is moving in the *same* direction as the variable it is shown by an arrow to influence, the relationship is indicated with an "S." When a factor is moving in the *opposite* direction as the variable it is shown to influence, the relationship is indicated with an "O."

A loop in which the variables would naturally continue to increase or decrease is referred to as a *reinforcing* loop and marked with an "R." A loop in which the factors tend to resist or slow a pattern of movement is called a *balancing* loop and marked with a "B." In some instances, like this story, the effect of one variable on another does not happen immediately and that phenomenon is reflected in the diagram by adding the term "delay" to the arrow between the variables. Figure 3 uses a causal loop diagram to tell the chaplain's story.

Figure 3: The Chaplain's Burnout Story

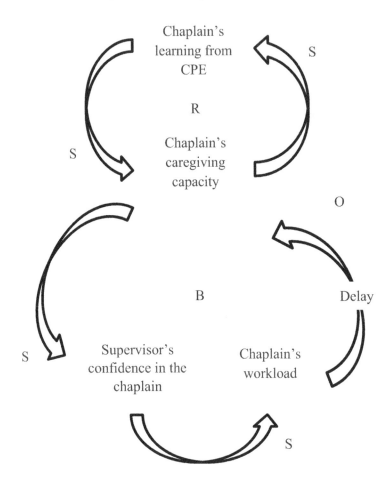

Valuable benefits of telling stories through CLDs include the opportunities to see key contributing factors and to practice feedback, disclosure, and dialog that stimulate clarity and shared perceptions. A CLD is often able to help an individual or group identify the points of highest leverage for positive change in the system. In the case of the chaplain's story, two opportunities for constructive intervention become evident: first, the Certified

Educator can appreciate the chaplain's increased abilities without excessively increasing her workload, and second, the chaplain can provide feedback to the Certified Educator more quickly, thereby reducing the delayed consequences of the change with its inordinate fatigue.

Strategists that refined the tool of causal loop diagrams also discerned that most organizations demonstrate many common patterns of behavior. Consequently, they developed a cadre of systems *archetypes* that depict these routine organizational patterns.[15] Leaders can effectively apply the archetypes to their groups or organizations.

Systems Thinking and Organizational Conflict

A few words are in order about conflict in organizational life. This section notes four ordinary ways that conflict is described or experienced in groups and how a systems perspective and related tools can help.

Problem People:

Many organizations include individuals who seem to have difficulty working well with colleagues. In many instances, those individuals become known as *problem people*, whether they exhibit abrasiveness, aggression, dishonesty, or other undesirable traits. When these behaviors are routine, *individuals* are commonly labelled as the source of the system's problems.[16] While people with personality disorders and destructive behavior can create challenges for a group, two key considerations are how the entire group contributes to the situation and what the participants choose to do about the circumstances.

In light of Systems Principle # 2, if the group chooses not to confront inappropriate action, then everyone in the system contributes to the condition and shares responsibility for the outcomes. In this case, passive modes of inaction are ultimately as destructive as the behavior of the people "acting out." Rather than invest so much time blaming others for apparent shortcomings, the high leverage opportunity for the group is for change in themselves and the ways they relate to one another.

Power Plays and Survival Modes:

When an organization does not have a common understanding of why disappointing patterns are repeated, or a clear, shared, and compelling vision of the future, individuals and subgroups are more likely to act on motives and goals that benefit themselves most directly. Without shared perceptions and goals, the resulting void may entice people to use whatever means and power are necessary to pursue their own objectives. If an organization experiences very high levels of disruptive chaos without healthy processes to re-organize that energy, the participants may adopt what they perceive to be necessary modes of self-protection or even survival. Acquiring consensus about challenges and opportunities can stimulate the systemic alignment encouraged by Systems Principle # 4.

When individuals or subgroups overlook the complexity, connectedness, or changes in the organization, they often fall prey to incomplete, competing assessments and strategies. Using group dialogical methods frequently reveals many plausible explanations and response options that foster group solidarity.

Miscommunication and Misunderstanding:

Minor or major conflict can grow from poor communication and the failure to understand or appreciate what others attempt to convey.[17] Individuals may perceive themselves to be slighted, unappreciated, or misled when the basic problem is inadequate communication. Disagreements about issues easily degenerate into interpersonal conflict. These dilemmas can be significantly decreased by learning from the Ladder of Inference and Johari's Window to strengthen clarity and constructive intent. Groups can develop more collegial assessments and aspirations though the practice of the Five Whys activity and Causal Loop Diagrams.

Polarity Management:

Many contested circumstances appear to be decisions between "either-or" *choices* when the opposing parties are simply attracted to different sides of a "both-and" *polarity*. When a caregiver prefers to emphasize the quality of care in the organization and a hospital administrator prefers to emphasize the quantity of persons for whom the system cares, the tension between quality and quantity may be needlessly overdrawn. Barry Johnson and Roy Oswald provide a helpful model and methods for *polarity management* which can re-frame and de-escalate interpersonal and organizational conflict.[18] Self-awareness, self-disclosure, and trust help individuals appropriately distinguish between decisions to make and polarities to manage.

Conclusion

Caregivers are positively and negatively affected by the patterns of behavior in their organizations. The press of life and a penchant for superficial responses often lead to unproductive reactivity in which problems are perpetuated and opportunities are missed. The perspectives, principles, and tools of systems thinking can empower caregivers to make more appropriate changes in themselves, their relationships, and their organizational systems.

James H. Furr

1 Jim Herrington, Mike Bonem, and James H. Furr, *Leading Congregational Change: A Practical Guide for the Transformational Journey* (San Francisco: Jossey-Bass, 2000), 144.

2 This chapter considers the systemic nature of organizations and the groups that comprise them. Likewise, references include both caregivers and the leaders of the groups and organizations in which those individuals serve.

3 Peter M. Senge, et al., *The Fifth Discipline Fieldbook: Strategies and Tools for Building a Learning Organization* (New York: Currency Doubleday, 1994), 6.

4 During the past several decades, systems thinking has been utilized by a variety of disciplines. This chapter draws primarily from the field of *systems dynamics* developed in the 1960s by M.I.T scholar Jay Forrester and further refined by thought leaders that include Russell L. Ackoff, John Sterman, Peter M. Senge, Daniel H. Kim, Donella H. Meadows, Dennis Meadows, Michael Goodman, Art Kleiner, Charlotte Roberts, Bryan Smith, Richard Ross, Rick Karash, David Peter Stroh, and Linda Booth Sweeney. Related concepts draw upon the work of Chris Argyris, Donald A. Schön, and Edgar H. Schein. See also Scott Cormode, *Making Spiritual Sense: Christian Leaders as Spiritual Interpreters* (Nashville, Abingdon, 2006).

A secondary resource for this chapter comes from the field of *family systems* and its adaptations to faith communities. Murry Bowen was the originator and later refinements were generated by Edwin H. Friedman, Roberta M. Gilbert, Peter L. Steinke, Ronald W. Richardson, and Israel Galindo. See also Jim Herrington, R. Robert Creech, and Trisha Taylor, *The Leader's Journey: Accepting the Call to Personal and Congregational Transformation* (San Francisco: Jossey-Bass, 2003).

5 Adapted from Herrington, Bonem, and Furr, 152-157 and Peter M. Senge, *The Fifth Discipline: The Art and Practice of the Learning Organization* (New York: Currency Doubleday, 1990), 57-67.

6 Margaret J. Wheatley, *Leadership and the New Science: Discovering Order in a Chaotic World* (San Francisco: Berrett-Koehler, 1999), 123-129; Richard T. Pascale, Mark Millemann, and Linda Gioja, *Surfing the Edge of Chaos: The Laws of Nature and the New Laws of Business* (New York: Crown Business, 2000), 229-232. Besides examining fractals, these authors explore the so-called *new science* which incorporates learning from complexity science, chaos theory, quantum physics, and the sciences of living systems. Pascale and his colleagues view *complexity science* as constructively moving beyond systems thinking. Their concern about systems dynamics is that when decisions are

made from the "top down" by organizational managers, the result is artificial and mechanistic *re-engineering* rather the processes of *re-organizing* they observe in complex living systems. The temptation to use systems thinking to manipulate rather than to empower people makes this a worthwhile note of warning but does not warrant the abandonment of systems dynamics.

7 Senge, *The Fifth Discipline*, 63.

8 Chris Argyris, *Overcoming Organizational Defenses: Facilitating Organizational Learning* (Upper Saddle River, NJ: Prentice Hall, 1990), 91-94. Argyris contrasts what he calls single-loop learning to addresses presenting questions with double-loop learning to assess why those problems existed in the first place. The latter considers the underlying values and beliefs that shape action.

9 Donella H. Meadows, edited by Diana Wright, *Thinking in Systems: A Primer* (White River Junction, VT: Chelsea Green Publishing, 2008); David Peter Stroh, *Systems Thinking for Social Change* (White River Junction, VT: Chelsea Green Publishing, 2015).

10 Argyris, *Overcoming Organizational Defenses*, 87-89.

11 Rick Ross, "The Ladder of Inference," in Senge and others, *The Fifth Discipline Fieldbook*, 242-246.

12 Ross, *The Fifth Discipline Fieldbook*, 242.

13 Ross, "The Five Whys," in Senge and others, *The Fifth Discipline Fieldbook*, 108-111. One need not complete five rounds, each with five factors, to generate 3000+ variables, but attempt to brainstorm as many factors as possible without taking time to amplify or justify the suggested reasons.

14 Michael Goodman, Jennifer Kemeny, and Charlotte Roberts, "The Language of Systems Thinking: 'Links' and 'Loops,'" in Senge and others, *The Fifth Discipline Fieldbook*, 113-120. Two websites provide many resource articles and guidelines: www.appliedsystemsthinking.com and www.thesystemsthinker.com.

15 Senge, *The Fifth Discipline*, 378-390; Senge and others, *The Fifth Discipline Fieldbook*, 121-150.

16 Edwin Friedman explains how the tendency to focus attention on an *identified patient*—the person in the system who bears the symptoms or "problems"—may reflect the dysfunctions of an entire family or group.

Generation to Generation: Family Process in Church and Synagogue (New York: The Guilford Press, 1985), 19-23.

17 The popularity of the following publications underlines the fundamental need for effective communication. Kerry Patterson and others, *Crucial Conversations: Tools for Talking When Stakes Are High*, 2nd ed. (New York: McGraw Hill, 2012); Susan Scott, *Fierce Conversations: Achieving Success at Work and in Life One Conversation at a Time* (New York: Berkley Books, 2002, 2004).

18 Barry Johnson, *Polarity Management: Identifying and Managing Unsolvable Problems* (Amherst, MA: HRD Press, 1992, 1996); Roy M. Oswald and Barry Johnson, *Managing Polarities in Congregations: Eight Keys for Thriving Faith Communities* (Herndon, VA: The Alban Institute, 2010).

8

THE IN BETWEEN

Susana McCollom,[1] MAT, BCC
Workplace Chaplain, LifeGift Organ Donation & Private
Practice Spiritual Counseling & Inquiry

W HEN THE PAGER GOES OFF at 4:00 a.m. it sounds like a siren. The chaplaincy office is not equipped for interns to sleep over, so the passage across the GW bridge gives me time to reflect upon the case information shared from the front desk. It is not a code, and there is no imminent physical danger. The patient's son has called in with a different kind of emergency: he needs to talk.

Upon arrival, the hospital corridors are weathered, with slow-brewing elevators. At the end of the cardiology hall a young man paces. It's Ben.[2]

We meet and step into the hospital room. Ben's mother, Ella, sits quietly in a corner chair, wistfully looking out the window. Harry, his father, is propped up in the bed, asleep. After some dialogue, Ben points to a picture he has taped to the wall. In it, Harry and Ella stand arm in arm with Ben, his wife, and their son, smiling wide in front of Rockefeller Center.

"That was my dad less than a year ago," Ben's voice cracks. He is their only child. Within months after the picture was taken, Harry had quadruple bypass surgery and has since grown thin and tired.

This is their fourth visit to the hospital. Each visit has been followed by Harry's long-term stay in rehabilitation. The question, which has become Ben's to answer, is whether his father should return to rehab or go home.

"Can I talk with you for a minute, outside?" Ben motions for us to move back into the hall.

"I'm confident it is the right decision to stop rehab." He resumes pacing, with a stern look on his face. "That means after this, my father will go home. The doctor says he may do fine there, with my mom. I'm not going to consider the other option, because I know what will happen."

Ben lays out the scenario like a set of instructions (in his life outside the hospital, he is a high school teacher). "He'll go to rehab, struggle, get better, and we will have hope. Then he will relapse and we will lose him all over again." A matter of fact statement, showing no emotion.

"And every time it happens, I have to leave work, take the train from Baltimore, leave my family. Is he going to get better? I just can't …" Ben's voice tapers with a twinge of anger, the type kindled by anticipatory grief. "So he will just go home. No rehab. That is the plan."

Then the pacing stops. For the first time during the visit, Ben lets go long enough to send a meaningful glance. "What do *you* think?"

There is a gust of silence. Vulnerability graces the space.

"I know it's the right decision to have him go home. I can't keep going through this. We can't keep losing him. So I'm confident."

Then his head drops, and eyes close. With a gentle exhale, Ben looks back up, his eyes watering. "The thing is, what if? *What if?*"

Personal Stories Reflect Public Opinion: Spiritual Care and Ethnography Narratives

That summer, and since then, I've reflected on Ben's experience, and his urgency—brought not by a code or last breaths, but by the potential of each, by the what if. Physical pain is unambiguous compared to the abstract nature of emotional or psychological pain.

For Ben's family, things were fairly steady and in order—on the outside. But internally Ben felt plagued by uncertainty, a sense of urgency, and the fear that ensued with their merging. *What if* he was being selfish? *What if* he could not take care of his family and his parents at the same time? *What if* he made a decision that led to his father's death? *What if* any painful outcome was single-handedly his fault? The ambivalence was suffocating.

Thought Leaders Talk About Ambivalence

Hospital rooms contain personal and family stories that weave throughout contemporary society. While Ben's ambivalence constellated around his father's physical illness, the nature of his struggle is prevalent.

There is the lawyer who wants the financial benefits of his career, but feels constantly stressed and dreams of a quiet life as a writer.

The parents who love their oppositional defiant son, but hate him for making their lives so difficult.

A happily married analyst who loves her family but longs to be with a woman.

The daughter who struggles to maintain a relationship with her father after he molested her sister.

The nurse who is thankful for the miracle of organ transplants yet struggles to reconcile the religious conflict she feels around it.

The young man who wants to travel the world but does not want to stray too far from his parents and siblings.

The woman who wants to heal her struggle with drug addiction but needs one more week before she quits.

Across health, illness, legal matters, marriage, politics, career, race, religion, and sexuality, from death to ordering a meal—at some point, most people will find themselves entangled in ambivalence. And chances are they will desperately seek a way out.

Interviews conducted with U.S. Thought Leaders[3] reveal textured feelings about ambivalence. Many feel that contemporary society is more interested in staying superficially busy than in being intimately present with another person's experience. "Society doesn't want to go there," says a Marketing Executive. "People listen to you as long as you talk about surface stuff. But when it gets into personal or deeper subjects, they get uncomfortable."

Throughout this crowd, there is a resounding opinion that American society is not a big fan of ambivalence, a condition that relentlessly creates self-doubt, worry, and confusion. In fact, several participants believe U.S. society perceives experiencing ambivalence as a weakness.

"Everyone has ambivalence, they just don't talk about it," says a Social Worker. "It's what keeps us in business as therapists."

Beyond research qualifiers, the participants are vibrant people moved by daily kindnesses. Most volunteer, know their neighbors, and have close friends and family. Yet for many of them, the mere mention of ambivalence about a job, marriage, friendship, or anything that matters, feels too risky; it suggests dissatisfaction or tentativeness, both unpopular qualities. An Environmental Business Leader says: "People don't share their ambivalence because socially, there's a pressure to be certain or right. To have your shit together."

In a society that affirms certainty, those who bravely express ambivalence can stir things up with three seemingly simple words: *I feel torn.*

Ambivalence: What It Is and How It Feels

"I remember, when I was in my early twenties, a girlfriend saying she was on the fence about getting married." Katherine peers over her left shoulder, scanning the café to make sure no one is listening.

"At the time," she continues, "I was horrified. It should be perfect, I thought there should be no doubt. That's when I still lived in the fairy tale, before I knew about life and relationships. I suppose it's ironic that years later, when I got married at 40, I felt the same way. Is this the right choice? Should I wait? Really, it was 50-50. I decided to marry him. But just because I got married, it doesn't mean my ambivalence went away. Now I ask myself every day, 'Should I stay married?'"

Katherine loves her husband, but these days she also can't stand him, or herself. Her struggle is quiet but painful. She is not sleeping and finds herself persistently preoccupied, unable to focus. She feels persistently distracted and isolated.

Like Ben, Katherine stays awake, pacing. Similarly, others experience sleeplessness, anxiety, back pain, stomach problems, depression, and fatigue. A Theology Professor says: "I have a lot of ambivalence about my career, and yet I could never express that at work, I could easily be fired for it. I resolve it by saying it doesn't matter whether I'm happy. Even if it's hurting my body, it could be worse. So I press ahead."

Which could be why some people stay quiet or "pretend," a word some participants use to describe a coping mechanism for dealing with mixed feelings. Some assume this is a unique kind of struggle, that everyone else has it together. At the same time, they know this can't be true. But just in case, better to post happy pictures and share all the good stuff.

There is also a tendency to hyper-focus on making a decision and doing it quickly. Ideally, the one that will produce the least amount of suffering. Yet placing all bets on one decision typically makes the experience worse. Any move feels like it will radically redirect the course of an individual's otherwise controlled life. Plus, the mounting pressure can end up tainting the choice that is finally made.

Ambivalence is sometimes confused with indifference. But it couldn't be more different. Whereas indifference is a bore, ambivalence sends us into overdrive: the tension of feeling both love and hate for the same situation, idea, or person (including one's self). Debilitating or intoxicating, there is nothing neutral about ambivalence, including the ambiguity around what we want. A Psychiatrist says: "People think ambivalence is some kind of amorphous thing. It's not. Ambivalence always has some component of something you don't want to do."

It's true. When a person is mired in ambivalence, they often know exactly what they want. It is simply not a choice. Katherine wants a husband who can financially support the family and help care for their child. She also wants passion. But right now, that's not what the relationship looks like. Katherine shares her internal conflict: she could leave, and has thought about it. But, in her words, that would be "disastrous." Or she can stay and try to find peace.

Visions of the worst-case scenario thrust people into the grittiest corners of anxiety: Abandonment. Hurting loved ones. Loss. Yet in the throes of ambivalence, the very thing we fear is already happening. The inner life starts to look like a building on fire, and so does the response: grab all valuables and run.

Decision, Distraction, and Shifting the Question

"Be careful when you hear questions like *What should I do? What if? Are you sure?*" says a Psychologist. "It's a set up. The very nature of them implies guilt and self-doubt. We beat ourselves up with those questions."

Why does this matter? Because this line of questioning is not only diminishing, it is distracting. And it's not really about the decision. It's about asking more insightful questions such as: What is my life trying to teach me? How can I be loving to myself and others during this discernment? How can I cultivate strength and trust?

This kind of investigation helps us live with reverence. It shifts a process of interrogation into one of discernment.

For many participants, particularly leaders in fields of spirituality and psychology, ambivalence is an essential part of what it means to be human.

A Chaplaincy Director pauses, mindfully choosing words that will honor variations of religious beliefs and non-beliefs. "We live in flesh and in spirit, in love and in hate," he says. "To use a Paulist image, we live with the tension of being a saint and a devil."

By denying our experience, we are essentially denying our nature—our human nature, and where it conjoins with our spirit. But the high social value placed on certainty distracts us from the deeper experience asking for our attention. It may be as clear as what the ambivalence indicates: facing a difficult time in a marriage, or considering a new career. But it's not always that straightforward. A Non-Profit Director says: "It's like going to the beach, and stressing for hours about whether to take sandals or sneakers. It's not really about the shoes."

The space in between the black and white of certainty beckons us to stay for the shades in-between. Interview participants as well as personal stories—at work, in the hospital, in any day-to-day context—reveal ambivalence as an invitation to delve into the internal chambers of our life.

"We may think the ambivalence is about getting married, but it's actually about a childhood trauma that is asking to be healed," says a Contemplative Prayer Leader.

Trying to understand the confusion can feel bewildering. So we begin to question ourselves—what we feel, what we think, and what we do. A Buddhist Leader says: "Ambivalence suggests someone is doubting what they know. It's a discursive thought loop. There are times in my life when I used ambivalence as a mindfulness bell, like an alarm clock. When it shows up, it means something is not being accepted, or really known. And I need to investigate that."

These can be painful revelations. We may not have access to our knowing quite yet, and we may never come to understand it. Or we may be fully aware of what's going on, but honoring that might bring some kind of loss. Almost all scenarios call for exploration, and this takes time. Which is tricky. Feeling torn comes with a potent sense of urgency—it's the last place we want to hang out.

The Beauty of Our Nature

Ambivalence asks us to connect with the experience, which is rarely easy, but almost always meaningful. By sticking around we may actually uncover parts of ourselves that were disowned somewhere along the way. We can contemplate the murkiness rather than avoid it.

Several participants describe a radical shift that comes with delving into their lives. They feel more embodied, and a greater sense of personal authority. "From here," says a Chaplaincy Director, "you can access your humanity, and become more vulnerable and transparent. Then, you can truly touch others."

Participants also describe a deepened trust in a divine force greater than ourselves, be it love, God, friendship, or a universal benevolence. A Technology VP reflects on seventeen years of discernment within an ambivalent marriage: "I used to think making career choices and working on my marriage meant I was in control. But I was just going through the motions, as if my life was not really my own. I saw a fork in the road like this: you make a decision, and force yourself onto one path or the other."

While several participants describe the exhilaration that comes with making a decision, it usually stems from hard work. The deepest relief rarely emerges from a journey of certainty.

"Now I realize you can take a lot more time to get to that fork in the road. I worked through a lot personally. I do things more consciously than I did before. I finally realized it was about having faith and trusting in a bigger plan. It's not like I don't have my eyes wide open, or that I'm surrendering my free will. But I look for what God wants, because before I only focused on what I wanted."

The most valuable external move can start by sharing the story. When this is done with a person most intricately tied to the struggle, like a spouse, the experience can be profoundly liberating. It can be healing for the individual hiding their feelings, and bonding for the couple.

Interestingly, the majority of participants do not personally espouse negative attitudes towards ambivalence. To the contrary, they consider the ability to engage it as emotional and intellectual acuity. Many appreciate the need for certainty in high-stakes situations, particularly around politics and business decisions. But interpersonally, they prefer to be around others who are willing to traverse the murkiness of doubt.

The Contours of Presence and Authenticity

Ana is in a sterile hospital room, receiving treatment for a second experience with cancer. Though the possibility of a recurrence always hovered, it still came as a surprise for the whole family; an interruption to an autumn filled with plans of travel and creativity.

Ana's daughter Sandra has requested a chaplaincy visit for her mother. Sandra and her sister leave the room to create some privacy. Ana rests on her side, and asks for help with the pillows. Her eyes are heavy.

"I feel like I am less human each day. I can't do anything by myself, I can't even get up to go to the bathroom. I have to totally depend on the girls, the nurses." Her voice fades. "I don't feel God here. I know Jesus is with me, I just don't feel him here. It's lonely here."

Ana's life is filled with family, friends, colleagues, and purpose. Yet around the room, the walls are bare. The view from the window is a concrete parking lot. There are no visual reminders of the fullness of her life and the love that surrounds her.

She continues: "I should look ahead, but I only focus on memories. Like the road trip this past spring with my husband. When I look ahead, I don't see myself getting better. I thought I would see my grandkids grow up. Now I can't imagine that. But I am resigned to it. I am okay with death, with not getting better. I have lost hope. The chemo, the treatments, they have helped."

Her daughters return. "Can we come back in?" Ana waves her hand gently, toward the door. "Not yet, you can go for a little longer." The girls smile, closing the door with an expression of reverence that I imagine weaves through the daily contours of their family dynamics, particularly with their beloved mother.

Ana stays quiet for a minute. "I don't know," she sighs. Yet she does know. She has expressed clarity around everything she feels, and the difficulty of feeling it. Here, she has dispatched the strength to say it.

"Ana, how does it feel when you think about healing? To look ahead and imagine yourself going home?"

Her eyes close, and she lets out a breath with the sound of cleansing. "It's too difficult. I think about my townhouse. Three floors. About how I will maneuver around three floors. Everything about it—going home feels difficult. It's just too hard. I don't want to do that."

Wrestling, Reverence and Awakening

Ambivalence opens a window to personal narratives around illness, loss, uncertainty, and a deep desire to live well and love fully. It transcends demographics, reminding us that no one is spared major life choices or changes and the emotions that accompany them. Sharing the experience gives birth to a tender dialogue as people disclose their voyage through the corridors of *what-ifs* and *then-whats*. Whether we are the ones sharing or listening, a lot can transpire when we are willing to brush aside the veneer and let people in.

Letting go of control unearths one of our most primal fears: death. This starts with small deaths, including daily markers, rituals, and relationships that shape our identity and orientation to life, and extends into the concrete passage of our physical death.

The emotional or psychological aspects of ambivalence can seem trite in the face of physical loss and mortality, yet the two are often entwined. Thought Leaders and those who share their experiences teach us that being present to the suffering in the midst of either space is where the transformation transpires.

"What do I really want? I want a lot of things. If I say yes to this one thing, I say no to all the others. It's a sacrifice to make a decision. It's a death," says a Presbyterian Minister.

Underestimating our capacity to suffer, heal, and grow propels us to grasp more tightly. But what if we were to loosen our grip? The very experience we stifle is often the one longing to emerge.

Spiritual traditions share stories of waiting: sitting in the tension of life with compassion and inquiry, wrestling with dualities of joy and sorrow; birth and death; humanity and divinity. Prophets step into a life of discernment, leaving behind daily reminders of individual identity such as wealth, family, and schedule. We hold onto these things dearly. It is the hero's journey and all of the suffering, bliss, and renewal that comes with it.

"There is a spiritual component to ambivalence. Trusting in God, or in even in myself, that whatever the answer is that I will be okay," says the President of the Environmental Corporation. "It's like the yoga savasana pose, practicing death, surrendering."

Ambivalence is not an interruption to life. Nor is it a mistake asking to be fixed. It is potential, if we allow it to be. A creative energy that rouses us to awaken, and to integrate. Sometimes, it means coming to terms with hard discoveries or decisions.

Does this sound weak? No. But it sounds hard. Because sometimes letting go can mean coming undone, so that we may become more fully ourselves. How this shows up is uniquely, beautifully, specific to each one of us.

---

1 www.susanamccollom.com.

2 All names have been changed or omitted to respect confidentiality.

3 Observations, findings and analysis are based on 1-1 chaplaincy sessions and scores of in-depth interviews (IDIs) conducted for various projects and organizations across the United States between 2015 and 2020. Approximately 40 of the IDIs were conducted with Thought Leaders across fields of psychology, spirituality, and religion; others are professionally engaged in corporate business, non-profit work, the arts,

humanities, or government, with a specific focus on the topic of ambivalence.

CULTURAL COMPETENCIES

9

THE SIGNIFICANCE OF PRAYER LANGUAGE IN INTERCULTURAL DIVERSE SETTINGS

Rev. Charles Abuyeka, MDiv, ThM, BCC
Emergency Department Staff Chaplain
at Houston Methodist Hospital

RAYER IS ONE OF THE MOST COMMON and widespread faith practices in the world today. It is as old as mankind, as universal as religion, and as instinctive as breath. It is also complex and multifaceted, especially in pluralistic healthcare settings. Why is prayer so important? Can prayer really change things? Does talking to God have any effect whatsoever on what happens to those in crisis? At first glance one might think these are either silly questions or just a theological waste of time. But prayer comes from deep within a heart with a need greater than mankind's ability to meet. It connects people with the divine, with their communities, and with each other. It allows people to realize that they are not alone in the world or in their experiences.

Spiritual support is a vital resource for those in crisis. A patient perhaps afraid to face a risky surgery may not want to express fear in front of their loved ones. But he or she might find it very comforting to share it with a spiritual caregiver. Spiritual caregivers in health care have the privilege of sharing in these meaningful experiences on a daily basis with patients, their families, and staff. In an intercultural setting, prayer provides the possibility of reaching across religious divides in relevant and meaningful ways. While this chapter focuses mainly on the idea of God in prayer in Christianity, Islam, Hinduism, and Buddhism, other faith traditions find prayer significant and meaningful as well. This chapter attempts to show that the idea of the divine greatly informs an individual's prayer. It explores different aspects of prayer and their impact on spiritual and emotional well-being. Finally, it focuses specifically on the language of prayer as well as the dos and don'ts in prayer.

Spiritual caregivers find themselves in significant positions when attending to care seekers' requests for prayer. Historically, Christians view prayer through God's attributes and His relationship to the world. Christians view God as an all-powerful, all-knowing, and all-present personal being. As a result of God's omnipresence, Christians have an assurance that God will hear their prayers no matter where they are, even in the belly of a fish (Jonah 2:1). Prayer, according to the Christian faith, is an expression of faith in God.[1]

The Christian God has revealed Himself in three persons—Father, Son, and Holy Spirit. The ultimate reality of this triune God is fully realized in Jesus Christ. He came to this world; He lived, died, and rose from the dead. These human aspects allow this God to relate to humanity in a very personal way. Since nothing is impossible with this God, He will not overlook our prayers because He knows everything (Psalm 139:2-4; Matthew 6:8). Christians view God not only as the one who really cares about the universe, but also for each person. He is not a deaf god, but a caring and active God. He transcends His creation, and He is immanent—or active—in it. No prayer is too small for Him to hear, nor is any prayer too large for Him to handle.

When spiritual caregivers understand the characters of the Christian God, they can make meaningful spiritual connections with Christians who view prayer as an essential part of their faith journey.

The Lord's Prayer is perhaps the most common prayer among Christians. According to Gospel accounts (Matthew 6:9-13; Luke 11:2-4), Jesus taught His disciples to pray using this model. The first words of the prayer focus on the relationship with God. These words demonstrate the human dependence on God for providence and protection. Prayer played a significant role in the ministry of Jesus. He repeatedly withdrew to lonely places and prayed (Luke 5:16). He encouraged his disciples to pray with others (Matthew 18:20) as He did Himself (John 17:9, 20). Jesus wanted His disciples to be aware of other people's needs and to provide comfort as needed. When Jesus chose to leave the realms of heavenly glory to walk among people, His connection to God was prayer. Jesus was constantly in prayer with his father.

Prayer is an art anyone can learn. It was so important that Jesus taught His disciples how and when to pray. Christians are urged to pray constantly and in an unceasing manner (1 Thessalonians 5:17; Philippians 4:6). When prayer is patient or need centered it enriches spiritually as well as emotionally. A patient-centered prayer follows the patient's lead. It is respectful of and responsive to individual patient preferences, needs, and values. It ensures that the patient's values and needs guide the whole visit encounter. This provision of care empowers patients to discover exactly what they need or might not need in the moment. Christian care seekers find that there is purpose, promise, provision, and often praise in prayer. This proceeds out of their attitude of deep dependence on God.

165

Christian prayer is not just asking and receiving, it is seeking and finding, knocking and opening closed doors (Matthew 7:7). Prayer expresses trust and deepens an individual's fellowship with God. The creator-creature relationship in Christianity makes that fellowship possible. It is the pattern by which everything else is measured. Such a center is God. When God made Himself known to humankind, He found no better word than "I AM" (Exodus 3:14). God speaks of Himself in the first person and says, "I AM." When Christians speak of Him they say, "He is. But when they speak to Him in petition or supplication they say, "Thou art" or "Father." When in crisis, Christians look to God for their moral bearing, meaning, and purpose in life.

Muslims also believe in one God, whose name is Allah. Allah has seven characteristics. He has absolute unity, that is He is "one" and there is no such thing as a Trinity. He is all-seeing with infinite wisdom, all-hearing, all-speaking, all-knowing, all-willing, and the all-powerful one to build and to destroy.[2] No one is equal to Him for He is exalted above everything. He is magnificent and almighty. He is the living one, ever existing, everlasting, eternal, creator of everything out of nothing by the strength of His word. He creates life and causes death (Sura 7:44). He saves whom He wills and condemns whom He wishes (Sura 7:44, 8:27, 16:35, 76:32). Above all He is the compassionate and merciful one.

Since Allah is the center of everything, prayer is one way Muslims obligatorily demonstrate their total submission to Him. Muslims are expected to pray five times a day facing Mecca with prescribed washing, ritual, and gestures. Allah judges all human beings for their submission to Him. All Islamic faith and practice is based on the understanding of Allah and His attributes expressed in the Qur'an. Prayer is an integral part of

Islamic practice and worship. It is a righteous act by which an individual may accumulate good deeds. Everyone who serves Allah hopes to receive a reward from Him. For whoever calls on Allah, Allah will answer them (Qur'an 40:60). Likewise, whoever fears Allah, "Allah will find a way out for them [from every difficulty] and provide for them from sources that they could never have imagined." (Qur'an 65:2-3). Those who perform prayers expect to receive earthly or heavenly blessings. Muslims pray to keep the law and for the goodwill of Allah to be bestowed on them.

In Islam it is mandatory for an imam or spiritual leader to visit the sick in the hospital when called upon. But when an imam is unable to make a visit, prayers from a Christian spiritual care person may be accepted, because Jesus is the only healing prophet mentioned in the Qur'an (Sura 3:40; 5:110).[3] When the name of Jesus is mentioned in Islamic writings, it is usually followed with the expression 'May peace be upon Him.' When spiritual care providers understand characteristics of Allah they can provide meaningful spiritual support to Muslims. For example, incorporating phrases such as, "May Allah answer your secret prayers," "May Allah wipe away your secret tears," "May Allah erase your secret fears," or "May Allah lift you to the position you so dearly desire" can be very comforting to a Muslim patient. A dying Muslim patient may desire to sit or lie down facing Mecca while reciting the Qur'an. Repositioning the bed to face in that particular direction might seem an insignificant gesture, however for a Muslim patient it is very comforting and deeply appreciated. So, when caregivers pay attention to such characteristics in Islam, they can provide meaningful spiritual support to Muslims, who view prayer as an essential pillar of their faith in Allah.

In Hinduism, prayer focuses on the personal forms of God such as Shiva, Vishnu, or Vishnu's avatars, Rama and Krishna. For some Hindus, Jesus was an avatar or incarnation of God— one among many avatars. As in Islam, prayer is an integral part of Hindu spirituality. Mantras are the heart and soul of Hindu ritual tradition. They are the most popular form of worship. A mantra is a sacred sound in the form of a syllable, word, prayer, phrase, or hymn. They are used as spiritual conduits or magical chants that produce a desired result either in the mind and body or in the life of an individual. While the language of chants might not be understood, it provides deeper connections to Hindus than can be conveyed through words alone.

The human condition in Hindu is *samsara*. Samsara is the flow of reality in which souls are continually dying and being reborn.[4] For Hindus the present existence is an illusion. Hindus believe that people are unaware of their oneness with God. The goal of life is liberation from the cycle of reincarnation. This entails passing beyond illusion to become one with the divine (Ultimate Reality) by following the proper yoga. The desired ultimate state of existence is *moksha*, the final release.[5] To understand the language of Hindu prayer, one must first understand that Hindu prayers seek divine assistance in attaining moral purity and spiritual progress. Hindu beliefs and practices seek to make sense of the limitations of the human condition and to relieve the emotional and physical suffering that accompanies it.[6]

Unlike Christians and Muslims, Buddhists do not pray to anyone or for anything. Instead, they pray to connect with compassion, with self, and to achieve awakening. Buddhist practice is a way of letting go of everything. For Buddhists, the human condition is suffering caused by attachment to things and the craving (desire) accompanying this attachment. The solution to the human condition is eliminating attachment, particularly by following the Eightfold Path, which stresses moral virtue, including right action, right vocation, and right conduct. This includes loving kindness, selfless giving to others, and efforts to alleviate human hurts. Nirvana, negation of suffering, is a state of being realized by eliminating desire.[7]

The concepts of God outlined above show that intercultural awareness poses a significant challenge to spiritual care providers. Caregiving in multicultural settings invites caregivers to conform to plurality with humility. It also offers spiritual care providers and seekers an opportunity to celebrate God, who created diversity. Diversity drives ideas, enriches communities, and spurs innovations. Knowing something about a person's idea of the Divine opens a window into their worldview, allowing one to see the world from their perspective. This kind of knowledge can be described as empathy. It seeks to see through an eye of another, hear through the ears of another and feel through the heart of another. It reminds us of our own vulnerability to unpleasant things that happen in life. Empathy expressed in prayer ministers in the context of complicated issues with sensitivity and respect. It pays attention to the ways people are different. It does not intrude; it does not control or force itself on the needs of others. Instead, it trusts people to find their own ways as they need to in their own faith journeys. As a result, it does not *have to*, *need to*, or even *get to* fix anything in people. Instead, it comes alongside others in comfort as shepherds, midwives, and intimate strangers or as wounded healers. It sits with others in pain as they find quiet spaces inside themselves to discover what they need spiritually. It brings a non-judgmental attitude along, while facilitating what is happening in the moment rather than what it thinks ought to be happening. It comforts with silence and enters the pain of another at the level it enters its own.

Spirituality is the human aspect by which individuals seek to express their own meaning and purpose in life. It is also the way people experience connectedness to the moment, to self, to others, to nature, and to the significant or sacred.[8] In some circumstances, spiritual care providers act as intermediaries between God and people who feel they cannot or must not approach God personally. These people may be atheists or agnostics. They may be angry with God or feel unworthy of God. They might never have considered God as approachable at all. They might have been ashamed, embarrassed, afraid, or even intimidated by the idea of God.[9] Upholding other people's spiritual views prevents caregivers from imposing their own spiritual values or beliefs on them. When prayer is sensitively tailored to the uniqueness of an individual's experience it empowers patients and their families. It gives them the choice of whether or not to accept the spiritual caregiver's offer of emotional or spiritual support.

People's belief about God, the divine, or a higher power shapes their prayer language. People come to prayer with many different motives—altruistic or selfish, merciful or hateful, loving or bitter. Whatever the reasons might be, to pray is to commune with God. And language plays an important role in such communication. Language can intimidate, inspire, inform or even influence decisions. Language uses words, and words have the power to convey healing or harm. The same holds true for the language of prayer. It can bring healing or cause harm. Knowing how to pray and what to pray for fosters intimacy and growth with God. Prayer is more than a language. It is waiting, listening, thinking, imagining, but mostly just being present spiritually or emotionally with another. Prayer is a conversation with another about the most private or intimate feelings. It powerfully unites hearts in the acknowledgment of the mysteries of life and sacred values held in common.[10] A spiritual caregiver who understands the language of prayer can foster spiritual growth and intimacy and support others. When neglected, the absence of prayer can cause spiritual harm and discomfort for the patient.

There are two types of prayer languages: the command language and the compassion language. The command language speaks in the exercise of power, while compassion language speaks in a relational, empathetic exercise. Christians tend to embrace the command language in prayer more than other faith traditions. This is perhaps an attempt to emulate or mimic the language of Jesus as expressed in the gospels. For example, while Jesus was being tempted in the wilderness, He used scriptural commanding language against Satan. In His preaching, teaching, and healing ministry Jesus rebuked and cast out demons, calmed the stormy seas, and healed the sick by the power of His name. Christians acknowledge that there is power in the name of Jesus. It makes sense when Christians invoke the name of Jesus in a commanding way in their prayer. There is nothing wrong with this kind of language as long as it meets the care seeker's needs.

Spiritual caregivers must pay attention to the fact that prayer for many people is sacred and very personal. If approached inappropriately, prayer can be viewed as an invasive or insensitive act causing more harm than good. The casting out of demons, the wrestling against principalities and powers (Ephesians 6:10-18), the judging of the fallen angels (1 Corinthians 6:2-3), the crushing of Satan under our feet (Romans 16:20), or the tearing down of strongholds in the name of Jesus Christ might not be a comforting language for everyone. Likewise, while ending prayers in the name of Jesus might be comforting for Christians, others might see it as an act of proselytism. Removing the reference of the name of Jesus for non-Christians or those of unknown faiths can increase their comfort level. It shows respect for their faith journeys. It also demonstrates that the care provider has no ego or a hidden agenda invested in the process.

On the other hand, compassionate or relational language invokes feelings and empathy. It involves feeling for another and co-suffers with others in the painful place life has put them.[11] It mobilizes and engages others in a non-anxious manner, providing sacred space where people feel loved and heard. It examines wounds, evaluates losses, and does not provide unhelpful guidance when life is at its tattered edges.[12] It embraces God, who is willing to suffer alongside yet allows people to find meaning and purpose in their own existence, which they hold sacred. The sacred space is where beauty and the holy embrace each other. Some envision the sacred as God the father or God the mother, but the sacred could also be the transcendent, family, nature, or community.[13] When a sacred space is carefully created, it becomes a place of beauty persons will want to enter to address the isolation and loneliness often felt by patients. This aspect is especially important for those who work in pediatrics or in some long-term or elder care facilities. Sacred space compassionately helps care seekers feel secure in more private moments such as prayer or meditation. Compassion language in prayer does not come across as evangelistic or exclusive. Instead it is empathic and nurturing. It accommodates and comforts spiritual care seekers more than power language in prayer does in their crises.

Praying through the names of God is another practice that compassionately expresses intercultural sensitivity. When properly incorporated, the attributes of God can also convey comfort. The Holy Qur'an documents ninety-nine names by which Allah describes himself in divine attributes. Muslims believe studying Allah's attributes effectively strengthens a person's relationship with Him. It nurtures consciousness and humility that enhance good actions. In their supplications, Muslims are encouraged to call upon Allah by the most appropriate names that relate to what they are requesting (Qur'an 7:180).[14] For example, He is the God Who creates; He is the Compassionate, the Beneficent, and the Merciful One. He is the King, the Sovereign Lord with complete dominion. He is the source of peace and free from every imperfection. He is the most gracious; most merciful; most beautiful God is He (Qur'an 59:23-24).[15]

In Christianity, God is the divine presence, the refuge in times of trouble. He shepherds those who are estranged or lost. He is a compassionate Samaritan who does not injure, hurt, or neglect others. He is the wounded healer who sits among the poor, binding their wounds. He is the intimate stranger familiar with the unknown and a midwife who attends to people in their travail, in any kind of tribulation or anguish.[16] In his classic book on the attributes of God, A.W. Tozer states that "What comes into our minds when we think about God is the most important thing about us."[17] He continues on to say that "Man's spiritual history will positively demonstrate that no religion has ever been greater than its idea of God. For worship is pure or abases as the worshipper entertains the high or low thoughts of God." Even though Muslims and Christians disagree on some doctrinal issues such as Jesus being the Son of God, or the Trinity, they both find it meaningful to pray through the attributes of God. It must be noted; Christians and Muslims, as well as Jews, worship the one God, Whose roots and inception go back to the time before Abraham, who is their common link.[18]

One of the biggest misconceptions about Hinduism is that Hindus worship many gods. But in fact, I discovered from a Hindu patient that Hinduism believes in only one God, who allows people to worship Him in many forms, such as nature (including trees, sun, idols, or animals) and in persons such as Lord Krishna, Lord Rama, Lord Shiva, or Lord Vishnu. These celestial beings are called *devas* or deities and they are likened to Jesus and Buddha as messengers of God. Devas are not to be confused with the One, the Supreme God. Another way to look at Hinduism is as a philosophy of pantheism. This idea considers everything, living and non-living, as divine and sacred. Hindu patients accept prayers from spiritual caregivers of other faiths because Hindus view human beings as manifestations of God. Integrating the oneness of God in Hindu care can be very comforting to Hindu patients in healthcare settings.

The uniqueness of Buddhism among world religions is very noticeable. Buddhism does not have a place for God in its practice. Although beliefs in Buddhism vary, a core belief common to almost all Buddhists involves "taking refuge" in Buddha.[19] Even though Buddhists pray to Buddha, Buddha is not a deity or Supreme Being comparable to the God of monotheistic religions. Buddhism strongly rejects the notion of a Supreme Being as irrelevant. Instead, Buddhists concern themselves with a method of escape from worldly ills. This involves undertaking a mental method of discipline and a code of conduct, which sufficiently satisfies the spiritual requirements. As previously referenced, the Buddhists' Eightfold Path stresses moral virtue. Although Buddhists reject the concept of a Supreme Being, integrating the language of morality while providing spiritual care can be very comforting to them. For instance, allowing Buddhists to reflect on their actions of kindness, mindfulness, selfless giving to others, or their efforts to alleviate human hurts conveys meaning and the purpose stressed in their moral virtue. For that is the ancient path travelled by the rightly self-awakened ones of former times.

The dos and don'ts in prayer inform spiritual care providers in an intercultural setting, as do the idea and the attributes of God. When a patient requests prayer, the guiding principle is never to overstep boundaries in the caregiving relationship. These requests must be handled thoughtfully, compassionately, and professionally. As previously stated, prayer requests are always personal, sacred, and patient-centered. Allowing the patient to initiate the need for prayer is a safe place to start since the journey belongs to them. When caregivers follow the lead of the patient it is very empowering. It shows respect, expresses trust, and honors the patient's sacred space. As providers, we do not intrude, control, or abuse this individual space. Instead, we are invited into it to look, to listen, and to learn about the patient's relational, emotional, and spiritual needs. The main role as an invited caregiver is to facilitate the patient's story. Any deviation from that task intrudes and disrespects the patient's process by denying them the ability to access their own faith beliefs to find meaning, peace, and comfort.

Therefore, as clinically trained spiritual care professionals, we tread carefully when offering prayers. We do not want to obligate patients to accept prayers or rob them the chance to say "No" to us if they don't feel comfortable with it. Handling such moments thoughtfully indicates a sign of humility in the provision of care. It embodies compassion and avoids what could be termed as "spiritual malpractice." Instead, the spiritual caregiver can ask, "Is there anything else I could do for you before I leave?" At this point, the patient can choose whether or when to ask for prayer or any other spiritual intervention that is meaningful to them.

The dos and the don'ts in prayer come with religious boundaries. Just because a person claims a particular faith tradition does not necessarily mean their prayer language is the same as others of that tradition. For instance, Christians from more liturgical or ritualistic traditions might find comfort in reciting the Apostles' Creed or reading from a common book of prayer, while Pentecostals find comfort in the power language in the name of Jesus, and Catholics in reciting the Lord's Prayer or saying the Hail Mary. The fact that a spiritual care provider would take the time to approach these requests with thoughtfulness empowers the patient and demonstrates humility, compassion, and professionalism. So when care seekers request prayer, it is incumbent upon spiritual caregivers to identify the care seeker's spirituality in order to use the appropriate prayer language when providing them with spiritual care. If the patient's spirituality is unknown, seek permission by simply asking the patient.

The challenge comes when providers initiate prayer without the patient's permission. This can be interpreted as the spiritual care provider feeling uncomfortable sitting with patients in pain. In such a scenario, prayer becomes an exit strategy for the care provider. When prayer becomes an exit strategy, the spiritual caregiver fails to be present. The art of presence requires the care provider to listen to the patient's account of their immediate crisis and consider how it relates to the care seeker's larger story. It also listens to the testimony and counter testimony that appear in the way a person presents their problems and life.[20] Being present in the discomfort of others can be very comforting to them. It demonstrates that the caregiver is aware of and comfortable with his or her own discomfort. This awareness helps the spiritual caregiver not to gloss over the patient's pain nor to emotionally abandon them at the time of their greatest need. It avoids minimizing or intellectualizing people's pain, and instead remains present. It acknowledges and validates their feelings without trying to talk them out of their pain so quickly.

The quest for inclusiveness in healthcare arises from a spiritual care imperative to treat each individual or faith tradition with dignity and respect. The appropriate use of prayer is one of the primary ways to achieve this goal. Unlike clergy persons, who minister to groups of people with similar religious beliefs or common cultural identities, spiritual care providers minister in the context of complicated issues, which demand both cultural and religious sensitivity. They include ministry to people with different religious beliefs or none at all. Such diversity requires a genuine theological integration of spiritual care with a theory that respects all religious differences. As care providers, we can learn from the example of the Apostle Paul. To the weak he became weak, that he might win the weak. He became all things to all men so that by all possible means he might save some (1 Corinthians 9:22). The message is not to win all, but to win some. With that mindset, we can use our time, talents, and treasure to provide meaningful spiritual care support that is sensitive to diversity, respectful, and comforting.

When prayer is offered appropriately, it can bring spiritual healing. On the other hand, when prayer is insensitive, it can cause spiritual harm. When spiritual care providers pay attention to spirituality in an intercultural setting, it allows them to become all things and to relate to all others without compromising their own beliefs. It is therefore necessary for spiritual care providers to try to find common ground with everyone, doing everything they can to provide emotional and spiritual comfort to all, without criticizing the faiths or beliefs of other people.

If there is a single experience shared by all people around the globe, it is the language of pain and comfort. Pain transcends all people, cultures, races, and creeds. It has no respect for the rich or poor. It does not matter whether you are young or old, black or white, male or female, spiritual or unspiritual, religious or non-religious—pain strikes us all. And during those moments of crisis, illnesses, and suffering, all it takes is the comfort of a seasoned spiritual care provider who wisely chooses the appropriate ministry intervention for the situation. He or she initiates ministry to all people, regardless of age, gender, ethnicity, or faith tradition. Such care approaches cultural, religious or spiritual differences with humility and willingness to learn and apply new information.[21] This kind of effort is ultimately committed to providing inclusive care for all patients, families, and healthcare staff. It does so with compassion and respect for human dignity.

---

1 Wayne Grudem, *Systematic Theology: An Introduction to Biblical Doctrine* (Grand Rapids: Zondervan, 1994), 376.

2 Ron Rhodes, *Reasoning From the Scriptures with Muslims* (Eugene, OR: Harvest House Publishers, 2002), 95.

3 Nervile A. Kirkwood, *A Hospital Handbook on Multiculturalism and Religion: Practical Guidelines for Health Care Workers* (Harrisburg, PA: Morehouse Publishing, 2005), 33.

4 Harold G. Koenig, *Hinduism and Mental Health: Beliefs, Research and Applications* (Middletown: Center For Spirituality Theology and Health Duke University, 2017), 12.

5 North American Mission Board. Interfaith Witness Division, *Comparative Belief Charts* (Alpharetta, GA: North American Mission Board, 1998).

6 Koenig, *Hinduism*, 83.

7 Mission Board, *Comparative Belief Chart*.

8 Christina Puchalski, et al., "Improving the Quality of Spiritual Care as a Dimension of Palliative Care: The Report of the Consensus Conference," *Journal of Palliative Medicine*, 12, no. 10 (Oct. 2009), 885-904.

9 Naomi K. Paget and Janet R. McCormack, *The Work of the Chaplain* (Valley Forge: Judson Press, 2006), 17.

10 Ted Brownstein, *The Interfaith Prayer Book* (Lake Worth: Lake Worth Interfaith Network, 2014), i.

11 Frederick W. Schmidt, *The Dave Test* (Nashville: Abingdon Press, 2013), 7.

12 Schmidt, *Dave Test*, 8.

13 Paget, *Work of the Chaplain*, iv.

14 www.whyislam.org/allah/god/names-and-attributes-of-allah/

15 Rhodes, *Reasoning*, 95.

16 Robert C. Dykstra, *Images of Pastoral Care* (St. Louis, Missouri: Chalice Press, 2005), 66 ff.

17 A.W. Tozer, *The Knowledge of God* (San Francisco: HarperCollins, 1978), 1.

18 Kirkwood, *Handbook*, 28.

19 John Ross Carter, Mahinda Palihawadana, *The Dhammapada: the Sayings of the Buddha* (Oxford: Oxford University Press, 2000).

20 John Patton, *Pastoral Care: An Essential Guide* (Nashville: Abingdon Press, 2005), 32.

21 Paget, *Work of the Chaplain*, 8 ff.

10

ENHANCING CULTURAL COMPETENCE THROUGH IMMERSION

Satoe Soga, DMin, BCC
ACPE Certified Educator,
Houston Methodist Hospital

I N THIS CHAPTER, I discuss the importance of using experiential learning to enhance cultural competence. The chapter is based on a study of a pilot clinical pastoral education (CPE) program called "Cultural Immersion CPE" that was conducted in an urban hospital in Dallas, Texas. The students were embedded in neighboring minority faith communities during their CPE training while serving as hospital chaplains. I present qualitative data collected from stories shared by the participants in this program to reflect on the effectiveness of enhancing cultural competence and increasing empathy through experiential learning.

Cultural Competence and Self-Awareness

Cultural competence is a requirement for health care professionals serving a patient population from diverse sociocultural and religious backgrounds. It is broadly defined as "the ability of providers and organizations to effectively deliver health care services that meet the social, cultural, and linguistic needs of patients."[1] If one looks more deeply into the competency of the professional care provider, however, one cannot deny that an important element is the care provider's self-awareness.

Self-awareness in the helping professions means being aware of one's thoughts and feelings and one's status and power and how they impact one's interaction with others. None of us is exempt from having preferences and biases. We are all socialized within our respective cultures with values, thought processes, and behaviors. We have the tendency to believe that the ways we speak, act, and behave are culturally appropriate—are, in fact, the cultural standards—especially when our language, culture, or religious practice is accepted as the norm by the society we live in. When our cultural practices are accepted as the norm in our society, at a subconscious level we may dislike anything that is different and judge other ways of being as abnormal or inferior. As health care providers who are in a position of power, we need to become aware of our cultural practices so we do not impose personal bias on the care receiver and participate in cultural oppression.[2] As Geri-Ann Galanti states, cultural competence "begins with understanding your own culture and biases, becoming sensitive to the culture of others, and appreciating the differences."[3] When we appreciate differences, we help patients from diverse backgrounds to feel at ease when receiving care.

Empathy and Experiential Learning

Cultural competence requires not only the awareness of culture and appreciation of differences but also the ability to imagine the experiences of another person. It requires empathy. Empathy is an entering into another person's experience. It is the ability to use one's intellect, memory, and imagination to understand another's thoughts and feelings.[4] It imagines what the other is feeling and what the other might need, and responds in caring ways.[5] Without empathy, health care providers may focus mainly on technical actions and questions. They may ask, "Has everything been done correctly?," without asking the care-ethical question, "Has everything been done to benefit the care receiver?"[6] Derald Wing Sue and David Sue also emphasize the importance of understanding the emotions. "[Cognitive] understanding and intellectual competence are not enough. Concepts of multiculturalism, diversity, race, culture, ethnicity, and so forth are more than intellectual concepts. Multiculturalism deals with real human experiences, and as a result, understanding your emotional reactions is equally important in the journey to cultural competence."[7]

One of the best educational methods to enhance one's ability to empathize is immersion. Immersion is a model of experiential learning through which students develop knowledge, skills, and values from direct experiences. It enables students to experience course content outside the classroom, where concepts can be better integrated into their lives.[8] Patients from various cultural, linguistic, or religious backgrounds come to the hospital, inevitably bringing their diverse life experiences and their emotional reactions to injury, illness, and other people. In order to meet them where they are, the healing team must be equipped to understand how they feel. If the health provider has empathy, an emotional understanding of how to enter the other's experience, then it can be an effective therapeutic element for patients that results in better communication, greater treatment satisfaction, and increased quality of life.[9]

Immersion as Experiential Learning

Cultural Immersion experiences have been used as a pedagogical approach to multicultural learning in disciplines related to the helping professions.[10] Positive outcomes of this experiential training include enhanced cultural awareness, self-awareness of one's own culture, cultural empathy, critical consciousness, commitment to change, and social justice advocacy.[11] Cultural Immersion CPE moves regular cultural immersion pedagogy one step further. It creates an environment for chaplain students to experience what it is like to be a minority. When a chaplain is in a cultural group that is different from his or her own cultural group, the chaplain becomes "the designated minority," who inevitably runs into barriers such as language or culture and challenges such as confusion, misunderstanding, or exclusion, which are common experiences minorities encounter in everyday social interactions. As the chaplain experiences what it is like to be a minority through social interactions, he or she cultivates an attitude of empathy that enhances professional knowledge. When serving patients from minority backgrounds in the hospital, rather than just focusing on technical knowledge to address the illness itself, the chaplain is equipped to address the health and feelings—the holistic health—of the patient, taking into consideration the patient's cultural, religious, and spiritual needs.

Educational Contexts

The contexts we used for this immersion were the neighboring minority faith communities of our hospital. The four faith communities involved were located in the Dallas-Fort Worth area. These were an African Presbyterian church with a mostly Nigerian congregation, a Latino Baptist church with a Spanish-speaking congregation, a Latino Methodist church with both English- and Spanish-speaking congregations, and an Islamic center.

The CPE center used the 20-week extended part-time program as the bedrock for this training. At this particular CPE center, the extended program requires students to complete at least 320 clinical hours and at least 100 hours of education to meet the Association for Clinical Pastoral Education (ACPE) accreditation requirements. For cultural immersion, each student is required to complete 300 hours in the hospital, and the remaining 20 hours are to be fulfilled through immersion with a host family within a faith community. While the student is embedded in a particular faith community, the host family agrees to help each CPE student to develop relationships, to understand the community's experiences and concerns as a minority group, and to ask questions they may have about obtaining necessary health care in America.

Rules of Engagement

Since the Cultural Immersion CPE program was a pilot program, we explored various cultural immersion models and came up with some rules of engagement for the students and the host families. We allowed each intern and the respective host family to decide how they would spend their time with each other for the 20 hours within the 20-week period. Each session could last four, three, or two hours, depending on the nature of the activity. The host family received guidelines during the orientation about what to do and what not to do. They were asked to go on with their daily life without significantly changing their routines and activities to accommodate the student. They were told they could encourage the student to attend events sponsored by their faith community, such as Bible study, worship services, lectures, or festivals. They could invite the student to their home for lunch or dinner, most of the minority communities value hospitality and develop friendships over meals. As for the chaplain students, they were to be open to what this immersion process could teach them and to explore and imagine the most effective ways to offer health care for minorities in a culturally sensitive and helpful manner.

Student Reflections

Nine students participated in the pilot Cultural Immersion CPE training. Five students participated in the 2017 program and four students participated in the 2018 program. At the conclusion of the units, all students presented their experiences and taught their CPE peers about things they had learned concerning the faith community in which they were immersed. Sheryl A. Kujawa-Holbrook states, "Personal narratives are at the root of how we experience differences, as well as how we experience God."[12] As a chaplain educator who discovers God in human experiences, I present the following excerpts collected from chaplain students from the two programs. For the sake of confidentiality, I have used pseudonyms to protect the identity of each participant.

Case #1:

Daniel was a monolingual European American male student immersed in a Spanish-speaking faith community. As he interacted with the congregation, he started to realize that he had a tendency to engage with people who were similar to him. After several engagements with the Spanish-speaking faith community, Daniel got in touch with his feelings of loneliness and anxiety. This caused him to imagine how non-English speakers might feel in a hospital setting. He considered:

The gravity of the loneliness, confusion, and the potential fear a family can feel as they enter into the intimidation of the ICU and are unable to formulate relationship(s) with the staff team unless an interpreter steps in. But even so the intimacy is lacking, because the directness of the common mutual language is lost ... This is the first time I ever considered something of a cultural difference not only with my mind but with my emotions.

Daniel later ministered to a Spanish-speaking patient with suicidal ideation. Rather than letting the language difference move him away from caring for the patient, Daniel used a Spanish-speaking staff member as an interpreter and listened to the patient's despair. As a result, Daniel enabled the suicidal patient to have an important conversation with his son, which dissipated the patient's desire to end his own life.

Case #2:

Anthony and John were immersed in the same Spanish-speaking church during the fall extended unit. Anthony was an African American student, and John was a Nigerian student. They each had a different host family within the same congregation. At the beginning of the unit, while their colleagues were scheduling their 20-hour immersion with their host family, Anthony and John had a difficult time getting responses from their host families. Anthony shared with the group his feelings and assumptions about his host family during an interpersonal relations (IPR) session:

I wonder if my host family does not like me. I took the initiative to talk to them and engage with them, but they seem to be distant. The two daughters of my host family speak English, so they serve as the translators between myself and the parents of the host family, but I am not sure if they are interested in me.

Thinking that people did not like him was not foreign to Anthony. In his personal history, Anthony shared that he experienced disapproval from his father, so the lack of contact he experienced from his host family reinforced his familiar assumption of not being wanted. John, however, had a different perspective. John invited Anthony to consider the following:

Just like you are struggling with the language and the culture, your host family is experiencing the same struggle. The parents for the host family are not English speakers. They may have difficulty speaking to you, not wanting to make mistakes in English. They may have difficulty knowing what to talk about, because they have not found something in common with you to talk about.

John proceeded to share about the tendency people have to congregate with those who speak the same language and have similar life experiences. As a Nigerian minister who had done missions in other countries, John had observed members of faith communities not knowing what to do with visitors from other countries. He encouraged Anthony to keep working on it and be patient with the host family. John's input helped Anthony to interpret the behavior of his host family from a different angle.

Anthony's concern prompted me, as the program educator, to seek clarification and counsel from the pastor of the Latino congregation. When I brought Anthony's concern to the attention of the pastor, she acknowledged the need to encourage the host families to spend time with the chaplain students. Nonetheless, she also clarified that the women from both host families were busily involved in the women's retreat as leaders of the church. She further noted that, in her experience with Latino families, women were the drivers. When the woman was away, there was no centralized influence to mobilize the family for any activity. This was reflected in both students' experience of a lack of contact. The pastor's clarification helped Anthony to realize how his assumptions based on his personal history impacted his interpretation of the behavior of the host family. He also learned the importance of clarifying and understanding the story of the other party so he would not let his own assumptions influence his attitude toward his host family (ACPE Outcome L1.2).[13] Due to his tenacity and his fun-loving personality, Anthony persevered, and his relationship with the host family improved.

Case #3:

Pearl was a European American Christian chaplain who was placed in the Islamic community for her cultural immersion during the Fall Extended Unit. She had received theological training at a seminary that emphasized the inerrancy of the Bible, and her upbringing also stressed the importance of finding the correct answer to matters related to life. While she was open to engaging people who are different and excited about the opportunity to learn from them, she did not expect the treasure she would receive and the turmoil she would go though.

At the beginning of their interaction, Pearl was surprised to discover the access she had as a woman to the woman in the

Muslim family in which she was embedded. According to the guidelines of Islam, men and women are to show modesty through their attire. In the presence of the opposite gender, being modest in both actions and appearance are means to maintain and elevate human dignity. When the mother of the host family showed Pearl her face without her hijab (veil), she told Pearl that the previous male chaplain student had never seen her face. Having a history in her own family of not been seen and heard, Pearl was elated and touched by the honor given to her to engage with the mother of her host family and "see her" without any visible barrier. Pearl also learned from the mother of the host family that wearing the hijab and covering her face was her own decision. The mother of the host family had had a conversation with her husband about whether to cover her face or not. Her husband acknowledged that the decision was between her and Allah and that he would support her decision. The mother of the host family decided to cover her face in the presence of men who were not relatives. Pearl was moved by the opportunities granted her to see her host mother. She also treasured the moments she engaged in theological conversation with the host family openly and freely. She was excited to see and hear every member within her host family, and she cherished the way they saw and heard her in return.

When she was exposed to various lectures and observed several prayer meetings, Pearl was brought to a place that shook her theological foundation. As she listened to the teachings of Islam that encourage believers to serve, as she engaged with her host family in intellectual conversation regarding God and creation, as she observed those who believed in their faith deeply and practiced its teachings in their everyday lives, Pearl began to wonder if she was the same Christian she had been before the immersion experience. The experience with her host family and the friendship she built within the Islamic community created difficult emotional, intellectual, and spiritual challenges for Pearl. She had to reconstruct her own faith and pursue God and the creation from a different angle, taking into consideration the perspectives of non-Christians (ACPE Outcomes L2.2, 2.3, 2.6, 2.7).[14]

At the end of the unit, Pearl spoke of an experience of heart break she had when she saw a man praying in the hospital chapel:

> I was in our chapel and I saw a man standing there ... I thought he was a Christian man worshipping God. But immediately he bent his body in a certain way, and I realized that he was a Muslim man praying. It was about 12:30 or 12:45, so the man was doing his noon prayer. At first, I was excited about recognizing what he was doing, and I had a deeper appreciation for that. And very quickly my excitement turned to heart break. Because here was this man trying to honor God and pursue connection and worship, but one of the people in front of me was on his cellphone, and there was another woman in the chapel beside myself ... The whole set-up was not what he would encounter at a mosque. On the one hand, I felt very glad that he did feel welcome in the chapel, because he was welcome, but on the other hand, he did not have a rug to pray on, and he was praying on the carpet. I felt so bad that he was bowing down and placing his face on the carpet. My heart broke. I wanted to be able to

provide something for him that showed a little more that "Yes, this space is here, and let's make this space even more accommodating for you, because we do want you to be here and we do want you to get what you need to worship, and we do value you."

Pearl went through a process of "theological empathy," in Doehring's term. According to Doehring, "Theological empathy occurs when spiritual caregivers stand in the shoes of those theologically different from them and appreciate how their lived theology can be a home for them in troubled, challenging times." It is an experience of "affective mentalizing, in which spiritual caregivers imagine the kinds of lived theologies or spiritual orienting systems generated by the emotions that the other seems to be experiencing."[15] Because of the increased empathy Pearl felt toward the Muslim man praying in the chapel, she became an advocate for the Islamic community within the Department of Pastoral Education at our institution. She encouraged the department to provide space and prayer kits that would assist the Muslim patients and family members to maintain their spiritual practice.

These are a few examples that demonstrate ways in which the immersion experience influenced students' learning. Some students became aware of their assumptions and had their perspectives modified; some gained the courage to engage with people they normally would not encounter (ACPE Outcome L1.7)[16]; and some students developed deeper connections with patients who resembled the culture of their host families. The program helped the students achieve ACPE objectives and outcomes. The program also cultivated empathy and understanding among some of the students. Daniel recognized the loneliness and confusion a non-English speaking patient may face in the hospital; Pearl was deeply moved by the discomfort the Muslim man might have experienced in the chapel.

Further Reflection on Program Outcomes

We celebrated our program's success, but we also examined challenges the program encountered. Principal among these was the immersion of a minority student with a family from a different minority background. When we reviewed the experience of Anthony, an African American student, and his Latino host family, the family's pastor and I discussed the barriers existing *between* minority groups. Anthony's host family assumed that they would feel more comfortable with Anthony as another minority than with Daniel, an Anglo student. They thought their common experience with discrimination would bond them better. In this case, contrary to everyone's expectations, it was actually more difficult for a minority student to be immersed in another minority community.

All minorities have engaged with the dominant European American culture, so engaging with people from the dominant culture is not a new experience. When Anthony engaged with his Latino host family, both parties had to work with a culture with which they were not familiar. It took more effort for the parties to experiment with how best to relate to each other, to test their comfort zone with one another, and to build the relationship. At one point, we considered whether it would be easier to place a minority student with a European American host family in the congregation, and one minority student made this particular request for the future.

Yet I am not convinced that this kind of arrangement would serve the purpose of Cultural Immersion CPE. One of the goals of the program is for the students to understand the plight of minority patients and to offer culturally appropriate care. This facilitates connection points between people who do not normally interact with one another.[17] It is as important for minority students as it is for students from the dominant culture to increase empathy toward patients from other minority groups in order to achieve cultural competence. What I will do in the future is to better prepare the minority students and the host families for the immersion experience. I will help them become aware of the possible discomfort that may arise since both parties need to adjust to another culture with which they normally would not interact.

Limitation of the Data

The data from our pilot program and study are limited because (1) the number of participants was small, nine chaplains and five host families from various faith communities; and (2) the impact of the program on participants was self-reported.

Future Research and Development

The data from this project are people's subjective experiences, i.e., self-reported data. I hope to identify an appropriate assessment tool that can effectively measure students' cultural competency before and after the training. Possible models, used by students in behavioral health care and intercultural competence, include Bennett's Developmental Model of Intercultural Sensitivity (DMIS; 1986, 1993)[18] and Hammer's Intercultural Development Inventory (IDI; 2013).[19]

I also want to consider ways this program might mobilize students to have a greater impact in intercultural interactions and social transformation in whatever context they work.

Lockwood-Stewart states the importance of critically examining and assessing immersive learning on an ongoing basis.[20] Kushner also warned against the danger of "tourism," which does not change the places one visited or is immersed in for the better.[21] I hope that Cultural Immersion CPE will not only enhance students' appreciation for diversity, equality, and inclusion, I hope it will also motivate them to improve relationships with minority communities and improve intercultural relationships. As Rhodes states, "The key to personal and social transformation is post-immersion work and creating infrastructures that support that work."[22] If Cultural Immersion CPE can contribute to personal and social transformation even on a small scale, we will have achieved a great deal.

Conclusion

The hospital chaplain students who participated in our pilot experience learning program of cultural immersion increased their awareness of the loneliness, confusion, and exclusion minority patients and families go through in a dominant culture; grew in empathy toward people from an ethnic, cultural, and linguistic background different from their own; and subsequently made deeper connections with diverse patients in our hospital. Finally, sponsoring the Cultural Immersion CPE program began to change our institutional relationships with surrounding minority faith communities, making our staff and leadership more aware of the power relationships in play. Experiential learning can enhance cultural competence.

1 Emily Ihara, *Cultural Competence in Health Care: Is It Important for People with Chronic Conditions?* (Washington, D.C.: Center on an Aging Society, [2004]).

2 Derald Wing Sue and David Sue, *Counseling the Culturally Diverse* (Hoboken, NJ: John Wiley & Sons), 23.

3 Geri-Ann Galanti, *Caring for Patients from Different Cultures* (Philadelphia: University of Pennsylvania, 2015), 2.

4 Elisa Magri, "Some Remarks on For-Me-Ness and Empathy," *International Journal of Philosophical Studies,* 23, no. 5 (2015): 625-29.

5 Carrie Doehring, "Intercultural Spiritual Care," *Journal of Pastoral Psychology,* 67, no. 5 (October 2018): 461-74.

6 Linus Vanlaere, Trees Coucke, and Chris Gastmans, "Experiential Learning of Empathy in a Care-Ethics Lab," *Nursing Ethics,* 17, no. 3 (May 2010): 325-36.

7 Sue, *Counseling the Culturally Diverse,* 6.

8 George M. Slavich and Philip G. Gimbardo, "Transformational Teaching: Theoretical Underpinnings, Basic Principles, and Core Methods," *Educational Psychology Review,* 24 (July 2012): 569-608.

9 Melanie Neumann, et al., "Empathy Decline and Its Reasons: A Systematic Review of Studies with Medical Students and Residents," *Academic Medicine,* 86, no. 8 (2011): 996-1009. Doi:10.1097/ACM.0b013e318221e615.

10 Kyoung Mi Choi, Richard W. VanNoorhis, and Audrey E. Ellenwood, "Enhancing Critical Consciousness through a Cross-Cultural Immersion Experience in South Africa," *Journal of Multicultural Counseling and Development,* 43 (October 2015): 244-61.

11 Judith A. Burnett, Dennis Hamel, and Lynn L. Long. (2004). "Service Learning in Graduate Counselor Education: Developing Multicultural Counseling Competency," *Journal of Multicultural Counseling and Development* 32 (2011): 180-91. Doi:10.1002/j2161-1912.2004. tb00370.x.

12 Sheryl A. Kujawa-Holbrook, "Love and Power: Antiracist Pastoral Care," in *Injustice and the Care of Souls,* ed. Sheryl Kujawa-Holbrook & Karen Montagno (Minneapolis: Augsburg Fortress, 2009), 19.

13 Association for Clinical Pastoral Education, *ACPE Standards and Manuals* (Decatur, GA: Association for Clinical Pastoral Education, 2020). https://www.manula.com/manuals/acpe/acpe-

manuals/2016/en/topic/objectives-and-outcomes-for-level-i-level-ii-cpe. Accessed November 7, 2020.

14 Association for Clinical Pastoral Education, *ACPE Standards and Manuals*.

15 Carrie Doehring, "Teaching Theological Empathy to Distance Learners of Intercultural Spiritual Care," *Pastoral Psychology*, 67, no. 5 (October 2018): 465.

16 Association for Clinical Pastoral Education, *ACPE Standards and Manuals*.

17 Alida Miranda-Wolff, "Experiential Learning through Cultural Immersion: Is Cultural Immersion the Next Wave in Leadership Development and Diversity, Equity and Inclusion?" Jan. 28, 2019, *Chief Learning Officer*, http://www.clomedia.com/2019/01/28/experiential-learning-through-cultural-immersion/.

18 Milton J. Bennett, "Becoming Interculturally Competent," in *Toward Multiculturalism: A Reader in Multicultural Education*, ed. Jaime S. Wurzel, 2nd ed. (Newton, MA: Intercultural Resource Corp., 2004), 62-77.

19 Mitchell R. Hammer, Milton J. Bennet, and Richard Wiseman, "Measuring Intercultural Sensitivity: The Intercultural Development Inventory," *International Journal of Intercultural Relations*, 27 (2003): 421-43.

20 Odette Lockwood-Stewart, "Immersive Formation: Reflection on Dislocation and Transformation in Seminary Education," *Reflective Practice: Formation and Supervision in Ministry*, 37 (2019): 169-84.

21 Jacob Kushner, "The Voluntourist's Dilemma," *The New York Times*, March 22, 2016.

22 As quoted in Lockwood-Stewart, "Immersive Formation," 172.

SPIRITUAL CARE OF SPECIFIC PATIENT POPULATIONS

11

SPIRITUAL ABUSE: THE ROLE OF THE HOSPITAL CHAPLAIN IN RECOGNIZING PROFOUND SPIRITUAL TRAUMA

Hilary Chala
Senior Staff Chaplain, Houston Methodist Physician Organization

THE MOST PROFOUND HURT a person will experience will be a hurt to the soul.[1] There are many life experiences that pain our souls, grief being the most recognizable.[2] When a person's soul is hurt with intentionality, the pain is far reaching. Spiritual abuse is often difficult to recognize and less often screened for. Reviewing the different spiritual assessment tools, one recognizes the immediacy of the presenting spiritual concerns, pains from the past may be missed. The purpose of this chapter will be to define spiritual abuse for the clinical chaplain's use, demonstrate suggested ways to screen for and identify spiritual abuse, provide clinical examples of the chaplain encountering spiritual abuse, and examples of addressing spiritual abuse once identified.

Defining Spiritual Abuse

What is spiritual abuse? For the purpose of my work as a chaplain I have been using the following definition: "Spiritual abuse, spiritual trauma, spiritual terrorism, or spiritual holocaust is the act of intentionally using one's faith, or spiritual or religious beliefs to hurt another individual, group, or population." This definition has been useful to other treatment team members who were unfamiliar with spiritual abuse and requested a chaplain's perspective.

One does not have to be religious or spiritual to be a victim of spiritual abuse. The reverse is also true, the abuser does not have to be spiritual or religious to inflict spiritual abuse.

It is imperative for chaplains to be aware of spiritual abuse and its signs and symptoms. As the spiritual advocate for our patients, we must discern whether or not people we minister to have experiences of this in their history and maintain a spiritually safe environment within the clinical setting to prevent spiritual abuse from happening at the bedside.

Screening for Spiritual Abuse

The foundation of professional clinical hospital chaplaincy began with Anton Boisen.[3] In reviewing the spiritual histories[4] Boisen developed for patients over his career there is a depth most professional chaplains today cannot achieve, due to the limited time they can devote to each patient. However, the gift of the depth and breadth of the history used by Boisen naturally addresses whether or not the person was a victim or perpetrator of spiritual abuse. A better screening tool would be one that is less cumbersome and more flexible in light of chaplains' constraints, allowing for either a shorter screening process or addressing deeper issues such as spiritual abuse. Screening for spiritual abuse is not regularly done, yet if the chaplain suspects abuse or if the person receiving ministry verbalizes abuse, it is the responsibility of the chaplain to determine the level of spiritual hurt, whether or not the person is ready or able to experience spiritual healing, and what that spiritual healing would be for the person.[5]

Regardless of the spiritual assessment tool the chaplain uses when one decides to screen for spiritual abuse, some additional questions in the spiritual assessment to consider may include:

1. Have you always been [this form of religion or spirituality]?
2. Did your family of origin have the same religious beliefs as you while you were growing up?
3. Was your family's faith a source of support, stress, or both for you while growing up?
4. Were you forced to participate in any form of ritual while growing up?
5. Did anyone in this faith tradition hurt you, either a family member or a spiritual leader or member of the community?
6. About how old were you when you decided "This isn't for me"?
7. Why was that?
8. What religion(s) or belief(s) did you decide to investigate at that time?
9. How is your faith now?
10. What do you normally do to pray?
11. Have you been able to participate in religious observances recently?
12. Do you feel spiritually safe when you are outside of the hospital?
13. Do you feel safe now?

Key points for the chaplain to remember while completing the screening include:

1. The person may have experienced spiritual abuse in multiple settings, in which case the chaplain should consider repeating the questions regarding the history of spiritual abuse and spiritual safety for each episode of abuse.

2. It is possible that even with the patient answering all the questions to the best of their ability, the chaplain may not understand everything being said or remain confused about some complicated aspects of the history. Be open to the possibility that the chaplain may discover a complex spiritual history which may be difficult to understand.

3. The chaplain may hear about international crises such as genocides and holocausts that have spiritual impact; the overt political circumstances may cause the chaplain to miss nuances of the spiritual trauma.

4. If the chaplain discovers that the person has been a victim of sexual abuse in the context of spiritual abuse, the chaplain should follow a guideline for how to ask questions about the sexual abuse in a way that prevents the person from being traumatized again and the chaplain receiving secondary trauma.[6]

5. To whom is the spiritual trauma disclosed?[7] Do not assume, if the patient has a history of trauma, that the treatment team is aware of the trauma or the person will have disclosed this to their care providers. It is possible, because of how intimate the pain is, that the person will identify all manner of other hurts to clinicians, but keep the spiritual abuse private and only disclose it to one

specific provider, which could be the chaplain. Prior to speaking with the treatment team, confirm with the patient whether or not these aspects of their history are to remain under pastoral confidentiality, or if the patient is comfortable with the treatment team being informed. It has happened on a few occasions that the patient has asked me to keep the information confidential. In every case I have respected the patient's request and upheld our role as guardians of the secrets of the soul. In one instance I felt the information was pertinent to the care of the patient. In this one case I encouraged the patient to consider sharing the history herself with the team and educated her on how the information could positively improve her treatment.[8]

It is the duty of professional chaplains, when aware that someone has been a victim of spiritual abuse, to discern how the pain is being interpreted by the person. How will the person define healing? Is the person ready to experience any part of this healing right now? When the patient is discharged, where in the patient's community will they have a spiritually safe place to continue to explore areas of healing and growth beyond the trauma?

Identifying Spiritual Abuse

The victim of spiritual abuse may disclose this to only one person on the treatment team. This might not be the chaplain if the person has negative transference towards religious persons. However it is not uncommon for the person to disclose to a chaplain if the chaplain is effective in creating a spiritually healing environment for the patient. Regardless, some markers that may indicate that the person should be screened for spiritual abuse include (but are certainly not limited to):

1. An unhealthy relationship with their faith or spirituality
2. An aversion to anything spiritual
3. An aversion to or avoidance of very particular religious or spiritual things—this may include an aversion to meeting with the chaplain
4. A spiritually negative sense of "self"
5. Spiritual distress regarding specific aspects of self
6. Spiritual distress regarding familial and intimate relationships and sexuality

The clinician should also be aware of spiritual or religious themes surrounding other forms of abuse the patient may disclose.

While there are many different ways spiritual abuse may present in the clinical setting, below are just two glimpses of what the clinical chaplain may encounter.

Case Study 1: Political Spiritual Abuse

A man presents to outpatient therapy for support. He is an immigrant from another country. He has been fairly happy and successful with his new life in the United States. Everything suddenly came to a stop when he found himself unable to complete his work, his daily tasks, and his interactions with his loved ones. He was referred to our group, which includes a spiritual care component involving optional individual meetings with the chaplain or group sessions. The patient said he chose our program within Houston Methodist because of the optional spiritual care component we advertised on our website. He met with me his first week.

During the history portion of his assessment he told me he was brought up in a country that does not have a separation of religion from the government. Indeed, in his home country there is a regulated state religion. In his early twenties, his very intellectual and artistic family began secretly exploring other religions under the guise of studying "philosophies." In his mid-twenties he decided to convert to a different religion. This had to be done in secret, but government officials somehow found out about his conversion and he was imprisoned for "treason to the state," which depending on how the court rules against the guilty could be punishable with a fine, imprisonment, or execution. The patient was given a prison sentence, which he served. Upon his release, he and his entire family fled to the United States, completely abandoning his country of origin and the hills, waters, and skies he and his family had known for generations. He converted to the religion he had chosen and was practicing safely before his presentation to our outpatient clinic.

Symptoms (or areas of the story that speak of spiritual abuse):

1. There is a regulated state religion
2. His entire family had to study other thoughts and belief structures in secret
3. When he decided to convert to a new religion, this had to be done in secret
4. In his native country's court of law he was found guilty of having committed treason
5. He was threatened with execution for treason
6. He served time in prison because of his religious beliefs
7. He and his entire family had to flee to the United States for safety

Identifying Spiritual Trauma:

1. He had to flee for his life

2. Against his will he had to leave the geography he felt such a strong attachment towards
3. He understood all his relations' lives were also at risk
4. Recently, the trauma he endured prevented him from living his daily lifestyle

Patient Strengths:

1. His immediate family is supportive of him and each other
2. His loved ones encouraged him to seek mental health treatment
3. He had the courage to engage in mental health treatment
4. He had spiritual resiliency, the insight that he needed to meet with a chaplain to help him process and make sense of the spiritual components of what he had endured

The chaplain in this case will be able to listen to the patient and identify areas he associates with spiritual trauma or abuse. This patient is also able to articulate how much and in what ways he needs healing. While being threatened with execution by his government is an example of profound spiritual trauma, addressing it is still part of the chaplain's daily work of listening, validating, and spiritual empowerment.

This patient's future was wonderful. He was able to slowly resume his prayer and spiritual rituals at home. Over time he connected, first on the internet and then in person, with a spiritual community. This is particularly important. As the chaplain, I want him to have resources in his own community where he can access spiritual guidance, support, and help when needed, so as not to foster an unhealthy reliance on me for these things. He will be empowered to become his own spiritual advocate. The patient also was able to connect with people from his country of origin who had similar experiences. It was meaningful for him to be able to share with others the spiritual hurts he endured. This helped him deal with and make sense of his story.

Case Study 2: Intimate Partner Violence and Spiritual Abuse

A young lady is in the emergency room. One of the treatment team member's gut instinct is telling her to consult the chaplain, yet the patient is identifying as an atheist. In the context of the treatment team member's moral distress,[9] the chaplain is consulted. The nurse writes the consult, justifying herself by saying the patient is a victim of domestic violence and a spiritual history will be useful to the team.

When the patient is about to be transferred to another care facility, the chaplain meets with her. Consistent with the report to the treatment team, the patient identifies herself to the chaplain as an atheist. She grew up in a very religious household. The female figures in her home were spiritual inspirations, heroines, to her. No one in her religious community ever harmed her in any way. She enjoyed her faith.

When she was still young, around six years old, one of the men in her family raped her and a history of sexual abuse began. Her religion and faith became a consolation and refuge for her during a period of life that was absolute torment. When she was around seventeen, she ran away from home with a man who promised to marry her. She believed he was rescuing her. He did marry her and they have three children together. He is very brutal to her and she moved from one horrific situation to another.

While in her family of origin the men seemed indifferent to the women's faith, in her current home her husband is jealous of God. He does not allow her to say she is religious—she is an atheist. If he finds her praying, he beats her. He threatens the children. She had hidden in a secret place a porcelain statue of a religious figure. When she was able, she would secretly complete a prayer and ritual with this figurine. Knowing that she had this secret faith gave her strength to overcome all the sorts of abuse she endured. One day the patient's husband found the figurine, destroyed it, then beat her. As she described all her suffering, this is the only part of her story where she wept, her body rocking as she sobbed.

Symptoms (or areas of the story that speak of spiritual abuse):

1. There is a conflict of faith in the home of her family
2. Her current husband forces her to say "I'm an atheist"
3. Her faith must be secret for her own physical safety and that of her children
4. When her husband finds her praying he beats her, threatens the children, and destroys whatever religious items he finds
5. The instinct of the treatment team[10]

Identifying Spiritual Trauma:

1. Even when the patient's husband is not present, she does not feel safe enough to share her true beliefs
2. While she did not cry when she spoke of physical and sexual abuse, she cries when she recounts a spiritually painful moment that profoundly wounded her soul
3. The confusion of the treatment team

Patient Strengths:

1. The patient has the courage to pray in secret
2. Shrouding herself in atheism, the patient secretly shares her story with the chaplain

Four reasons make this a much more challenging case for the chaplain than the first study. First, the patient told the treatment team she was an atheist, which fostered a sense of confusion in the team member who referred a chaplain to an "atheist." While atheism does not preclude anyone from receiving a chaplain's visit, for most treatment team members this is counterintuitive and will often discourage the nurse or doctor from consulting their chaplain. Second were the physical safety concerns of the patient. Our first patient was in a safe place and ready to receive help, this woman's life is still actively in danger as soon as she is discharged from the hospital. Within this situation of domestic violence, the patient was not ready to receive help, nor was she willing to consider leaving her husband to go to a shelter for victims of domestic violence. Her spiritual safety was very poor, and the patient felt safest identifying herself and the team labeling her as "atheist." Third, she is not yet in a position where she is willing to experience change. The majority of her life has consisted of abuse and the thought of change must seem overwhelming to her.[11] Finally, contrasting with the first case where the patient was part of a program where he was seen regularly for a period of time, this patient is imminently being transferred to another care facility. This time constraint can create a sense of urgency and possibly a sense of performance pressure on the chaplain.

With these challenges, the spiritual medicine she experienced was unique to her needs and desires.[12] The chaplain should validate her identification of "atheist" and continue using the label. Yet conversely her story communicates a desire for prayer which should also be validated. Again, this is precarious because of the patient's safety concerns. A chart note for a visit like this might appear as: "Pt identifies as atheist, Prayer with Pt."

This prayer is perhaps the only prayer she experienced with another person for years and perhaps for an additional undetermined time in the future. There is no place in her immediate community where she will be able to pray safely again.

This patient's future appears very dismal. She does not have the freedom, beyond dwelling within her own soul, to access any spiritual support to nourish herself or to help her soul heal or grow.

Addressing Spiritual Abuse: Suggested Tools for the Clinical Chaplain

The chaplain will orient him or herself to the "living human document,"[13] the patient is our docent or tour guide and our map.

The key items to be established are:

1. Present: Immediate spiritual safety
2. Future: Theology of afterlife
3. Past: Theology of forgiveness

This is not to reduce the tools the chaplain can use. Rather if we consider spiritual care as spiritual medicine and therefore art, these three items are our primary colors on our palette, from which will spring a myriad of tools and options the clinical chaplain can use. Indeed it is my belief that searching for discovery of all the nuances of the soul led Boisen to his incredible spiritual intake of hundreds of questions for each person. This is not reductionism but rather simply a place to begin. These three points will be the foundation of the patient's personal tools, the chaplain will facilitate the patient's engagement with these to grow towards healing.

First, a clinical chaplain must create and maintain spiritual safety, including for patients, visitors, and staff. In the second example, a treatment team member was anxious that she was going to hurt the patient further by consulting a chaplain when the patient was an atheist. This staff member will need to be included in the chaplain's visit as well as the patient. The staff's anxiety can become spiritual hurt, depending on how the chaplain approaches the case. If the chaplain chooses not to visit the patient because of the atheist identification, the staff may feel spiritually abandoned because their patient is not receiving some form of spiritual care that they sense the patient needs. At the same time, if the chaplain makes the patient feel worse, or adds to the spiritual hurt, the team will react as having failed the patient's safety and contributed to her abuse. Continuing and fostering the spiritual safety of the treatment team will foster the spiritual safety of the unit for the patient.

Reviewing the suggested questions for the spiritual abuse assessment, we encounter the importance of the question: "Do you feel safe now?" The immediacy of this question is important: is there something *right now* I as the chaplain need to do to help this person be safe? Is there something in this hospital room I am unaware of? I have learned many things about staff and the immediate hospital environment by asking this question. It is relevant and timely to remember that abuse and spiritual abuse can happen anywhere, even at the hospital bedside.

Second, consider how the person articulates a theology of the afterlife. This can be helpful to the chaplain to understand how the person relates eternally with their faith and if the abuser has affected or manipulated in any way the patient's beliefs. For example, the two case studies presented offer very different belief constructs between the victim and the abuser. By allowing the person to articulate and sort out their own beliefs in a safe place, the chaplain can help the patient take ownership of their own chosen beliefs.

Third, how does the person give and receive forgiveness? In the first case, because the patient had weeks of individual and group sessions, the chaplain had more time and was therefore better able to address and discuss this at a pace dictated by the patient. In the second case, because of the immediacy of the spiritual and safety needs, including the perpetuation of the abuse, time constraints, and the fear of prematurely addressing forgiveness (which can be more hurtful than helpful in some cases), forgiveness was not addressed in the session at all.

Reflection of the Clinical Chaplain While Engaging Spiritual Abuse and Hope

Chaplains have a tremendous amount of power,[14] so subtle because it is spiritual that they can be unaware of it. The spiritual caregiver must be cautious not to inadvertently use this authority with someone as vulnerable as a victim of abuse, particularly spiritual abuse. In this case the chaplain will unwittingly step into the role of abuser and reinforce the victim's inability to proactively and safely pursue their own spiritual safety. This is where the chaplain engages spiritual humility before the victim.[15]

It is not uncommon to be uncomfortable with theologies that differ from our own, particularly theologies that we can clearly see are experientially damaging or abusive.[16] It is helpful for the chaplain to be mindful of this and maintain boundaries and set clear goals for the session, consonant with our governing ethics.[17] The patient's theology will grow and mature when the patient's soul is able and ready.

The clinical chaplain must also pursue self-supervision. Questions to ask people receiving ministry to help the spiritual care provider to grow include: "Is there something you wish I had said, that I did not say?," and "Is there something I said, that you wish I had not said?"

Personal reflections and reflections with mentors are valuable, but are influenced by the personal perceptions of the chaplain. Yes, the person I ask may be too intimidated by my pastoral authority to be honest, yet I have received feedback from patients and have changed what I say and do based on their recommendations. Ultimately my goal is to be a spiritually healing presence and advocate for those to whom I minister. Therefore the best indicator of my competence will be those individuals. Also, these questions are an opportunity for me to help the person to safely exercise a spiritual freedom, their voice.

Finally, the amount of pain patients have suffered, and to which they may return after discharge, can tempt the provider to despair. Just as the person is a thread in the tapestry that is our life, so we are in theirs. In other words, the chaplain is not the culmination of the person's healing. The chaplain may help the person begin healing or give some guidance towards a healthier form of spiritual healing, however the person's spiritual journey is going to transcend the limits of our work. This capacity for transcendence should be something effective chaplains integrate within their ministry.

1 Gerōn Porphyrios, *Wounded by Love: the Life and Wisdom of Elder Porphyrios* (Limni, Evia, Greece: Denise Harvey, 2005).

2 Tim VanDuivendyk,*The Unwanted Gift of Grief: A Ministry Approach* (Routledge, 2006).

3 Perry N. Miller, Raymond J. Lawrence, Robert C. Powell, "Discrete Varieties of Care in the Clinical Pastoral Tradition: Continuing the Dialogue," *Journal of Pastoral Care and Counseling*, 2003, 57 (2): 111–6; Anton T. Boisen, *Out of the Depths: An Autobiographical Study of Mental Disorder and Religious Experience* (New York, NY: Harper and Bros., 1960).

4 Glenn Asquith, "The Case Study Method of Anton T. Boisen," *The Journal of Pastoral Care,* June 1980. http://www.metro.inter.edu/facultad/esthumanisticos/coleccion_anton_b oisen/Case%20Study%20Method-Glenn%20Asquith.pdf.

5 Hierotheos Vlachos, Pelagia Selfe, and Effie Mavromichali, *The Science of Spiritual Medicine: Orthodox Psychotherapy in Action* (Levadia, Greece : Birth of the Theotokos Monastery, 2010).

6 Al Miles, *Responding to Domestic Violence and Spiritual Abuse* (Waco, Texas: Institute for Faith and Learning, Baylor University. 2016), https://www.baylor.edu/content/services/document.php/264319.pdf.

7 "Priest-penitent Privilege," https://en.wikipedia.org/wiki/Priest%E2%80%93penitent_privilege#cite_ note-ChildWelfareClergy-7. Accessed November 22, 2017.

8 "Standards of Practice for Professional Chaplains," http://www.professionalchaplains.org/content.asp?contentid=514. Accessed November 22, 2017.

9 Michael Guthrie, "A Health Care Chaplain's Pastoral Response to Moral Distress," *Journal of Health Care Chaplaincy*, 20:3-15, 2014.

10 Ibid.

11 Hugo Tristram Engelhardt, "Suffering, Meaning, and Bioethics," *Christian Bioethics*, 2(2):129-153 (Aug. 1996).

12 Gerōn Porphyrios, *Wounded by Love.*

13 Glenn H. Asquith, "Anton T. Boisen and the Study of 'Living Human Documents,'" *Journal of Presbyterian History*, 60, no. 3, Fall 1982, 244-265.

14 James Newton Poling, *The Abuse of Power: A Theological Problem,* (Nashville: Abingdon, 1991).

15 Hugo Tristram Engelhardt, *The Foundations of Christian Bioethics* (Taylor & Francis, 2000).

16 Stephen Arterburn and Jack Felton, *Toxic Faith: Experiencing Healing from Painful Spiritual Abuse* (Colorado Springs: WaterBrook, 1991).

17 Hugo Tristram Engelhardt, "The Foundations of Bioethics: Liberty and Life with Moral Diversity," *Reason Papers*, Fall 1997, (22):101-108.

12

SIGNIFICANT ASPECTS OF THE LGBTQ+ COMMUNITY AND THE IMPLICATIONS FOR SPIRITUAL CARE

Rev. Lynette Ross, MDiv
Ordained Minister in the United Church of Christ

"Our job is to love others without stopping to inquire whether or not they are worthy. That is not our business and, in fact, it is nobody's business. What we are asked to do is to love, and this love itself will render both ourselves and our neighbors worthy if anything can."
— Thomas Merton[1]

PROVIDING SPIRITUAL CARE is sacred work and it is needed now more than ever. We live in a wounded, wounded world, and the physical, emotional, and spiritual wounds we carry impact every area of our lives, whether we know it or not. We also live in a world that has become increasingly divisive, underscoring our wounds and their impact on our lives and the lives of those with whom we live as friends, families, neighbors, and communities. The good news is that we have also become increasingly enlightened and open to the myriad complexity of human life. As a result, knowing how to provide spiritual care to the LGBT community has become increasingly critical and relevant.

This chapter is not about the origins of homosexuality or what is considered the morality of homosexuality. Nor does it address the origins or morality of the transgender component of the LGBT community. Both topics are vitally important, but neither can be adequately addressed in a single chapter. You will find at the end of the book a brief bibliography that includes resources that address homosexuality and, specifically, homosexuality, Christianity, and the church.

It is tempting to begin this chapter by stating that providing spiritual care to those who are members of the LGBT community is no different than providing spiritual care to anyone. In some respects that *is* a true statement and at the same time, it is *not* true. As a member of the LGBT community,[2] I would like to begin by clarifying what the LGBT community *is* and what the LGBT community is *not*.

First, there really is no such thing as an LGBT community, just as there is no such thing as a Black community or a Hispanic community. The word community, by definition, assumes people live in the same city or neighborhood and that is not the case for those who are LGBT. Those who are LGBT can be found in the country, in the suburbs, and in metropolitan areas. The word community, by definition, also assumes a set of common interests. Certainly, people who share commonalities like race or sexual orientation may share certain viewpoints and concerns, but those who are LGBT do not all think alike or have identical viewpoints or concerns. There are lesbian, gay, bisexual, or transgender persons who do share common interests and think of themselves as a "community," but their common interests and unity derive from the separateness and marginalization they have experienced. In addition, members of the normative culture often assume all LGBT persons know each other and that is not the case. Neither do all LGBT persons in a neighborhood or city socialize together.

Keep in mind that we do not refer to heterosexuals as being part of the heterosexual community. We know you cannot lump all heterosexuals into a single community. Neither can you do so with those who are homosexual, bi-sexual, or transgender. It is called the LGBT community just as it is called the Black community because the normative culture sees those who are LGBT or those who are Black as separate and apart.

Second, there is no singular way to aggregate and title this marginalized group of people. The letters LGBT or GLBT have been used for many years. Recently, they have been superseded by the letters LGBT*Q*[3]. Some even use the letters LGBT*QIA*[4]. The understanding of sexuality and gender continues to evolve, and what may appear as "alphabet soup" underscores this fact and underscores the reality that those who do not easily fit into the normative culture, by virtue of their sexual orientation or gender identity, are perceived as separate and different. For the sake of discussion I will use the phrase LGBT community as we address significant aspects and the implications for spiritual care.

It is important to keep in mind that sexual orientation and gender identity are significant components of spiritual care precisely because they are components that either make someone a part of the normative culture or make them separate from it. It is the result of being separate and apart, marginalized and discriminated against, that makes sexual orientation and gender identity significant components for those who are LGBT. Sexual orientation and gender identity cross most, if not all, of the other components. Persons who are LGBT are members of all races, hail from all countries, are rich and poor, practice all faith traditions, deal with disabilities and diseases, and all face loss and death. They are your lawyer, physician, mechanic, stylist, your pastor, and your children's teacher.

Your ability to provide spiritual care to those who are LGBT will be greatly enhanced if you understand what you believe theologically about LGBT persons. It is not that your theology needs to change or that your theology is wrong, but if you come to the ministry of providing spiritual care with a belief that homosexuality is wrong or sinful, without remaining aware and cognizant of what you believe, more than likely it will impact the effectiveness and appropriateness of your spiritual care.

Ideally, it would be valuable to take the time to reflect on what your theology is regarding those who are LGBT. What is it you believe? What are the sources of your theology? Who or what influenced your theology? You may want to do some journaling or speak with a trusted friend or colleague. As stated earlier you will find a brief bibliography at the end of the book that you may find useful as you explore and examine your theology regarding those who are LGBT.

David K. Switzer in *Pastoral Care of Gays, Lesbians, and Their Families* tells us that "It is difficult to talk intimately, pastorally helpfully, with people we don't like, of whom we are afraid, whom we see as being very different from ourselves, who we believe are 'bad people.'" He goes on to write though that "We are all just people, people who need to grow beyond where we are in order to become increasingly effective in all of our personal relationships, including our pastoral care and counseling, with a greater number of different kinds of people."[5]

The reality is that we do *not* feel equally comfortable around everyone. We may feel uncomfortable with those who are mentally ill, uneducated, the dying, the angry, or those who are homosexual. There is nothing wrong with being uncomfortable, especially if we can own it and know it may impact what we say and what we do if we are not careful. It is essential that we do not shrink from offering spiritual care simply because we are uncomfortable. If you are uncomfortable around those who are LGBT, you might want to explore why you are uncomfortable. Again, journaling or speaking with a colleague or friend may help you in this area. Coming to know persons who are LGBT is the best way to eliminate the discomfort.

Often it is not our theology that keeps us from accepting those who are LGBT, but homophobia and heterosexism. Homophobia is the "irrational fear of, aversion to, or discrimination against homosexuality or homosexuals."[6] This fear plays itself out in the form of prejudice, anger, hatred, discrimination.[7] Today there is a whole gamut of homophobic reactions: outright bashing, psychiatry's attempt to 'cure' the homosexual, discriminatory laws and employment practices, inability on the part of social service agencies to deal with the homosexual, the media's demeaning and stereotypical images of the homosexual, and the tolerance of the homosexual so long as she or he remains invisible. All these reactions come from a combination of ignorance and fear.[8]

There are many people who will say that they are not homophobic. They do not hate homosexuals, nor do they treat with them anger, hatred, or discrimination. As the world has been willing to explore this topic, we have come to understand that often what is present is heterosexism, which Alia E. Dastagir defines as a "system of oppression that considers heterosexuality the norm and discriminates against people who display non-heterosexual behaviors and identities."[9] Our entire culture is organized on the basis of heterosexuality and we know that the majority "always wants to keep the people of the minority separate, apart, down underneath if possible."[10]

Those of us in the LGBT community have experienced the ramifications of the hetero-normative culture in the workplace, the community, in our families, and in the church. Those of us in the LGBT community know that most people we encounter, especially those in the church, would prefer it if we changed. We must be sensitive to the history of alienation caused by decades of negative statements and actions directed toward the LGBT community by church officials and ministers.

Churches and denominations often make their stance for or against homosexuality clear up front. Churches that take a stance against homosexuality have alienated the LGBT community as well as others who find the stance offensive. Other churches attempt to mitigate what they believe by saying they "love the sinner but hate the sin." Many people do not consider homosexuality a sin and those in the LGBT community are hurt and insulted when someone states that they *"love the sinner but hate the sin."*

Other churches do not make clear up front what their stance is regarding homosexuality, but in time it becomes known. For example, Ecclesia Church in Houston, Texas, has an outreach to the LGBT community, but their underlying theology is that being homosexual is a sin. They believe you "cannot possibly affect someone's morality without introducing them to Jesus,"[11] and their hope is that with time and the power of the Gospel of Jesus Christ the homosexual will be changed. One of the pastors, Chris Seay, maintains "Christians must be smart, wise, and educated. We should not be treating people differently based on their sins. Scripture is clear that no sin is greater than another. Grace is big enough for homosexuality ...

it just takes time. Redemption and sanctification don't take place overnight."[12]

Ecclesia is not unique in their stance and they provide a powerful example of why the LGBT community is distrustful and wary of organized religion and, in particular, Christianity. Consequently, anyone associated with organized religion, such as chaplains or clergy, may not be trusted or welcome. The many have been harmed by the few.

Whatever you believe, whatever your faith tradition, God has called us to love. In the Christian tradition we hold fast to the words found in 1 John 4:7-8: "Beloved, let us love one another, because love is from God; everyone who loves is born of God and knows God. Whoever does not love does not know God, for God is love." Our spiritual care must embody and reflect that LGBT people are equal to other people in worth and dignity. However, if you discover that your theology prevents you from being spiritually supportive to those who are LGBT, do what you need to do to make a referral without causing harm.

Sexual orientation and gender identity have been viewed by various segments of society as moral issues, which has exacerbated the shame and sense of marginalization and discrimination experienced by people who are LGBT. The sense of marginalization and separateness experienced pervades every aspect of the life of someone who is LGBT. It is so pervasive that one has no idea what it would feel like *not* to be marginalized and separate from the rest of the world. The sense of marginalization and separateness becomes ingrained, it becomes second nature so that often we are not aware of how different we feel living in the world from our heterosexual family member, friend, neighbor, or co-worker.

The day after the Supreme Court of the United States affirmed marriage equality[13] I marched with my church in the Houston pride parade, one of the most exhilarating experiences of my life. Early the next morning I had to catch a flight to attend my denominational General Synod. I was in the Nashville airport waiting for my connecting flight and as I sat in the waiting area looking at people, as I have done in airports for decades, I realized that for the first time in my life I did not feel different or less than everyone around me. I felt a sense of belonging, of connectedness, and equality that I had *never* experienced before in my life. I did not know until that moment how I had always felt a sense of not belonging, a sense of being on the outside looking in. It was an overwhelming feeling of joy that is difficult to articulate. Ironically, there is not a person in my life, including myself, who would not have been completely surprised at my admission, because I had never been aware of, or more precisely had never been able to articulate, the underlying sense of disconnectedness and alienation I had felt since I first realized I was sexually attracted to women. That's how deep and pervasive marginalization can feel to someone who is LGBT, and it influences every aspect of a person's life.

You may think you have no experience ministering to someone who is LGBT. Chances are you have already ministered to LGBT persons and did not know it. People who are LGBT do not have markings that make their sexual orientation obvious. During my time in CPE I realized that I ministered to people who did not know I was a lesbian. I also realized that if they had known, they might not have wanted my spiritual support. I learned that the need for spiritual support and sustenance can transcend all differences, all human prejudices and fears.

If you are providing spiritual care to someone who has identified themselves to you as LGBT, you would be wise to assume that the patient is going to be skeptical that you will support them, even if you know they are LGBT. Do not be afraid to let the person know that you don't want to say anything to offend them or make them uncomfortable. The LGBT person will sense you are uncomfortable, whether you verbalize it or not, and your willingness to be open and vulnerable may give them permission to be open and vulnerable as well.

No one likes to be ill and it can be a difficult circumstance for anyone, but when you are LGBT and seriously ill you become hypervigilant. You are no longer in a safe environment and you have no idea how you will be treated or what people will say to you. This is especially true if you are transgender. Transgender people have a gender identity or gender expression that differs from their assigned sex at birth. Gender identity is a person's internal, personal sense of being a man or a woman (or boy or girl.) Like everyone else, transgender people have a sexual orientation. Transgender people may be heterosexual, lesbian, gay, or bisexual.[14] If you are transgender, but your gender markers on your legal documents have not changed, or you have not transitioned physically, the heath care staff may use incorrect pronouns or refuse to use the pronouns you prefer. This can be disheartening and only serves to further alienate those who are transgender. It may happen out of a lack of knowledge, but it can also come from a place of bias or prejudice.

We may not think we define someone by their sexual orientation, but there is a pervasive assumption of heterosexuality in our culture. We assume everyone we meet is heterosexual unless we are informed differently. I am lesbian, and I assume when I meet a stranger that they are heterosexual. The assumption of heterosexuality is a cultural norm. In our work of providing spiritual care it would benefit us to be aware of that cultural norm when we meet people to whom we are offering spiritual care.

In this culture we may presume that everyone is heterosexual, but we do not *define* heterosexuals by their sexual orientation. That is not always the case with those who are lesbian, gay, or bi-sexual. Sexual orientation does not define who we are, but rather who we are attracted to sexually, which is only one component of our humanity. Along those lines, it is important to note the difference between sexual orientation and sexual preference. Being lesbian, gay, or bi-sexual is not a sexual preference, it is an orientation. As a provider of spiritual care, it would be beneficial to learn to use the term sexual orientation rather than sexual preference. In the African American LGBT community, the term same gender loving is often used rather than same sex attraction.

Using the phrase sexual preference rather than sexual orientation with those who are LGBT assumes they had a choice about whom they are attracted to sexually, which is not the case. To assume that whom we are sexually attracted to is a choice, a decision, begs the question, if you are heterosexual, when did you make the choice, the decision, to be heterosexual? When people who are heterosexual are asked that question they are either rendered speechless or they laugh. They laugh because they know it is an absurd question, they know they never decided or made a choice to be heterosexual, yet we think it an accurate description of what takes place in the life of someone who is lesbian, gay, or bi-sexual. There is no doubt that there are those who are attracted to the same sex or gender who are not willing to live a homosexual lifestyle, but that is not the same thing as sexual orientation, nor is it sexual preference.

When providing spiritual care be careful not to fall prey to the stereotypes our culture has attached to those who are LGBT. Not all lesbians look masculine and not all gay men are effeminate. The stereotypes we have in our heads about what a homosexual looks like and how they act are not only old ideas from a different era, but they are inaccurate and only serve to reinforce homophobia and heterosexism. Older generations of lesbians and gays may have acquiesced as to how they perceived they needed to dress or act as a homosexual, but that is no longer the case. In addition, gender expression has become fluid and it is no longer always possible to neatly put people in boxes labeled heterosexual, lesbian, gay, or transgender.

We are taught that God meets people where they are, and the use of inclusive[15] or gender-neutral language tells the other person that you see them as they are, and you are not imposing artificial cultural norms that can be exclusionary and divisive. What does that mean and what does it look like when you are interacting with people? For example, if the person you are providing spiritual care to is male and you know they are married, rather than asking "What is your wife's name?" or "Is you wife coming to visit you?" use language such as "What is your spouse's name?" or "Is your spouse coming to visit you?"

When you use inclusive language or gender-neutral language you send the message that you are not defining or pigeonholing the person, or assuming their sexual orientation. You send the message that you are being inclusive and accepting. If the person is LGBT, they will *hear* that acceptance and it creates a space for them where they may feel safe to be honest with you.

As sad as it is, do not assume that the LGBT person to whom you are offering spiritual care has family support. When you want to find out what kind of support the person may have you might ask "Do you have support at home?" rather than "Do you have family support at home?" It may be difficult to understand, but many LGBT people have been rejected by their families of origin. Some are fortunate enough to have a network of loving and supportive friends, but their parents, and often their siblings, have cut off all contact. In many cases their families have rejected them because the religious faith they embrace holds that homosexuality is a sin. This rejection may only increase their reluctance to accept spiritual care from someone they identify as sharing the same belief as the family that rejected them.

Marriage equality has dramatically changed the landscape, especially in the health care arena. Prior to marriage equality, same sex partners were not protected, they had no spousal rights, regardless of their length of their relationship. There are endless horror stories of loved ones kept from the bedside of a dying partner by family members of the dying partner. Consequently, you may see couples in the hospital setting, both young and old, make it abundantly clear to the medical staff and the spiritual care providers that they are married. You may see same sex married couples behave in a way that says they expect everyone to honor and respect their marriage. You may also see the spouse or the partner, whether they are legally married or not, be vigilant and protective, shielding their loved one from anyone, including a spiritual care provider, if they fear their loved one will be disrespected or harmed.

Older LGBT persons may be more closeted, dismissive, or angry and not willing to accept any spiritual care. If as a spiritual care provider, you understand the marginalization and discrimination at the hands of clergy or the church that older LGBT persons have experienced throughout their lives, or that they have witnessed or know of, you will understand their anger and dismissiveness. Many older LGBT persons were taught growing up that God thinks they are sinful and depraved. They have been deeply wounded and may not be able to accept spiritual care even if they desperately need it.

At the same time, older LGBT persons may be the most receptive if they had a positive experience with organized religion growing up. They may welcome the offer of spiritual care and see it as a sign that they are being seen and accepted as equal to others. They may have remained active in a church, even a church that did not readily accept them, or they may have found a home in the growing number of churches that are affirming and accepting of all people.

Younger LGBT persons are often the most open and unashamed about their sexual orientation or gender identity. At the same time, they may be the most dismissive of spiritual care. More than likely they will be friendly and gracious, they just may not want any spiritual support. Younger LGBT persons may not have grown up being a part of a faith community and what they know about organized religion, especially Christianity, they learned from the media. Therefore, they identify spiritual care as something that is a part of organized religion, or more specifically, Christianity, and they view Christianity as marginalizing, discriminatory, and irrelevant.

You will discover LGBT persons, both young and old, who see themselves as "spiritual but not religious." Consequently, they will be open and receptive to your offer of spiritual care and find it meaningful and valuable. You may discover among LGBT persons a strong interest in Buddhism. For them Buddhism fills a spiritual need but does not contain the discrimination and marginalization they believe present in Christianity.

As noted earlier, you will find that those who are transgender are the most guarded, even fearful. It is fair to say that our culture does not know how to accept and embrace those who are transgender, even in a health care setting. Transphobia may be rampant and if you are to succeed in being able to provide spiritual comfort and care it is essential to be cognizant of how guarded and fearful a transgender person might be.

Regardless of their age, if the LGBT person you are providing spiritual care to is terminally ill they may ask you "Does God really hate me because I am LGBT? Am I really going to hell when I die?" You must find a way to answer those questions, regardless of your theology, in a manner that is supportive and loving.

We are called by our faith and our profession to minister, not just to those who may be ill, we are also called indirectly to minister to their families and friends as well. However, when the patient is LGBT there are emotional landmines you may witness or find yourself having to navigate with family members.

It may become clear that the family does not know their loved one is lesbian or gay or does not acknowledge it. Do not feel that you must inform the family or ask them to acknowledge the sexual orientation of their loved one. There is a saying "There are no secrets, there is only denial." Families will talk about the reality of having an LGBT loved one when and if they are ready. Our responsibility is to maintain a non-anxious presence.

There might be an occasion when you witness the family of someone who is LGBT be disrespectful to the partner/spouse and/or the friends of their loved one. This can be an uncomfortable situation and if the space and time presents itself it would be appropriate to talk with the person who is LGBT about how they feel about how their family member behaved. They may be accustomed to it or they may want to talk with you about how it made them feel. Our first obligation is to support the patient.

Even more difficult is when the family does not accept their loved one being LGBT and the family is open about their non-acceptance. In those circumstances an effort should be made to provide spiritual care to the person who is LGBT. Regardless of how you may feel about someone being LGBT, no one who is a provider of spiritual care wants to see someone marginalized and disrespected, especially by their own family members.

Last, there may be the rare instance when the family seeks you out as a spiritual care provider because they want you to intervene and help convince their loved to one see the sinfulness of their sexuality. Again, regardless of how you feel about someone being LGBT, you do not want to be part of any such discussion with the person who is LGBT. Try and help the family focus on their love for the family member and their desire to see them well. It would be appropriate to refer them back to their own pastor regarding their struggle with their loved one's sexuality.

In the end we see, do we not, that providing spiritual care to those who are members of the LGBT community is no different than providing spiritual care to anyone. Like all human beings, those who are LGBT want comfort and reassurance. Like all human beings, those who are LGBT want to tell their stories. Like all human beings, those who are LGBT want to be seen and recognized and validated. Like all human beings in moments of uncertainty, illness, or impending death, those who are LGBT want to believe that there is a God and they want to believe that God loves them. Our sacred duty as providers of spiritual care is to provide comfort and reassurance, to listen to their stories, to let them know they are seen and recognized and validated, and to assure them there is a God who loves them.

---

1 Letter to Dorothy Day, quoted in *Catholic Voices in a World on Fire* (2005) ed. Stephen Hand, 180.

2 The author is the Rev. Lynette Ross, a United Church of Christ minister who is a homosexual and identifies as a lesbian.

3 LGBT stands for lesbian, gay, bi-sexual, transgender, LGBTQ add Q for queer or questioning

4 LGBTQIA adds I for intersex and A for asexual. The expansion speaks to the evolution of the understanding of sexuality and gender.

5 David K. Switzer, *Pastoral Care of Gays, Lesbians, and Their Families* (Minneapolis: Fortress Press, 1999), 68.

6 The Merriam-Webster online dictionary (https://www.merriam-webster.com/dictionary/homophobia)

7 Switzer, *Pastoral Care of Gays, Lesbians, and Their Families*, 69.

8 Colorado Pride Resource Center, https://prideresourcecenter.colostate.edu/resources/homophobia/.

9 Alia E. Dastagir, "LGBTQ Definitions Every Good Ally Should Know," *USA TODAY*, June 15, 2017.

10 Switzer, *Pastoral Care of Gays, Lesbians, and Their Families*, 70.

11 Chris Seay, "Without Christ We Are Incapable Of Dealing With Our Own Sins" quoted in David Kinnaman and Gabe Lyons, *Unchristian, What A New Generation Really Thinks About Christianity* (Grand Rapids: Baker Books, 2007), 113.

12 Seay, "Without Christ," 114.

13 On June 26, 2015 in a landmark civil rights case, Obergefell v. Hodges, the Supreme Court of the United States legalized same-sex marriage throughout the United States, including its possessions and territories.

14 https://www.glaad.org/transgender/transfaq.

15 Inclusive language avoids the use of certain expressions or words that might be considered to exclude particular groups of people, especially gender specific words.

Bibliography

Bawer, Bruce. *A Place At The Table, The Gay Individual in American Society.* New York: Simon & Schuster, 1993.

Chellew-Hodge, Candace. *Bulletproof Faith, A Spiritual Guide for Gay and Lesbian Christians.* San Francisco: Jossey-Bass, 2008.

Helminiak, Daniel A. *What the Bible Really Says About Homosexuality.* New Mexico: Alamo Square Press, 2000.

Johnson, William Stacy. *A Time to Embrace, Same-Gender Relationships in Religion, Law, and Politics.* Grand Rapids: William B Eerdmans Publishing Company, 2006.

Jung, Patricia Beattie and Ralph F. Smith. *Heterosexism, An Ethical Challenge.* Albany: State University of New York Press, 1993.

Martin, Dale B. *Sex and the Single Savior, Gender and Sexuality in Biblical Interpretation.* Louisville: Westminster John Knox Press, 2006.

Minor, Jeff and John Tyler Connoley. *The Children are Free, Reexamining the Biblical Evidence on Same-sex Relationships.* Indianapolis: Found Pearl Press, 2008.

Myers, David G. and Letha Dawson Scanzoni. *What God Has Joined Together, The Christian Case for Gay Marriage.* San Francisco: Harper Collins, 2005.

Rogers, Jack. *Jesus, The Bible, and Homosexuality, Explode the Myths, Heal the Church.* Louisville: Westminster John Knox Press, 2006.

Scanzoni, Letha Dawson and Virginia Ramey Mollenkott. *Is The Homosexual My Neighbor, A Positive Christian Response.* San Francisco: HarperSan Francisco, 1994.

Vines, Matthew. *God And The Gay Christian.* New York: Convergent Books, 2014.

13

HUMAN TRAFFICKING AND IMPLICATIONS FOR SPIRITUAL CARE

Kimberly Williams
Program Director Anti-Human Trafficking Initiative and
PATH Collaborative at St. Luke's Health, Houston, Texas

I N THE LAST FEW YEARS the term "human trafficking" has taken our country by surprise. Many have not heard the term and have little idea of its meaning. Crime, talk and radio shows have done investigative reporting to help us identify the problem. Organizations have developed around the world to address the issue, but there are still many people who are unaware of these harmful acts happening in our community.

So, what is human trafficking and why is it important for us to know about it? "Human trafficking is a form of modern slavery—a multi-billion-dollar criminal industry that denies freedom to 20.9 million people around the world, from the girl forced into prostitution at a truck stop, to the man discovered in a restaurant kitchen, stripped of his passport and held against his will. All trafficking victims share one essential experience: the loss of freedom," according to Polaris Project, an organization that "leads in the global fight to eradicate modern slavery."[1]

United Against Human Trafficking, an anti-human trafficking organization located in Houston, says victims range in age from young children to adult men and women and can be U.S. citizens or immigrants. Trafficking can occur in businesses, schools, malls, or even in homes. "No person is exempt from falling victim. Diversity in Houston, the fourth largest city in the country, makes it easy for trafficking victims to blend in with the general population."[2]

The City of Houston Office of Human Trafficking and Domestic Violence reports that the problem is prevalent locally as well as internationally. Sadly, Houston has been identified as a hub for human trafficking. However, Texas is considered a leader in the fight against this issue, having been among the first states in the country to pass a statute criminalizing human trafficking. The department notes that Houston-area lawmakers have championed anti-trafficking legislation.[3]

Recently the Statewide Human Trafficking Mapping Project for Texas (2018) reported that there are more than 300,000 victims of human trafficking in Texas.[4] This statewide research effort, published in "Human Trafficking by the Numbers: The Initial Benchmark of Prevalence and Economic Impact for Texas (Final Report December 2016)," noted, "From sex trafficking within escort services to labor trafficking of farmworkers, the ways humans are exploited differ greatly. Each type has unique strategies for recruiting and controlling victims, and concealing the crime."[5] (See graphic.)

HUMAN TRAFFICKING IMPACT IN TEXAS

APPROXIMATELY
79,000
MINORS AND YOUTH
ARE VICTIMS OF
SEX TRAFFICKING
IN TEXAS ★ ★

APPROXIMATELY
234,000 WORKERS ARE VICTIMS OF LABOR TRAFFICKING

THERE ARE CURRENTLY AN ESTIMATED **VICTIMS OF**
313,000 HUMAN TRAFFICKING IN TEXAS ★ ★ ★ ★ ★

TRAFFICKERS EXPLOIT **$600 MILLION** FROM VICTIMS OF LABOR TRAFFICKING ★ ★ ★ ★ ★ IN TEXAS

MINOR AND YOUTH
SEX TRAFFICKING COSTS
THE STATE OF
TEXAS
APPROXIMATELY
$6.6
BILLION

It is essential for us to focus on human trafficking because freedom is a basic human right. When human rights are violated by one group of people at the expense of another group, it creates an imbalance in our world. It creates a group that preys on another, with abuse in the form of force, fraud, and coercion. Human trafficking consists of these three components. First, we see force, when an individual is made to do things against her will. Forcing individuals to work and function under the control of a manipulative individual or group of people is a sign that human trafficking is occurring. Second, fraud happens when promises are made and then broken, and the individual is trapped in a circumstance to which she did not agree. The trafficker often lies and convinces the individual to believe one set of rules and then maneuvers to another set of expectations that leaves the victim without recourse. Third is coercion, when individuals are strong-armed into a vulnerable situation, oppressed and burdened with unreasonable expectations, leaving the victim worried, troubled, and filled with anxiety and fear. This fear causes the victim to act in ways that are irrational and illogical to those of us on the outside looking in, but when one digs beneath the surface, one can see the signs of an abused and mistreated individual who in most cases is fearing for her life and the lives of her loved ones.

The Trauma of Slavery

In most cases the victim was seeking a better life, a safer environment, or a meal, things most of us take for granted each day. Victims fear their captors and will do little to instigate trouble in an already tense and volatile position. They are beaten mercilessly and left without proper care or food. Basic necessities are limited and are often used as a tool to keep the victim captive and trapped. Bargaining and rationalizing with traffickers is of little use for the victim, because this one-sided relationship only benefits the trafficker. The victim has no rights, privileges, or claims for anything. Everything is always in the control of the trafficker. From the time the person wakes up until it's time for bed, the trafficker has complete control and influence over every move the victim makes. The victim is so consumed with her safety and survival that little thought is given to anything else. Opportunities to run, escape, and remove oneself from the trafficker's grip are horrifying just to think about, much less act upon. A victim's life is constantly in danger and any slight infraction can have horrifying ramifications.

Therefore, victims spend all their time consumed with following instructions and staying alert. They become masters of reading and interpreting their environment and discerning danger and threats to safety. Staying alive is the priority in most cases and whatever it takes to stay "safe" is the goal for the moment. Truly it's a moment-by-moment reality. Dreaming, visioning, planning and goal-setting are not their realities. Fear, alarm, terror and dread are their daily companions, and this creates worry, anxiety, concern and nervousness.

Victims believe nothing is safe and have little trust in a system they believe has manipulated and trapped them into a life of slavery—slavery that causes apprehension when they meet someone new. They wonder whom they can trust, who has their best interest at heart, and who will listen to their story and share their sorrow, grief, and loss. They trusted the trafficker to be there. They shared with the trafficker their desire for a better life. They expressed their aspiration and longing for love and care, and the trafficker twisted that vulnerability and openness for their own gain. The victim is left defenseless and helpless after initial thoughts of promise and hope. "Fear, shame and trauma frequently prevent disclosure. Repercussions of disclosure may be both swift and violent."[6]

Hope has been shattered and crushed. The victim has exhausted all her means and is emotionally and spiritually beaten down to such a degree that she only sees despair. Her prospects for life and freedom seem out of reach. She has given up any hope for a better life, because the last time she was hopeful, it ended with her being trapped.

How can victims trust again? How can they share their traumatic circumstances with others? This is where we as health care professionals have an incredible opportunity to help form a new reality for the victim. We not only give a touch of the tenderness the victim has seen so little of, we also share compassion, empathy, and kindness. The victim has not felt a loving touch and doesn't expect anyone to care. Feeling worthless and desperate, the victim has landed in the emergency room or clinic, a setting with different standards and expectations that conjure feelings of vulnerability.

It's altogether strange and unexpected that a victim might end up away from the trafficker's control for a moment. She never thought this situation would happen. And now she sits before a provider who is asking about her feelings, the pain level, and the duration of the problem. Before this visit, no one has taken the time to ask questions as if she were human. The reality has been demand after demand, threat after threat, attack after attack. Now she is in a new setting that is clean, sterile, and well lit, which causes a flood of emotions and thoughts she has suppressed for months.

As care providers, we have an amazing opportunity to show care and concern to one of the most vulnerable populations in our community. Care can transform and draw the victim from the margins toward the prospect of change. It must not be rushed or hurried, but be a gentle and peaceful stance toward hope for a future without violence and control.

Our Approach, Stance, and Posture
Until now, the victim has seen a plethora of abuse and interrogation covering every aspect of her life. In some cases, she had to ask to go and relieve herself. The freedom to make decisions and have choices can be a valuable tool to show opportunity and possibility. It gives the victim a chance to think, and to develop and entertain options.

A barrage of questions and a frustrated provider will hinder communication and the exchange of information that can be helpful in assessing and caring for the victim. Staying composed and observing the signs the victim displays with respect and professionalism, without coldness and judgment, can break down many barriers and move toward an interruption of the trauma for the victim. Creating a break in the pain and suffering can make just enough space for the victim to see potential and possibilities.

As the provider, your openness to treat the victim says more than you can image. Your honesty and genuine attention to the victim reveal your willingness to serve. The service that you offer is different and distinctive because it gives the victim a glimpse into her emotional and spiritual health, which up to this point has probably been so neglected and mistreated that the victim has overlooked this method of coping.

The guilt and shame of the trafficking experience is emotionally and spiritually devastating to the victim. Many of our major religious practices frown upon immorality, crime, and wrongdoing. The victim is left to think that God has forgotten about her, that her sin is so bad that she cannot approach the sacred. She is embarrassed, guilt-ridden, and filled with dread. Some may be able to articulate that God loves them, but still believe their wrongdoing is far beyond God's love and ultimate provision.

The victim's spiritual health has been shattered and hope is lost. Providing care encourages the victim to express her feelings about what has happened to her. Listening with empathy as she rehearses the trauma, without losing sight that we are a conduit to establishing or re-establishing a relationship that has been severed, is imperative. We are reintroducing the possibility that hope is not lost and the Sacred is ready to respond to the need in a way that will help the victim cope in the now. Establishing an atmosphere where the victim is safe and feels she can trust the provider is a chance for her to sense a presence greater than her circumstance. She gets to reflect on her experience and see how she has survived to this point and how her survival is a picture of a greater authority or a higher being. Our reactions and responses to the victim's story-telling can enhance or hinder their progression toward healing. We are aiming to move toward healing, not re-traumatizing nor harming the victim further.

The FAITH Model

A model I developed to help me as I work with trafficking victims is the FAITH model.

"F" is for **Focus**. Remain present with the victim. Some victims are familiar with being overlooked and undervalued. Your goal as the provider is to let the victim know that she is the most important person in the room and her story, no matter the circumstance, is important enough to be heard. Hearing her story, the story that she wants to share, is valuable to the recovery. Remember, we are not aiming for interrogation, but to show true interest rather than engaging in fact finding. The problem with fact finding is that the provider can get caught up in the story and become traumatized by taking in all the information. Sometimes that's a tactic that the victim uses to create a wall. This wall is a safety mechanism to keep people from getting too close. Focusing helps remind you of your role in the encounter. When there is genuine concern and empathy, the victim feels cared for and the provider is effective in providing treatment.

"A" is for **Assess**. Assessing the victim's situation helps you better evaluate the need. Consider the perspective of the victim and the circumstances that brought the victim into your presence. Was this an attempt to run away or another effort by the trafficker to manipulate the health care system for their gain? "Trafficking victims pass through our doors every day, undetected, because health professionals do not know how to identify them," said Dr. Hanni Stoklosa, Emergency Medicine physician at Brigham and Women's Hospital, Harvard Medical School and Executive Director, HEAL Trafficking.[7] We have learned of cases where the trafficker repeatedly abused the victim and brought them to the emergency room, just to get pain killers for the trafficker. The victim never received any relief from the pain inflicted. You as the provider have an opportunity to gauge the vulnerability of the victim and measure the risk factors.

"I" is for **Initiate** encouraging words and thoughts. Initiating positive and encouraging language and expression bridges gaps in communication and interaction. Keep in mind that the trafficker does not share positive words or uplifting thoughts to raise the spirits of the victim. The trafficker's goal is to discourage the victim and promote fear and panic. The provider's goal is to be reassuring and nurturing, in opposition to the trafficker's plots of destruction. Therefore, providing a juxtaposition that creates an opportunity for the victim to compare and evaluate the character of the provider versus the character of the trafficker. We want to be a total contrast to what she has experienced from the trafficker.

"T" is for **Trust** your training and know that the victim is the expert on her experience. It is important to realize that all trafficking situations are different and vary from victim to victim. If the victim shares information that seems unfathomable to the provider, it's the provider's job to listen, which is what we are trained to do, and allow the victim to reveal what is important to her. It may seem irrelevant to us, but to the victim it's an opportunity to share her story on her terms, from her heart. What a disservice if we interrupt, re-write, or ignore the victim, which is what the trafficker has been doing the entire time the victim has been in bondage. Remember that we are not to emulate the trafficker's responses or actions. One-on-one conversations are an opportunity to establish trust with the patient, and may lead to disclosure.

"H" is for **Hope**. A foundational piece in care, recovery, and spirituality is the concept of hope. Hope builds confidence and courage for the victims and enables them to look forward to a different outcome. It gives them a chance to see the world with optimism that things will work out for the better. Just the prospect of having a different outlook can bring anticipation, potential, and promise to a gloomy, dark, and miserable existence of bondage. Hopefulness is an essential component for the victim to heal spiritually and emotionally. Regaining a sense of purpose, determination, and perseverance to reclaim her life as her own and to begin to think anew will contribute to rebuilding.

Focus, Access, Initiate encouragement, Trust your training and Hope demonstrate to the victims that all is not lost and that they can begin to dream again with the expectation that things can change, plans can be developed, and the past can be behind them.

Spirituality is an essential part of a person's being and therefore must be addressed in the healing and recovery of any victim. To overlook the spiritual care of the victim is to leave a huge gap in the recovery. Even victims have a way of coping with life and the challenges that arise while living. When opportunities for spiritual growth, development, and practice are eliminated from the victim's life there is a sense of wandering, of a life without an anchor, detached from the divine or holy. Note that what is holy or sacred to one victim can be totally different for another victim and may also be different for you.

Therefore, it's important not to push our religious agenda or program, but to let the victim decide where she wants to go with her spiritual life. If the victim copes by attending church, but has been prohibited from attending worship services by the trafficker, the victim may feel guilt or shame for not being able to attend regular worship services.

We have heard of instances where the pimp gathered the victims together each night to pray for their success on the streets. In this case, the victim's sense of religion and prayer may be skewed or distorted. We want to make sure the victim notes that our religious preference or desire does not have to be theirs. We let the victim choose the best mechanism and coping skill for herself.

Working with victims is challenging work. No two victims are alike or have the same experience. Each circumstance is different and bears multiple trauma-related injuries. It's essential for us as caregivers to remember that the victim is recovering from trauma and it may take years for her to develop coping skills. Therefore, skilled care and training is crucial to her care and recovery.

The importance of identifying resources and organizations that support victims is key to providing referrals, recommendations, and suggestions. When encountering a victim who needs housing, medical care, and other essentials, the process whereby your institution refers and consults with partner organizations will help facilitate a seamless transition for the survivor.

Fortunately, Houston has several organizations that provide support and assistance. These resources deliver trauma-informed care and assist survivors with the necessary tools to overcome their obstacles. Providing smooth relocation from one facility to the next with safety, precision, and caution reduces the possibility of harming the victim more. As stated previously, the goal is to provide care that heals and not to harm further. This includes relationships with law enforcement, health care providers, shelters, nonprofits, and city and county governments. This type of informed care wraps around the victim to prevent additional hurt. A coordinated effort among a group of qualified professionals ensures that progress is made toward the goal of ending human trafficking. Our aim should be that everyone on our team is aware of human trafficking, trained to identify a victim, and able to pinpoint where resources are that can be used to further support the victim.

---

1 "United States of Human Trafficking," https://www.theodysseyonline.com/united-states-human-trafficking.

2 "List of Charities," https://pearlandhouseconcerts.com/charities/.

3 "City of Houston Mayor's Office, Office of Human Trafficking and Domestic Violence," http://humantraffickinghouston.org/what-is-human-trafficking/.

4 "Statewide Human Trafficking Mapping Project for Texas (2018)," https://socialwork.utexas.edu/projects/statewide-human-trafficking-mapping-project-for-texas/.

5 Noël Busch-Armendariz, et al., *Human Trafficking by the Numbers: The Initial Benchmark or Prevalence and Economic Impact for Texas*, https://ic2.utexas.edu/pubs/human-trafficking-by-the-numbers-the-initial-benchmark-of-prevalence-and-economic-impact-for-texas/.

6 S. Bessell, et al., *Human Trafficking and Health Care Providers: Lessons Learned from Federal Criminal Indictments and Civil Trafficking Cases*, Human Trafficking Legal Center and HEAL Trafficking; 2017. https://www.htlegalcenter.org/wp-content/uploads/Medical-Fact-Sheet-Human-Trafficking-and-Health-Care-Providers.pdf.

7 Lee Mannion, *Train U.S. Doctors and Nurses to Spot Victims of Modern Slavery, Say Advocates,* https://www.reuters.com/article/usa-trafficking/train-u-s-doctors-and-nurses-to-spot-victims-of-modern-slavery-say-advocates-idINL8N1NR4CU.

14

PASTORAL CARE TO PEOPLE DEALING WITH CHRONIC DISEASES

Rev. M. Oscar Hall, DMin
Senior Staff Chaplain at Houston Methodist Hospital

FOR TWENTY-EIGHT YEARS I have had the privilege of working with two groups of patients dealing with chronic disease and end-of-life questions. The first group of people I intend to cover in this paper is those suffering from end-stage renal disease. The second group is patients dealing with brain injuries and severe brain damage caused by motor vehicle accidents, ruptured aneurisms, brain tumors, and a series of other causes. Over the years I have developed deep friendships with many of these patients, whom I visit weekly as they come to the hospital for radiation therapy or with problems related to infected grafts and other complications that require hospitalization.

People suffering from end-stage renal disease (ESRD) or from any type of brain injury are dealing with severe life-changing issues, including recurrent hospitalization and pain associated with surgeries and diverse medical procedures. The unbelievable courage of these patients is a testimony of human strength and determination. I cannot help feeling that God has given me the privilege of learning from these people as I journey with them while trying to join them in their world of pain, suffering, and despair. During this time, they try to find answers and meaning in the catastrophic events that are threatening to change their lives or alter its quality forever.

Together with some of my experiences accumulated over the years of pastoral care ministry to these patients, I will provide vignettes from the words of patients dealing with their chronic conditions. Marshall Shelley, when he talks about the difficulty in finding literature about chronic diseases, says, "three of my favorite selections in world literature are about it: *The Metamorphosis* by Franz Kafka; *The Death of Ivan Ilyich* by Leo Tolstoy; and the book of Job in the Bible. They are incredibly honest about what it is like to have a serious, unavoidable disease."[1] This statement may help people see that suffering does not occur in some abstract world. It is personal and contextual. It happens to real people in specific settings.

Another thing this paper intends to do is to invite pastoral caregivers to meet people in the reality of their suffering. Pastoral care providers must meet, hear, and comprehend the stories people with chronic diseases have to tell of their suffering, and try to help them explore the meaning they attach to their suffering. If pastoral care providers have listened attentively and compassionately, they may earn the right to walk with people in a deep and meaningful way.

Finally, the paper will look at the social function of people dealing with chronic diseases to determine their relationship to the pastoral care process. It will include dialogues with patients, expressions and evaluations of patients sharing their moral and religious viewpoints about their condition. It will also share my theological interpretation, which includes my pastoral interventions and outcomes. Through this paper, I desire to capture some of the realities of spiritual despair, moral pain, and social confusion experienced by people dealing with chronic disease.

A Look at Chronic Diseases

The two chronic diseases selected for this paper are ESRD and the complications from brain injury or TIA (Transient ischemic stroke). The American Association of Kidney Patients offers a short definition for ESRD, "It is a total kidney failure. When the kidney fails, the body retains fluid and harmful wastes build up. A person with this disease needs treatment (dialysis) to replace the work of the failed kidneys."[2] The two main causes of kidney failure are diabetes and high blood pressure.[3] Myers defines disease as "An impairment of normal physiological or psychological functions associated with infection, imbalance, or deterioration."[4] For a person to come to the realization that their diseased condition is chronic, not curable with the medical science and technology available today, is a tremendously humbling realization.

Almost every chronic disease will eventually change a person's lifestyle and expectations. Little by little, the sick person begins to realize that at least some of their dreams and future goals may never be realized. It is difficult to accept that one may no longer be able to play one's favorite sport, that the energy a person had before the onset of the illness has been reduced, and consequently that one must set lower goals for their life. This difficult emotional exercise usually creates a tension that can lead to despair and hopelessness. It is the job of the chaplain to walk with patients experiencing the grief caused by chronic diseases.

There are many chronic brain diseases. One of the predominant ones is organic brain syndrome, which Webster's dictionary defines as "an acute or chronic mental dysfunction (as Alzheimer's disease) resulting chiefly from physical changes in brain structure and characterized especially by impaired cognition."[5] Another is Parkinson's disease, which Webster defines as "a chronic progressive neurological disease, chiefly of later life, that is linked to decreased dopamine production in the substantia nigra and is marked especially by tremor of resting muscles, rigidity, slowness of movement, impaired balance, and a shuffling gait."[6] Yet another is brain cancer. "Brain cancer is a disease of the brain in which cancer cells (malignant) arise in the brain tissue. Cancer cells grow to form a mass of cancer tissue (tumor) that interferes with brain functions such as muscle control, sensation, memory, and other normal body functions."[7] There are multiple types of brain tumors and multiple types of radiation therapy and chemotherapy to treat these different types of brain cancers.

José[8], one of my dialysis patients, reported "With me it was slowly. My doctor told me about three years ago that I was headed for dialysis." For Tomás, a young athlete, the disease came without warning. Even two years later Tomás remains puzzled and bewildered: "I was young and healthy. I have never been sick. I played football and basketball in high school, and I was very good at both sports. When I was playing I weighed 230 pounds. Now I am down to 160." Judy is a 40-year-old woman with two children who has just discovered that she has a brain tumor, a glioblastoma, one of the most aggressive forms of brain cancer. At the first pastoral encounter, this young woman was enthusiastically celebrating her faith. She appeared to be sure that divine healing was right around the corner for her. She said, "God is my doctor and I have the faith that Dr. God will heal me either miraculously or through the chemotherapy and radiation therapy treatment I am getting for my treatment."

Four months after her husband's death, Irene wrote,

> Grief, you are a rascal. You take our energy, our organizational abilities, our brains and do strange things with them ... I am impatient with it all. You take so much out of us when we really need to be able to function well. I do not understand why. I must confess you've done good things for me also. I am more compassionate, understanding, and tolerant. You have given me new ways to be of service and God will show those ways. Perhaps after I've had more time to look back I will feel differently about you, but for right now you are not one of my favorite friends. I am a better person because of you and I must not lose sight of that.[9]

People with chronic illnesses have to deal with adjusting their lives and feeling that they have become a burden to their loved ones. Slaby and Glicksman note, "Those afflicted often feel cheated, hopeless, and that life has been taken out of control."[10] Control is a basic need for all human beings throughout their lives.

The Experience of Loss

Perhaps the predominant feeling people with chronic diseases experience at the onset of the terrible news is a deep sense of loss. Their losses are many and varied, while touching almost every aspect of their lives. Most people dealing with chronic illness run the risk of eventually moving from a life filled with activity, including employment, recreation, sports, and mobility, to a life of inactivity and boredom.

Robert, a 50-year-old Black male, recalls the loss of his vocation as a jazz musician for a 20 year period. In his musical years he traveled, played in nightclubs all over the country, and even recorded music. "I had a very difficult time coming to terms with it," he says. "I tried for a while to continue my work, but I couldn't do it. Eventually, I ended up losing my wife too." Most of these patients seem to attempt to cope with their particular experience of suffering by trying to find a spiritual explanation for their pain.

Rebecca Chopp cites Johann Baptist Metz, in his book, *The Emergent Church*, as identifying three stages in the Christian praxis of the imitation of Christ, "Christians imitated Christ by accepting the world, and in the second stage they imitated Christ by criticizing the world. Now in the third stage … Christians imitate Christ through the acceptance of suffering and through a praxis of interruption and conversion."[11] People dealing with chronic illnesses understand the suffering of Christ and the cross of Christ more than the average Christian. Agnes, for example, shared about her loss of mobility, "I used to complain about my husband leaving his clothing scattered all over the bedroom. Now I would do anything for the chance to just be able to bend down and pick up his socks … You never know how much you will miss the little things in life until you cannot do them anymore."

One thing I have observed in some patients dealing with a chronic illness is exemplified in what Jerome said about the discharge of a patient who had just gotten a new heart, "Everybody who gets a transplant says they are coming back to visit the unit, but most of them never do." So, in addition to the loss of health, mobility, friends, and an independent lifestyle, there is sadness over the loss of friends who leave by death or by a transplant.

Issues of Control and Dependence

In addition to the very significant experience of loss among people with chronic diseases, there is a tremendous cost that comes from feeling sick almost all the time. Most patients' condition plays out in a dance of the dialectic between control and dependence. Dr. John Newman, who is also a patient dealing with chronic kidney disease, writes,

> We are all aware of the spoken and unspoken fears of death, pain, the uncertain future, and the consequences of cheating 'just a little' on the restricted diet. These feelings and attitudes are common and normal for someone attempting to live through a major life crisis, which often calls into question the viability and stability of one's entire life ... Against this charged atmosphere the patient is naturally tempted to give up and leave his fate in the hands of the busy, overworked staff, and settle for disabled status.[12]

Due to their loss of control, some patients dealing with chronic diseases may suddenly develop an ongoing pattern of dependency. For example Charles, a patient who has been on dialysis for six years, said "To those who use their illness as an excuse for not making something of themselves, I refuse to accept the label that I am sick. I rarely let others 'in' on the fact that I am on dialysis. I even try to control the machine, it doesn't control me." In this case, Charles' need to be in control occasionally spills over to what he perceives as a power struggle between himself, the medical staff, and even other patients.

Arguments over minor infractions like the regulation of a thermostat are illustrative of the deeper issues around the need to exert one's diminished options and choices and to reestablish or regain a sense of control, if not over one's body, then one's environment. Gaining a sense of control over even minor things becomes important to the patient when they feel like they've lost control of larger things.

A Search for Meaning

Up to this point I have attempted to articulate the experience of individuals living with chronic diseases. The big question to ask patients who seem to be coping with their condition is, "What keeps you going?" Or, "What is your source for coping with your condition?" Ninety percent of the respondents said they found strength and meaning in their faith. About 50 percent of the patients believed their illness had a purpose. For some, that purpose was to help bring some order and good into their lives, for others the illness was meant to teach them something. Other patients did not believe the illness was directed at them for any particular reason, but did believe that some good had come from it. For example, José called his disease a blessing. He said, "Before I got sick I was out all the time, running around with women and drinking heavily. Now, God gave me a second chance, especially to make it right with my son. My son is the joy of my life." Carlos, another patient, echoes this sentiment. He speaks of his meninggioma (benign brain tumor) as something God is using to turn his life around.

Another dimension of faith is found in these three patients, who linked their new awareness of God's spirit in their lives to that of the inspirational writing, "Footprints." In this writing, the author describes a dream in which he asks God why at life's most trying moments God has abandoned him. The evidence was only one set of footprints in the sand. God responds: "My precious, precious child, I love you and I would never leave you.

During your times of trial and suffering, when you see only one set of footprints, it was then that I carried you."[13] Those who expressed this view believed that God was present with them in their suffering. They did not expect that their faith would give them the strength to somehow deal with the real world, relieving their experience of suffering and pain. Specifically, in a moment of deep anguish and intense disappointment following her failed kidney transplant, Kathy was a witness to this faith, "I know that God has been with me through all of this." Kathy appears to have found consolation in the assurance that God is in control of her life.

Joyce Rupp in her book, *Praying Our Goodbyes*, talks about how patients with chronic diseases are able to find new meanings and new melodies. She notes, "There are people who felt that all the songs in their heart had died, that all the roads they knew were wiped out and they could go no farther. Then a kind of resurrection happened within them and they discovered 'new melodies' and the wonder of new roads."[14] The role that faith plays in the life of people dealing with chronic illness should not be ignored. It seems as though people will go with God as far as their image of God goes.

Recently, in a retreat led by Fr. Matthew Linn, he shared with his audience an equation that goes Pain + Love = Healing.[15] The love of God, love for life, love for family, friends, and a sense of purpose and mission make healing possible. Greg Anderson notes that, "Healing has at its roots the ability to give and receive nonjudgmental, unconditional love."[16] An example of this is Rev. Jones. He is a 71-year-old Baptist preacher who has been on dialysis for 26 years. Rev. Jones uses his 12 hours a week on the dialysis machine to read and meditate. He drives his Cadillac to the dialysis center and has managed to remain active as senior pastor of his church, preaching and teaching his congregation with a renewed understanding of the many ways God can be present with his people and answer their prayers.

Ministry Implications

The ability to be with people dealing with chronic diseases is a great privilege and blessing. The role of pastoral ministry in this context basically consists of affirming the patients' experiences and seeking to learn from the patients about the things that are important to them. This paper will propose five implications for pastoral care; however, this list does not pretend to be exhaustive.

1. The pastoral care giver should be careful in respecting the confidentiality of the patient.

2. Each patient has a unique story to tell. The pastoral care giver's role is to elicit, to hear, and to walk with the patient. In addition the pastor should help the patients in their quest to find meaning in their story.

3. Healing can occur, not only as meaning is found within the context of the patient's story, but also as the patient is given the opportunity to give expression and voice the experience of loss, particularly where those feelings have not previously been explored or vented.

4. In an interesting study led by Rittman and others of chronic renal patients, the researchers asserted, "The danger in our reliance on technology lies not only in our desire for control, but also in our failure to grasp the significance of human connectedness."[17] In the face of a very strong dependence on technology for patients with chronic illness, one implication for pastoral care will be to offer the human face of care and compassion through their active presence and listening skills.

5. Finally pastoral caregivers should exercise caution in their pastoral relationships. They should carefully seek to facilitate and encourage the development of independence and self-control on the part of the person dealing with a chronic illness.

Conclusion

This paper intends to encourage pastoral caregivers to consider ministering to individuals who are living with chronic diseases. It seeks to provide the reader with a look into the difficult, painful, and struggling world of these people, so that caregivers may be more open to walk with them through their valleys of despair, and hopefully bring caregivers and patients to a place where hope, death and life are celebrated and where miraculous healing does happen. I want to point out that healing does not always mean being cured, but may result in finding meaning. Many patients with chronic illnesses have learned to be more focused on living than dying. Victor Frankl's statement, "He who has a why can bear any how,"[18] is dramatically lived out by many of these patients.

The implications for pastoral care and the conclusions drawn from this study are meant to act as an invitation into the lives of people dealing with chronic diseases. The study also suggests that pastoral care givers should be present with patients in their living and in their dying. In addition, this study shows that patients suffering from chronic diseases are not looking for deep theological explanations as to why something is happening. What they are seeking is meaning, love, respect, and encouragement to make the best of what life has given them.

——————————————

1 Marshall Shelley, *Building Your Church Through Counsel and Care: 30 Strategies to Transform Your Ministry* (Minneapolis, MN: Bethany House, 1997)

2 www.aakp.org/AAKP/glossary.ntm.

3 Statement given to me by Dr. Juan M. Gonzalez, prominent nephrologist at the Methodist Hospital in Houston, Texas.

4 Allen C. Myers, *The Eerdmans Bible Dictionary* (Grand Rapids, MI: Eerdmans, 1987), 285.

5 *Merriam-Webster's Collegiate Dictionary* (Springfield, MA: Merriam-Webster, 2003)

6 Ibid.

7 http://answers.webmd.com/answers/1177544/what-is-brain-cancer?guid=1.

8 All the names that I'm using as examples throughout this paper are not the real names of patients. I've also changed details to make sure that confidentiality is preserved.

9 Bob Deits, *Life After Loss: A personal Guide Dealing with Death, Divorce, Job Change, and Relocation* (Tucson, Arizona. Fisher Books), 93.

10 Andrew E. Slaby and Arvin S. Glicksman, *Adapting to Life-Threatening Illness* (New York. Praeger Scientific), 7.

11 Rebecca S. Chopp, *The Praxis of Suffering: An Interpretation of Liberation and Political Theologies* (Maryknoll, NY: Orbis Books. 1986), 78.

12 John Newman, *Psychonephrology 2: Psychological Problems in Kidney Failure and Their Treatment* (New York: Plenum Medical Book Company), 27.

13 Famous poem, "Foot Prints in the Sand." Unknown author.

14 Joyce Rupp, *Praying our Goodbyes* (Notre Dame, IN: Ave Maria Press), 97.

15 Fr. Matthew Linn is a Jesuit priest, spiritual director, and author of many books.

16 Greg Anderson, *The Cancer Conqueror: An Incredible Journey to Wellness* (Kansas City. Andrews and McMell), 89.

17 M. Rittman, et al., "Living With Renal Failure," *American Nephrology Nurses' Association Journal*, 20, no.3.

18 http://andreaskluth.org/2009/09/15/frankl-he-who-has-a-why-can-bear-any-how/.

SPECIAL CONCERNS OF SPIRITUAL CARE

15

DUELING PROFESSIONAL OBLIGATIONS: THE HOSPITAL CHAPLAIN AS A VOLUNTEER CLINICAL ETHICS CONSULTANT

Adam Peña
Project Manager II, Biomedical Ethics Program
at Houston Methodist Hospital System

THE MODERN DELIVERY OF HEALTHCARE utilizes a multidisciplinary team approach that delineates specific responsibilities to individuals according to their respective professions. As a member of a multidisciplinary team, the hospital chaplain's role, while singular in purpose, is multifaceted. Consistent with professional standards,[1] the chaplain's primary task is to provide emotional and spiritual support to patients and their families. Furthermore, the hospital chaplain's scope of practice extends beyond patients to include the development of supportive and professional relationships with clinicians and other ancillary healthcare professionals. The hospital chaplain's charge is to establish a ministerial presence within the hospital unit in which they practice.

In addition to their work in the clinical units, hospital chaplains fulfill other roles within the larger healthcare institution. For example, hospital chaplains may be responsible for developing a strategic plan for the renewal of commitment to institutional values. Hospital administrations may ask directors or seasoned hospital chaplains of Spiritual Care Departments to chair ethics committees, function as a member of the bioethics committee, or serve as a volunteer ethics consultant for the healthcare facility. One seminal study concluded that of 519 hospitals surveyed, 70 percent utilize chaplains as a participating member of a bioethics committee or consultation service.[2] This study demonstrates that hospital chaplains actively interface with biomedical ethics issues in their day-to-day practice and participate in bioethical and medical decision-making for patients.

There is wide-spread agreement that hospital chaplains (and, more generally, those with training in theology or religious studies) participate in the multidisciplinary professional landscape of clinical ethics.[3,4,5,6] The *Core Competencies for Healthcare Ethics Consultation*, as a professional consensus report,[7] identified certain skills (e.g., interpersonal skills) and knowledge domains (e.g., healthcare law) necessary to demonstrate proficiency in ethics consultation. While there are some differences in professional standards between clinical ethicists and hospital chaplains, generally, the skill sets of hospital chaplains and clinical ethicists are complementary. For example, both chaplains and clinical ethics consultants are expected to demonstrate advanced interpersonal skills that include empathic and active listening.[8] Therefore, it is arguable that a hospital chaplain's skill set makes them well-suited for the role of a volunteer clinical ethicist. Given these similarities, there is some symmetry between the two sets of professional standards of practice.

However, the similarity between the two roles may raise some concerns. There may be significant role conflict for the hospital chaplain serving both in the role of chaplain and of volunteer clinical ethicist. Role conflict is a dynamic state where an individual is subject to competing professional obligations.[9] Consider a scenario where a hospital chaplain, Brian, provided pastoral ministry to a patient, Mr. A. As the on-call volunteer ethics consultant, Brian receives an ethics consultation request because Mr. A is refusing recommended treatment. It would be difficult for Brian to function in both roles simultaneously. Still more concerning is the potential for undermining the therapeutic relationship that Brian built with Mr. A as a hospital chaplain when later engaging Mr. A in the role of volunteer ethics consultant. With the uptick in support for professionalization of clinical ethics and development of an attestation process,[10,11] serving dual roles as hospital chaplain and volunteer clinical ethicist within the same institution raises concerns about competing professional obligations. Whether performing ethics consultations as a member of a small team or an independent volunteer ethics consultant, the hospital chaplain may feel compelled to recuse herself from either role when confronted with the situation described above.[12]

Herein, I briefly identify the different roles hospital chaplains fulfill within biomedical ethics programs. Then I address two areas where the professional role of the clinical ethics consultant is consistent with the professional standards and expectations for the hospital chaplain. I end with a discussion of certain aspects of the hospital chaplain's role that may be incongruent with a volunteer clinical ethics consultant's role.

Professional Role of the Hospital Chaplain

There is wide-spread professional consensus that, as a member of the interdisciplinary team, a hospital chaplain is primarily responsible for providing emotional and spiritual support to patients, patients' families, and clinicians or other healthcare professionals. The hospital chaplain's training uniquely positions her to fulfill the unmet spiritual and emotional needs of the patient and the patient's family. Spiritual assessment tools, such as the FACT LaRocca-Pitts spiritual assessment,[13,14] help hospital chaplains gather relevant information about the patient to develop a plan of care that will meet the patient's specific spiritual needs. For example, a hospital chaplain could facilitate a patient visit from a Roman Catholic priest to administer the sacrament of Anointing of the Sick for a dying patient.[15] The hospital chaplain's training gives her the skills necessary to support the patient (or patient's family) during the patient's hospitalization.

In addition to regular professional duties, hospital administrations often task hospital chaplains with bioethics-related duties. For example, hospital chaplains often chair the bioethics committee or participate on the ethics consultation service as a consultant. With technological advancements in life-sustaining treatment, ethical issues at the bedside are becoming increasingly complex and require nuanced ethical analysis. While it is common for those with religious training to participate in value-laden decision-making,[16] those charged with these types of responsibilities may feel ill-equipped to respond to substantive clinical ethics questions. Unless the hospital chaplain has education or training in bioethics or clinical ethics, bioethics-related roles may cause the chaplain to operate at the margins of her professional expertise, thereby creating a psychological and an emotional burden for the hospital chaplain when functioning as a volunteer clinical ethics consultant.

Areas of Convergence

Cultural Broker:

One component of a hospital chaplain's ministry is to act as a religious and cultural broker between the healthcare team and the patient. A cultural broker is one who helps bridge the gaps between two different groups through mediation and advocacy on behalf of certain cultural groups.[17] Said differently, in some circumstances hospital chaplains may need to interpret and advocate for the religious or cultural motivations that influence the patient's medical decision-making. Suppose Mr. A, mentioned earlier, notifies his treating physicians that he is a practicing Jehovah's Witness and he has an advance directive stating that he does not want to receive blood products under any circumstances. Now suppose that Mr. A does not have the ability to make medical decisions for himself and his family members ask Mr. A's treating physicians to administer blood products to Mr. A. The hospital chaplain would be able to explain the theological, religious, or spiritual reasons why the patient requested not to receive blood products. At the very least, the hospital chaplain would have ready access to available institutional or community resources to offer to Mr. A's family members. The hospital chaplain could help facilitate negotiation between two competing interests: the family's interest in preserving the patient's life via blood transfusion and the patient's interest in maintaining obedience to a specific religious teaching or practice.

The role of a cultural broker uses a skill set that will aid the hospital chaplain who also functions as a volunteer clinical ethicist. Generally, a volunteer clinical ethicist is charged with eliciting the moral perspectives of relevant stakeholders when responding to a clinical ethics consultation request.[18] As part of information-gathering efforts, the volunteer clinical ethicist frames open-ended questions to obtain ethically relevant information, which may include any religious and/or spiritual motivations for medical decision-making. The hospital chaplain's professional training will equip the hospital chaplain with the necessary skills for performing clinical ethics consultations because Clinical Pastoral Education fosters active listening skills and communication strategies to help the patient express her narrative. While information-gathering may seem like a low-stakes step in the clinical ethics consultation process, clarifying moral perspectives of stakeholders can be a daunting task because it asks the volunteer clinical ethicist to create a space where the stakeholder can feel at ease expressing her moral perspective in light of the patient's clinical realities.

Mediator:

The value-laden nature of clinical ethical issues lends itself to reasonable disagreement among those directly involved in the patient's care, and therefore, each person involved may think differently about which course of action is the most ethically justified. It is rarely the case that an ethical issue has an easy or "black and white" answer. Rather, values ambiguity, as the core of any clinical ethical issue, can cause distress for providers, ancillary healthcare professionals, and the patient or patient's family. Diagnostic and prognostic information can compound distress, potentially becoming a significant source of ethical conflict.

Given the hospital chaplain's active listening skills, she has the tools to help elicit the varying perspectives of both clinicians and other healthcare professionals. Beyond listening, the hospital chaplain would be able to provide a degree of understanding and respect for a stakeholder's ethical concern(s). The nature of a hospital chaplain's work gives her the opportunity to minister to all within her institutional setting.[19] The hospital chaplain is uniquely positioned to help mediate ethical conflict among the various stakeholders involved in an ethics consultation.

For example, consider a scenario where some treating physicians disagree about whether it is medically appropriate to honor a family's request for continued aggressive treatment (e.g., mechanical ventilation and dialysis) because the patient's family firmly believes in miraculous healings. In this case, the chaplain's active listening skills, which include the ability to formulate open-ended questions, are a foundational skill in bioethics mediation.[20] That is, the hospital chaplain could help facilitate discussion among those on the healthcare team about the ethical concern, clarify misconceptions and misunderstandings between team members, identify common goals, and ultimately, help the team achieve consensus about an ethically justified resolution.[21,22]

Areas of Divergence

The *Guidelines for the Chaplain's Role in Health Care Ethics*[23] offers several guidelines that identify the role(s) of the professional chaplain within the field of clinical ethics. In conjunction with this document, other authors suggest that one component of the hospital chaplain's role is to act as a patient advocate, representing the patient's theological or religious beliefs and values. Suppose a patient who has the ability to make medical decisions for himself, informs providers that he would like to defer *all* medical decisions to a family elder or a spouse. As a patient advocate, the chaplain might recommend that the multidisciplinary team respect the patient's cultural practice by approaching the patient and the patient's spouse together for medical decisions.

While this practice of patient advocacy is appropriate for the hospital chaplain, it may not always be appropriate for the hospital chaplain to advocate on behalf of the patient's cultural beliefs when functioning as a volunteer clinical ethics consultant. Imagine a case where adult children ask their mother's treating oncologist not to disclose a terminal cancer diagnosis because of a cultural belief that this type of diagnosis would hasten their mother's death. As a hospital chaplain, it may be appropriate for the hospital chaplain to explain the reasoning for the request and recommend adherence to the cultural practice. As a volunteer clinical ethicist, the hospital chaplain would need to consider ethically relevant variables (e.g., invasiveness of treatment) to determine whether there is strong ethical justification to honor the adult children's request. Given the strong ethical (and legal) consensus surrounding informed consent, it would be ethically concerning, and perhaps ethically inappropriate, for the hospital chaplain to recommend that the team categorically respect the cultural practice because it undermines autonomy-based principles.

National competencies for clinical ethicists require that professional and volunteer clinical ethicists maintain neutrality, to avoid a personal or professional bias that could jeopardize or short-circuit ethical analysis of an issue.[24] Despite the shift toward the professionalization of clinical ethicists, the *Core Competencies for Healthcare Ethics Consultation* does not articulate a different set of competencies and standards for volunteer clinical ethics consultants, therefore the expectation is that volunteer clinical ethics consultants, when acting as independent consultants, will demonstrate the same level of competency necessary to perform clinical ethics consultation as a professional clinical ethicist. Further, the *Core Competencies for Healthcare Ethics Consultation* require that those performing clinical ethics consultation foster awareness of their professional and personal biases to avoid skewing ethical analysis.[25] Clinical ethics is a high-stakes activity that generally has significant consequences for all relevant stakeholders. Therefore, hospitals chaplains may need to depart, to some extent, from professional guidelines when performing clinical ethics consultations. Maintaining neutrality while participating in the resolution of clinical ethics issues as a volunteer ethics consultant may pose a professional challenge for a hospital chaplain.

Competing Professional Obligations

Generally, professional organizations such as the Association of Professional Chaplains (APC) endorse a hospital chaplain's involvement in clinical ethics consultations and promote the hospital chaplain's participation on the institutional ethics committee.[26] However, these organizations also recognize instances where the hospital chaplain may encounter competing obligations between the professional duties of a hospital chaplain and duties of a volunteer clinical ethics consultant. Professional standards direct the hospital chaplain to recuse her involvement as a volunteer clinical ethicist when it compromises her ability to function as a hospital chaplain.[27] The purpose of this guidance is to maintain the professional integrity of the hospital chaplain.

It is not difficult to envision a scenario where a hospital chaplain may need to prioritize two different sets of legitimate professional obligations: when the hospital chaplain has already provided pastoral care to the patient (or the patient's family) involved in the clinical ethics consultation. Consider a case where Chaplain B, as the on-call volunteer clinical ethics consultant, receives an ethics consultation request for Mr. A because he, a devout Jehovah's Witness, is refusing blood products. However, Chaplain B is concerned because she has already provided pastoral counseling surrounding the decision to forgo blood products. Here, the hospital chaplain may find it difficult to act a volunteer clinical ethics consultant when she has already interacted with a patient as the hospital chaplain, because it may undermine the therapeutic relationship built with the patient and family. In this instance, it is appropriate for Chaplain B to recuse herself from performing the consultation.

From a different perspective, the dual hospital chaplain/volunteer clinical ethics consultant role may compromise the neutrality required for ethical analysis if the chaplain has already provided the patient or family with pastoral support. In congruence with professional standards for hospital chaplains, there is large consensus that professional clinical ethicists should cultivate and maintain awareness of their professional and personal biases so that those biases do not influence analysis. Given that a hospital chaplain must be endorsed by a particular faith/spiritual tradition in order to meet certification requirements,[28] the hospital chaplain's religious doctrines could influence ethical analysis and consequently, the ethical recommendations. Therefore, it is especially important for hospital chaplains to foster an awareness of explicit and implicit religious and personal moral biases that could unjustifiably influence ethical analysis and recommendations.

Creating the expectation that a hospital chaplain will recuse herself from a case presupposes that a chaplain is able to do so. In some instances, limited institutional resources (e.g., personnel) that support ethics consultation services may make it logistically difficult for a hospital chaplain to remove herself from the consultation. Prior to becoming involved in the patient's care, it is certainly advisable for the hospital chaplain to discern which role to prioritize. However, in some foreseeable circumstances, it may not always be professionally appropriate to do so. For example, if the hospital chaplain for an intensive care unit (ICU) was acting as a clinical ethics consultant prior to the patient's transfer into the ICU where the chaplain is assigned, then the hospital chaplain should consider asking a colleague within the department to function as the hospital chaplain for that patient.

Recommendations

While more robust guidance from professional organizations is necessary, the time needed to accomplish consensus is lengthy. Still, relevant institution-level stakeholders can take more immediate steps to help avoid potential future instances of role conflict.

1. *Call schedule*: An immediate and practical step that ethics consultation services could take is to create a call schedule that includes a second person who serves as a backup for the on-call volunteer ethics consultant. Those responsible for creating call schedules should pair the hospital chaplain with another volunteer ethics consultant who is readily available to respond to a consultant request when a hospital chaplain recuses herself from fulfilling the role of a volunteer ethics consultant.

2. *Education and training*: A number of large biomedical ethics programs offer intensive courses or certificate programs that provide short-term clinical ethics training. Given that clinical ethics consultation is a high-stakes activity, it is crucial that volunteer ethics consultants are competent to provide substantive ethics analysis and perform high-quality clinical ethics consultation. In furtherance of this goal, hospital administrators or directors of spiritual care departments should offer senior chaplains the opportunity to attend intensive courses or some other form of clinical ethics training.

3. *Clinical Pastoral Education*: To offset concerns related to a lack of exposure to or knowledge of bioethics issues, Clinical Pastoral Education sites should incorporate bioethics education into their internship and residency training programs. Some may suggest that bioethics should not be prioritized over other topics more relevant to the professional competencies of hospital chaplains. While a legitimate concern, implementation

of this recommendation can vary among different training sites. For instance, Clinical Pastoral Education curricula could require that each summer intern attend one bioethics committee meeting and resident trainees shadow a professional clinical ethicist for a day. Given some evidence demonstrating that professional chaplains regularly engage in bioethics decision-making, training programs should provide surface-level exposure to frequently encountered clinical ethics issues.

Conclusion

While the professional hospital chaplain's role is to provide emotional and spiritual support to patients, patients' families, and healthcare professionals, the skill set of the hospital chaplain is multifaceted. Healthcare institutions often utilize hospital chaplains as chairs of bioethics committees and as clinical ethics consultants. Hospital chaplains function as consultants, in part, because the skill set of the clinical ethicist and the hospital chaplain blend. Whether serving as a chair of a bioethics committee or as an ethics consultant, the shared skill set aids the chaplain's ability to participate in ethical decision-making. However, other professional roles and biases could jeopardize the neutrality necessary for robust ethical analysis. Therefore, it is important for hospital chaplains and chaplain ethicists alike to foster awareness of professional and personal biases that influence daily practice. In the absence of professional guidance, practical solutions could offset latent concerns about role conflict. Call schedules could be adjusted to avoid the need for a hospital chaplain to recuse herself from an ethics consultation request. Integration of bioethics training into Clinical Pastoral Education programs and staff chaplain responsibilities would increase the necessary competencies to fulfill bioethics-related roles in a healthcare facility.

1 Association of Professional Chaplains, *Guidelines for the Chaplain's Role in Healthcare Ethics*, http://bcci.professionalchaplains.org/files/application_materials/guidelines_for_chaplains_role_in_healthcare_ethics.pdf. Accessed 21 December 2017.

2 Ellen Fox, Sarah Meyers, Robert Pearlman, "Ethics Consultation in United States Hospitals: A National Survey," *American Journal of Bioethics*, 2007; 7(2):13-25.

3 Ibid.

4 James T. Wagner, Tami L. Higdon, "Spiritual Issues and Bioethics in the Intensive Care Unit: The Role of the Chaplain," *Critical Care Clinics*. 12, no.1 (Jan. 1996): 15-27.

5 M. L. Smith, D. Burleigh, "Pastoral Care Representation on the Hospital Ethics Committee," *HEC Forum: an Interdisciplinary Journal on Hospitals' Ethical and Legal Issues*, 1991; 3(5): 269-72.

6 A. L. Simmonds, "The Chaplain as Spiritual Moral Agent: Strengthening the Process of Bioethics Decision Making," *Humane Medicine*. 1994 Apr; 10(2):103-7.

7 American Society for Bioethics and Humanities, *Core Competencies for Healthcare Ethics Consultation*. 2nd ed. (Glenview, IL: American Society for Bioethics and Humanities, 2011).

8 Ibid.

9 T. Tarrant, C. E. Sabo, "Role Conflict, Role Ambiguity, and Job Satisfaction in Nurse Executives," *Nursing Administration Quarterly*, 2010 Jan; 34(1): 72-82.

10 Joseph J. Fins, et al., "A Pilot Evaluation of Portfolios for Quality Attestation of Clinical Ethics Consultants," *American Journal of Bioethics*, 2016; 16(3): 15-24.

11 Eric Kodish, et al., "Quality Attestation for Clinical Ethics Consultants: A Two-step Model from the American Society of Bioethics and Humanities," *Hastings Center Report*, 2013 Sept-Oct; 43(5):26-36.

12 American Society for Bioethics and Humanities, *Core Competencies for Healthcare Ethics Consultation*.

13 Mark A. LaRocca-Pitts, "Four FACTs Spiritual Assessment Tool," *Journal of Health Care Chaplaincy*, 2015; 21(5): 51-9.

14 Mark A. LaRocca-Pitts, "FACT: Taking a Spiritual History in a Clinical Setting," *Journal of Health Care Chaplaincy*, 2009; 15(1):1-12.

15 In the Sacrament of the Anointing of the Sick, a Roman Catholic Priest anoints a seriously injured or ill individual with oil blessed by the Bishop at the Chrism Mass.

16 Lindsay Carey, et al., "Bioethical Issues and Healthcare Chaplaincy," *Scottish Journal of Healthcare Chaplaincy*, 2006; 9(1):23-30.

17 Mary Ann Jezewski and Paula Sotnik, *The Rehabilitation Service Provider as Culture Broker: Providing Culturally Competent Services to Foreign Born Persons* (Buffalo, NY: Center for International Rehabilitation and Research Information Exchange, 2001).

18 American Society for Bioethics and Humanities, *Core Competencies*.

19 Wagner, "Spiritual Issues and Bioethics in the Intensive Care Unit."

20 Nancy N. Dubler, Carol B. Liebman, "Bioethics Mediation: A Guide to Shaping Shared Solutions," Rev. and expanded ed. (Nashville, TN: Vanderbilt Press, 2011).

21 Dubler, "Bioethics Mediation."

22 Haavi Morreim, "Conflict Resolution in the Clinical Setting: A Story Beyond Bioethics Mediation," *Journal of Law, Medicine & Ethics*, 2015; 43(4): 843-56.

23 Association fof Professional Chaplains, *Guidelines*.

24 American Society for Bioethics and Humanities, *Core Competencies*.

25 American Society for Bioethics and Humanities. *Core Competencies*.

26 Association of Professional Chaplains, *Guidelines*.

27 Association of Professional Chaplains. *Guidelines*.

28 Board of Chaplaincy Certification, *Common Qualifications and Competencies for Professional Chaplains*, 2016. http://www.professionalchaplains.org/files/2017%20Common%20Qualifications%20and%20Competencies%20for%20Professional%20Chaplains.pdf. Accessed 21 December 2017.

16

SEEING SPIRITUAL CARE THROUGH LEGAL LENSES

Rev. Mark C. Grafenreed, JD, MDiv
PhD Student at Southern Methodist University
Texas attorney and Elder in Texas Annual Conference of
The United Methodist Church

THERE ARE UNDENIABLE LINKS between law and healthcare. Session after session, federal and state congressional leaders enact laws impacting healthcare. While the Affordable Care Act, dubbed "Obamacare," has received the most congressional and media attention by far, it certainly is not the only piece of legislation that has had a notable effect on healthcare. In 2003, the Texas legislature transformed the healthcare landscape in Texas with the promulgation of House Bill 4 (HB4).[1] HB4, also known as Texas Tort Reform, contained many provisions. But much of HB4 was codified in response to physicians being dropped by their malpractice insurance carriers due to the increased number of medical malpractice claims. Such litigation is based on allegations of medical malpractice or medical negligence against hospitals, doctors, and other healthcare providers. The probability of losing a malpractice claim awarding millions of dollars to plaintiffs and their attorneys caused many Texas physicians to begin practicing defensive medicine.[2] Physicians practiced medicine with potential lawsuits at the center of their thoughts, not the patients. As a result of HB4, litigation against healthcare providers is procedurally and substantively more challenging, although not impossible.

Law and healthcare intersect in other ways. Attorneys often provide vital input in the development, implementation, and sometimes enforcement of policies and procedures for healthcare facilities. Healthcare facilities and providers often have standing legal teams help them focus on patient care, while maximizing profit margins and minimizing their legal risks. In June 2021, a Houston federal judge tossed a lawsuit brought by 117 employees of the Houston Methodist Hospital System. The employees were objecting to the hospital's requiring its employees to take the COVID-19 vaccine in order to protect its patients, constituents, and the general public.[3] Judge Lynn N. Hughes held, "Texas law only protect[ed] employees from being terminated for refusing to commit an act carrying criminal penalties to the worker, and that receiving a COVID-19 vaccine [was] not an illegal act."[4] In this instance, a healthcare institution's legal team can be vital to the organization's existence.

But what, if anything, do law and spiritual care have to do with the other? Admittedly, this question might not appear on the popular game show, "Who Wants to Be A Millionaire," but the answers might be surprising. When Dr. Luis E. Rodriguez, Clinical Pastoral Education (CPE) Manager in the Department of Spiritual Care and Values Integration at Houston Methodist Hospital in Houston, Texas, posed this question to me, I struggled for answers. I needed a lifeline[5] or more clues to help me identify any answers, particularly since I wore both hats![6] However, upon deeper professional and theological reflection, I soon discovered that the practice of law and the administration of spiritual care had more intersections than meet the eye. Repeatedly throughout law school, I heard *ad nauseam*, "Think like a lawyer! Think like a lawyer!" After nearly 20 years of practicing law, I have discovered that "thinking like a lawyer" is more about embodiment, about *being* a lawyer rather than *thinking* like one. This chapter seeks to articulate some of the aforementioned intersections between spiritual care and law and offer chaplains, regardless of their ministry setting, a useful perspective on these connections, demonstrating that being a chaplain is much more like being a lawyer than either might have suspected.

Caveats and Concessions

At the outset of this task, it is critical to begin with several pertinent caveats and concessions. First, as a licensed Texas attorney, I offer a perspective that is likely to be uncommon and may be unfamiliar to many members of my intended audience, in that the percentage of attorneys who also serve as chaplains is, in all probability, very small. Second, while I am not suggesting people need to apply to law school and spend three long years amassing tons of student loan debt to understand it, this chapter at times articulates detailed legal nuances and intricacies that might be confusing. My task is to simplify those details as much as possible, so that the crux of this chapter does not get overshadowed. Third, this chapter does not seek to speak *for* or *about* all attorneys or chaplains. Such an effort would not only be arrogant, but also futile. Finally, we live in a religiously pluralistic society and the administration of spiritual care is equally diverse. While recognizing and respecting other faith traditions and leaving room for their contributions to this topic, this chapter is written from the perspective of the

Christian faith. Against this backdrop, we now shift to the task at hand.

The L.A.D. Effect

While are there are a plethora of transferable skills common to law and spiritual care, this chapter examines three: 1) Listening; 2) Assessment; and 3) Discernment. I will call these "the L.A.D. effect." The L.A.D. effect, in my estimation, provides the foundation for minimal service standards by fostering effective patient interaction. It is critical to note that the application of the L.A.D. effect is not linear. There is no 1-2-3 step process. Rather, the L.A.D. effect is a dynamic process that may be likened to a circus juggler tossing and catching several balls at once, but with all in use and in motion. Thus, while it is quite possible to make a reasonable assessment before listening to the patient or client, the L.A.D. effect must feature all three because there are dangers in excluding any aspect of this process. Listening, assessment, and discernment are performative acts that are all inextricably intertwined, and each should occur during every patient visit or client consultation in order to facilitate a patient-centered or client-focused experience.[7]

In the Houston Methodist Hospital System, "Our commitment to our patients remains our priority. Excellent care is driven by our continued focus on unparalleled safety, quality, service and innovation."[8] In other words, our patients are our clients, and they are always at the center of everything we do. We achieve our commitment through the I CARE values. Each employee commits to the service standards of Integrity, Compassion, Accountability, Respect, and Excellence. However, such values are not always evident in the legal or medical professions. While the clients' interests *should* serve as the focus, ethical, personal, professional, and even financial dilemmas can determine the outcome at times in attorney-client and physician-patient relationships. This claim should not receive blanket application to every attorney or healthcare provider. Yet, from a legal vantage point, I have firsthand knowledge of instances where the attorney's needs and desires outweighed the best interests of the client, to the latter's detriment. Likewise, at times the I CARE values have either been non-existent or lived out sporadically or only when convenient. Regardless, in both instances, patients or clients are indispensable factors in the equation. Without them, the healthcare and legal professions would be defunct. For chaplains, the administration of spiritual care and meeting the needs of patients with Integrity, Compassion, Accountability, Respect, and Excellence includes at least the "L.A.D. effect." Thus, we now examine these three critical aspects in more depth.

Listening

At some point, practically every one of us has heard someone say, "You're not listening to me!" We may have heard this from a spouse, a child, co-worker, family member, or friend. But, what about hearing a patient or client utter this phrase? While patients or clients may verbalize this concern from time to time, often, they will use non-verbal cues to indicate, "You're not listening to me!" Failing to listen, or to take such verbal and non-verbal cues seriously, can threaten or end the relationship. If this occurs, both attorneys and chaplains will have missed their only opportunity to make the initial or *any* connection with their clients. Therefore, listening is absolutely non-negotiable. German theologian Dietrich Bonhoeffer described listening this way:

Many people are looking for an ear that will listen. They do not find it among Christians, because Christians are talking when they should be listening. He [or she] who no longer listens to his [or her] brother [or sister] will soon no longer be listening to God either. One who cannot listen long and patiently will presently be talking beside the point and never really be speaking to others, albeit he [or she] be not conscious of it.[9]

Clients and patients do not seek legal advice or become patients in doctor's offices and hospitals because they are bored. Rather, they are seeking attorneys and spiritual care providers because they need competent professionals to listen to their serious, and often dire problems and circumstances. Given the high levels of anxiety, fear, vulnerability, uncertainty, and apprehension that can accompany these encounters, the last thing clients and patients need is a disinterested or unengaged listener. Clients and patients are usually inviting total strangers into the very deep recesses of their existence, even if only for a moment. They desire someone who is "trying to understand their inner world."[10] Therefore, clients and patients need an actively engaged, empathetic listener. This type of listener demonstrates genuine concern about the client's or patient's needs and ultimately desires to offer assistance to the extent they are legally and ethically capable of doing so. Jean Stairs calls this "soul listening." That is, listening for the "holy in the ordinary."[11] Robert A. Kidd agrees, calling spiritually supportive listening "sacred work."[12]

What barriers prevent us from being good listeners? While this list is non-exhaustive, Howard Clinebell's reasoning in identifying such barriers is instructive. The first barrier is blind spots. Students taking driver's education courses are frequently prompted to "check their blind spots." Whether we are aware of them or not, we all have physical, spiritual, and emotional blind spots. In the context of spiritual care, our blind spots are usually shadows of our own insecurities, feelings, and unresolved emotional and spiritual needs.

The second barrier centers on our over-investment in our feelings and ideas. We live in a self-absorbed, self-aggrandizing, and selfish society. "Me," "my," or "mine" usually precede "you," "your," or "yours." This self-absorption not only prevents us from hearing ourselves, but also from hearing others, and more importantly, God.

The third barrier involves our preoccupation with techniques and theories. Protocols, policies, and procedures are guidelines that set the minimum expectations for performing any given task. However, when these same policies and procedures become rote, they also tend to become mechanical or robotic. Following the letter of the law also does not allow for movement within often very dynamic situations. Patricia O'Connell Killen and John de Beer might describe the second and third barriers as operating from standpoints of certitude and self-assurance, leaving little or no room to "test a new experience."[13]

Finally, the fourth barrier centers on our need to prove our competence by solving a problem. This result-oriented disposition can lead to disorientation and create other problems for the individual and the client. Sometimes, saying, "I don't have the answer to that question" can be the most reassuring thing. It also embraces the limitations of one's humanity.

It is often said, "You never get a second chance to make a first impression." Don't miss an opportunity to meet the needs of the client or patient because of a deaf ear. Even Jesus Christ exhorts, "Let anyone with ears listen!"[14] Jesus Christ is making an appeal to our hearts. It is impossible to spell "heart" without the letters "e-a-r." Therefore, every h*ear*t has an ear. Some of the best attorneys and chaplains have many gifts and talents, but the keen ability to listen with the ears of their heart to the stories they hear can significantly impact outcomes. Such active, compassionate, empathetic listening is a key ingredient in gaining what Killen and de Beer call "movement towards insight"[15] and providing effective ministry.

Assessment

We are constantly making assessments or judgments, whether consciously or subconsciously. Assessments occur whenever we encounter people, places, things, or situations that are new or have changed, and are thus in some ways unfamiliar. We can make assessments hastily, or after a time of contemplation. For example, if you encounter a person with tears in his or her eyes, there are several assessments you could make: the tears could be tears of joy, sadness, bereavement, fear, an allergic reaction, and more. In either case, we make judgments or draw conclusions based on either empirical information or presuppositions, or both. Spiritual assessments are no different. Spiritual assessments are the area of expertise often associated with pastors, clergy, and lay leaders. In hospital settings, spiritual assessments are reserved for the chaplains.

But how do we effectively make spiritual assessments? What are the critical tools and skills we might employ? Why are spiritual assessments important? When physicians make assessments, they use the L.O.E.D. technique,[16] reminding them to: 1) Listen to stories; 2) Observe their patients; 3) Evaluate the data; and 4) Determine the interventions. Physicians may also utilize the S.O.A.P. technique: 1) Subjective; 2) Objective; 3)

Assessment; and 4) Plan. The subjective element considers the problem from the patient's perspective. The objective element is the medical differential diagnosis based on the physician's observations and the patient's feedback. The physician combines the first two elements to make an assessment and then develop a plan of action. For example, if a patient describes his or her symptoms as nasal congestion, fever, and runny nose, the physician's differential diagnosis might include influenza, common cold, or strep throat. The physician asks key questions such as, "When was the onset of the symptoms?" "Have there been any changes in environment?" or "Does anyone else have these same symptoms?" and examines the patient's ears, nose, and throat. The physician gains a clearer picture of the situation based on the patient's responses, can make an assessment that the patient has strep throat, and prescribes ten days of antibiotics as the plan.

Attorneys use a similar methodology called I.R.A.C. This acronym means: 1) Issue-spotting; 2) Rule of law; 3) Analysis; and 4) Conclusion. While a client is presenting a problem, the attorney is listening for facts and asking and anticipating key questions and responses in order to help them uncover clues and spot issues. From one set of facts, several legal issues may arise, which assist the attorney in identifying the applicable rule(s) of law. The issues and rule of law form the basis for the attorney's analysis or assessment. The analysis may be immediate, or might require additional legal research. Ultimately, the attorney reaches a conclusion based on the totality of circumstances and is then in a better position to advise the client.

Discovery is an invaluable part of an attorney's assessment process. Litigation or prosecution is initiated when a party files a petition, complaint, or indictment in a civil or criminal court of law. Once the defendant files an answer or enters a plea, the parties engage in the discovery process. This is usually the most protracted part of litigation. Here, the parties engage in written and oral discovery, using discovery tools such as Requests for Admissions (requesting parties to admit or deny certain facts), Interrogatories (written questions geared toward fact finding), Requests for Production (requesting parties to produce tangible documents), Request for Disclosure (requiring parties to automatically disclose certain facts and claims), depositions (live or written questioning of a witness by an attorney under oath), and trials (final resort for a resolution).

The administration of spiritual care shares some hallmarks with the legal discovery process. Often patients, physicians, and nurses initiate patient visits through consultations with or referrals to chaplains. When chaplains answer the referral, they engage in discovery with the patient. Like attorneys, chaplains are engaging patients for the purpose of gaining disclosure, admissions, and production of information. One of the main differences between legal discovery and discovering a patient's needs is the timeframe. Courts of law routinely allot the parties three to six months to conduct discovery before trial. Unfortunately, chaplains usually do not have the luxury of time. In most instances, chaplains visit patients they will never see again, especially when ministry occurs in the Emergency Department. In rare circumstances the duration of inpatients' stay may rival that of legal discovery, but in most cases the length of stay will range from as short as a few hours to as long as one to two months. Therefore, chaplains cannot afford to miss any opportunities when engaging with a patient.

Given the urgency of many pastoral care situations, and the uncertain prospects of subsequent interaction, it is essential that chaplains employ a methodology for spiritual assessments like those used by physicians and attorneys. The pastoral task is to assess the degree to which the patient's emotional and spiritual equilibrium has been disturbed by a particular event, and determine which interventions would be appropriate to help the patient restore that equilibrium and when such interventions should be employed. The key is intentionality.[17] Nina Bryant-Sanyika, Association for Clinical Pastoral Education (ACPE) Certified Educator of Spiritual Care and Education at Houston Methodist Hospital, teaches CPE students that whenever they enter a patient's room, they should always be asking, "What is the spiritual need here? What is the spiritual need here? What is the spiritual need here?" Some needs may be in what the law calls "plain view," while others must be unmasked. Therefore, chaplains must act as the Ben Matlocks, Perry Masons, Cagneys and Laceys, and John Shafts in the patient's room during their visits.

Review the following hypothetical situation and consider how an attorney might respond to the client and the client's spouse.

A = Attorney, C = Client, and S = Spouse.

A1 Mr. P, hello. My name is Attorney Always Accountable. Good morning, S. Are you related to P?

S1 Yes, I'm his spouse. (handshake)

A2 Okay. Well, I'm one of the partners at the firm. My secretary scheduled this meeting for us. Is there any way I can help you today?

C1 (No response)

S2 (No response)

A3 Would either of you like to share with me what brings you here this morning?

C2 (No response)

S3 He tried to kill himself.

A4 [Response]

S4 (Crying) Yes ... this is the third time this month. I just don't know what to do. I don't have any answers.

A5 [Response]

S5 I'm so glad we're here because we just don't know what to do or where to turn.

A6 [Response]

S6 He's just not been the same. I noticed he's more withdrawn, doesn't talk much anymore, and he's missing work.

A7 [Response]

C3 (After a five to ten second pause, C shows Attorney Accountable his bandaged wrists)

A8 [Response]

C4 = I did this all because of her!

A9 [Response]

S7 How dare you?! What do you mean you did this because of me!?!?

A10 [Response]

C5 I can't live this way anymore! You control everything,   our   home,   my   money,   my investments, my retirement, my voice, and my whole life! It's been like this for 21 years. I thought you would change, but you never have and never will!

A11 [Response]

S8 You're just a hopeless and pitiful man! You're always blaming others for your issues!

A12 [Response]

C6 Thank you for giving me space to freely talk with you. I'm concerned she's stealing my money and would take my life if she could since she has general and medical power of attorney over me.

A13 [Response]

C7 (Nodding affirmatively)

A14 [Response]

C8 Are you sure that's the best thing to do?

A15 [Response]

C9 On one hand, this makes me uncomfortable, but on the other hand it feels freeing. It's been a long time since I felt like I had a voice to make my own decisions.

A16 [Response]

C10 Attorney Accountable, I would really appreciate it if you could take my case.

A17 [Response]

C11 Sir, I really appreciate it. You just don't know how much this means to me.

A18 [Response]

Now, make an assessment based on how a chaplain might analyze this fact pattern with some slight variations.

C = Chaplain, *P* = Patient, and *S* = Spouse.

C1   Mr. P, hello. My name is Chaplain Compassionate Caregood. Good morning, S. Are you related to P?

S1   Yes, I'm his spouse. (handshake)

C2   Okay. Well, I'm one of the chaplains in the spiritual care department here at the hospital. I was making my morning rounds and wanted to stop by and check on both of you to see if there were any spiritual or emotional needs I could meet for you today. Is there any way I can support you today?

P1   (No response)

S2   (No response)

C3   Would either of you like to share with me what brings you to the hospital this morning?

P2   (No response)

S3   He tried to kill himself.

C4 [Response]

S4   (Crying) Yes ... this is the third time this month. I just don't know what to do. I don't have any answers.

C5 [Response]

288

S5   I'm so glad you're here because we just don't know what to do or where to turn.

C6   [Response]

S6   He's just not been the same. I noticed he's more withdrawn, doesn't talk much anymore, and he's missing work.

C7   [Response]

P3   (After a five to ten second pause, P shows Chaplain Caregood his bandaged wrists)

C8   [Response]

P4   I did this all because of her!

C9   [Response]

S7   How dare you?! What do you mean you did this because of me!?!?

C10 [Response]

P5   I can't live this way anymore! You control everything, our home, my money, my investments, my retirement, my voice, and my whole life! It's been like this for 21 years. I thought you would change, but you never have and never will!

C11 [Response]

S8   You're just a hopeless and pitiful man! You're always blaming others for your issues!

C12 [Response]

P6   Thank you for giving me space to freely talk with you. I'm concerned she's stealing my money and would take my life if she could, since she has general and medical power of attorney over me.

C13 **[Response]**

P7   (Nodding affirmatively)

C14 **[Response]**

P8   Are you sure that's the best thing to do?

C15 **[Response]**

P9   On one hand, this makes me uncomfortable, but it feels freeing on the other. It's been a long time since I felt like I had a voice to make my own decisions.

C16 **[Response]**

P10   Chaplain Caregood, I would really appreciate it if you could say a prayer for me.

C17 **[Response]**

P11   Sir, I really appreciate it. You just don't know how much this means to me.

C18 **[Response]**

George Fitchett and Andrea Canada define spiritual/religious assessment as a "more extensive [in-depth, ongoing] process of active listening to a patient's story as it unfolds in a relationship with a professional chaplain and summarizing the needs and resources that emerge in that process. The summary includes a spiritual care plan with expected outcomes which should be communicated to the rest of the treatment team."[18] Assessments are key and can become even more effective when utilizing active listening, but a crucial game-changer is the gift of discernment.

Discernment

Every human being has been a child, and practically everyone has been dishonest at least once in his or her lifetime. Parents can attest to this fact. Parents seem to have the keenest sense of awareness of when their child or children are being dishonest. The fact that parents know their children and their proclivities also plays a huge role. They can listen to what is said, examine body language, and notice patterns of behavior. They also can listen to the real story behind the story to uncover the truth. Some call it intuition, but I will refer to this as discernment.

When it comes to the administration of spiritual care, Donald McKim defines discernment as "The process of assessing and evaluating, particularly in relation to trying to determine God's will in a particular situation or for one's life direction."[19] In law, the best attorneys are not always the ones who graduated at or near the top of their class and received about every award imaginable. The best attorneys display the ability to assess and evaluate situations and make decisions on behalf of the client's best interest. These attorneys can discern and dissect legal issues and reduce them to their most basic terms. They can assess a situation and discern factors such as motive, opportunity, duress, undue influence, coercion, and more.

William Stafford describes discernment well when he says, "Within people's voices, under their words or woven into the pauses, I hear a hidden soul."[20] The ability to "hear a hidden soul" is the gift of discernment. I intentionally speak of discernment as a gift. This is because not everyone possesses it. While we may be able to access and learn strategies and techniques to improve our listening skills and ability to make assessments, discernment is a gift from God. If one lacks discernment, yet desires this gift, Scripture provides reassurances that God will provide it: "I will do whatever you ask in my name, so that the Father may be glorified in the Son. If in my name you ask me for anything, I will do it."[21] The Epistle of James is also instructive, stating, "If any of you is lacking in wisdom, ask God, who gives to all generously and ungrudgingly, and it will be given you."[22] Proverbs likewise promises that wisdom will be found by those who diligently seek it:

> My child, if you accept my words and treasure up my commandments within you, making your ear attentive to wisdom and inclining your heart to understanding; if you indeed cry out for insight, and raise your voice for understanding; if you seek it like silver, and search for it as for hidden treasures—then you will understand the fear of the LORD and find the knowledge of God.[23]

Chaplains with the gift of discernment can "search for … hidden treasures" and "find the knowledge of God," possessing an understanding that enables them to hear the hidden soul within a person. This is the mission of patient-centered care.

Conclusion

This chapter has attempted to draw parallels between two distinct, yet compatible professions. Professionals in the legal realm and in healthcare both provide vital services to a diverse and growing population. Clients and patients are indispensable to the very existence of the legal and healthcare professions. The relationship between a patient and a healthcare professional, like that between a client and an attorney, is a symbiotic relationship that is constantly evolving in a fast-paced world fueled by cutting-edge technology and instant global connectivity. Despite these constant changes, there are certain factors that remain constant in this relationship: listening, assessment, and discernment. This chapter promotes the L.A.D. effect as a way to effectively identify and remember the set of basic, minimum skills essential to both professions. Admittedly, other combinations of skills may be equally and sometimes more vital, but the "L.A.D. effect" is one method of ensuring patient-centered care and, ultimately, patient satisfaction.

---

1 Medical Malpractice and Tort Reform Act of 2003, 2003 Tex. Gen. Laws 897-99.

2 Harold Scherz, and Wayne Oliver, "Defensive Medicine: A Cure Worse Than The Disease," *Forbes Magazine*, August 27, 2013.

3 The World Health Organization declared a global pandemic for the novel coronavirus, also known as COVID-19, on March 11, 2020. To date, there have been more than 177,547,061 cases worldwide and 3,840,406 deaths. The United States leads the world in cases and deaths with 34,353,097 and 615,770, respectively.

4 Jordan Frieman, "Federal Judge Dismisses Lawsuit from Texas Hospital Employees Over COVID Vaccine Requirement," https://www.cbsnews.com/news/covid-vaccine-lawsuit-dismissed-houston-methodist-hospital-system/. Accessed June 16, 2021.

5 Contestants on the game show could opt to eliminate answer choices, call a "lifeline," or accept the money they had already won, if any.

6 The author has been a licensed attorney and counselor in Texas since 2003 and has served as a chaplain in various capacities within the Houston Methodist Hospital System since 2015.

7 In the legal realm, attorneys do not serve patients. To do so would be engaging in the unauthorized practice of medicine. Attorneys serve clients. However, in healthcare settings, the patients are the clients. Accordingly,

clients and patients will be used interchangeably here since their satisfaction serves as the core of the relationship.

8 Houston Methodist Hospital, *Living Houston Methodist Values: A Handbook for Employees,* (2016), 17.

9 Dietrich Bonhoeffer, *Life Together* (San Francisco, CA: Harper & Bros., 1954), 97-98.

10 Howard Clinebell, *Basic Types of Pastoral Care & Counseling: Resources for the Ministry of Healing & Growth,* updated and revised by Bridget Clare Mckeever, 3d. ed. (Nashville, TN: Abingdon Press, 2011), 70.

11 Jean Stairs, *Listening for the Soul: Pastoral Care and Spiritual Direction* (Minneapolis, MN: Augsburg Fortress, 2000), 12.

12 Robert A. Kidd, "Foundational Listening and Responding Skills," in *Professional Spiritual & Pastoral Care: A Practical Clergy and Chaplain's Handbook,* ed. Stephen A. Roberts (Woodstock, VT: SkyLight Paths Publishing, 2012), 92.

13 Patricia O'Connell Killen and John de Beer, *The Art of Theological Reflection* (New York, NY: Crossroad Publishing, 2015), 5.

14 Matthew 11:15 (NRSV). Unless noted otherwise, all Scripture references are taken from the New Revised Standard Version.

15 Patricia O'Connell Killen and John de Beer, *The Art of Theological Reflection* (New York, NY: Crossroad Publishing, 2015), 53.

16 D.W. Donovan, "Assessments," in *Professional Spiritual & Pastoral Care: A Practical Clergy and Chaplain's Handbook,* ed. Stephen A. Roberts (Woodstock, VT: SkyLight Paths Publishing, 2012), 42.

17 Ibid., 44.

18 Ibid., 56.

19 Donald McKim, *The Westminster Dictionary of Theological Terms* (Louisville, KY: John Knox Press, 2014), 89, s.v., "discernment."

20 William Stafford, *Learning to Live in the World: Earth Poems,* selected by Terry Watson and Laura Apol Obbink (San Diego, CA: Harcourt Brace, 1994), 65.

21 John 14:13-14.

22 James 1:5.

23 Proverbs 2:1-5.

17

EMOTIONAL AND SPIRITUAL IMPLICATIONS
OF COVID-19

Luis Elier Rodriguez
Manager, System Clinical Pastoral Education,
Houston Methodist

IN THIS TIME OF WORLDWIDE PANDEMIC, we have experienced a systemic global loss and grief. Through the dynamics of COVID-19, we have begun to see ourselves and our world as an interdependent, global community. This has brought challenges in healthcare and society. It also creates change in our model of how we provide spiritual care in our hospital institutions. We began to form an awareness that we belong to a system of interactions, with certain patterns of where we were and are experiencing systemic grief and loss.[1] Maybe our global system and/or our mourning community will never be the same. This pandemic has created immense stress, suffering, uncomfortable feelings, material loss, the intrapsychic loss of losing an emotionally important image of oneself. Also, in this pandemic, we sometimes lost the possibilities of "what might have been," abandoned plans for a particular future, or watched the death of many dreams.[2]

Therefore, I believe this pandemic has created for us the following conditions and characteristics concerning our global grief and loss:

1. Our grieving is very complicated because this experience, both individually and collectively, created an enormous spiritual and emotional global imbalance characterized by countless deaths and the dissolution of relationships with many accompanying losses: job losses, physical and mental illnesses, political challenges, high stress, systemic racism, and increasing interpersonal and intimate partner violence. This global crisis is impacting each of us both in the short and long term. The manifestations include sleep disorders, higher blood pressure, depression, and anxiety.[3] We have embarked on a very difficult spiritual journey of heart and soul. In some cases, we have been deprived of our old normality: freedom, a sense of meaning in life, and the loss of our supportive community. It's like feeling one's soul darkening, or feeling homesick.

   This many-faceted grief came suddenly, we didn't have a chance to prepare. For example, many mourners were isolated and denied the possibility of saying goodbye to their loved ones. They didn't have the time or the people around them to help repair the disruption caused by their loss.[4] We have to be reminded that dialogue and empathy are at the heart of mourning in spiritual care. Throughout this pandemic, many people did not have time to experience the integrity or sacredness of the loss of their loved one, creating the possibility that their mourning process may be blocked, keeping them from being able to move forward, from moving on. We cannot imagine how complex this process of loss has been because for every person who died of COVID-19, nine loved ones are left behind.[5] A recent study found that at least 37,000 children in the United States have a lost a parent to COVID.[6] Also, many of us mourned the impact of COVID in other countries, but did not have a sufficient well of empathy or adequate spiritual and emotional support to mourn these vast losses.

Many times, I have felt deep sorrow for this global situation we have lived through, and I have experienced a feeling I have not been able to name or identify in my feelings list. It's an unfamiliar feeling. Adam Grant called this feeling "languishing." It is when you and I are not functioning at full capacity. Languishing "dulls your motivation, disrupts your ability to focus, and triples the odds that you'll cut back on work."[7] He also mentioned that languishing is a sense of stagnation and emptiness. It feels as if you and I are mudding through our days, looking at our life through a foggy windshield.[8] Talking to my CPE students, friends, neighbors, family, and medical staff, I have noticed that many of them are experiencing these symptoms today. I think it is extremely urgent to start talking about these feelings, produced by this global crisis of discomfort and global and collective grief and intense fear. This is a long road, but always a long road begins with a few first steps. In this case, it is identifying languishing and adding it to our feelings list as a new feeling to be explored because of this pandemic.

Another aspect that makes this pandemic complicated is the collateral harm to our mental health and spiritual development. According to Raquel Pelaez, the following faces of the pandemic can be identified:[9]

- Pandemic fatigue, demotivation, and tiredness
- Haphephobia or fleeing physical contact for fear of contagion
- Cabana syndrome, fear of going out and returning to "normal"
- Rupophobia, obsessive cleaning, and fear of dirt
- Anuptaphobia, fear of not having a partner and feeling that entering into a relationship will not happen in the near future
- Demophobia, fear of others as a danger or a phobia towards crowds
- Paranoidism, denying reality by experiencing deep anguish

To these phobias or faces of this pandemic identified by Perez, I add two more:

- The world of work is suffering from a loneliness epidemic. In fact, researchers discovered alarmingly high rates of employee isolation even before COVID-19 forced millions of people to switch to remote work. Such feelings can take a painful toll on employee health, retention, and productivity.
- Ultra-use of technology to the point of sacrificing or avoiding human contact. This has been especially seen with employees returning to the workplace and pre-COVID normality by overusing their phones or tablets. This creates a disconnect between employees and customers. It can create an impersonal customer service environment and can become a systemic

relationship pattern that is unhealthy for an organization that wants to serve personally and with good quality.

All of the above can be accompanied by excessive stress, mood swings, irritability, concentration problems, distress, and anxiety.[10] All these collateral faces and potential damages should be taken into consideration when we are giving and offering spiritual care. We've had many people with burnout syndrome symptoms related to the prolonged pressure of this pandemic, with emotional and interpersonal symptoms. Many have felt emotional and physical exhaustion and decreased personal and work fulfillment. I suspect it has started to be a global ailment, given the difficult challenge of coping with life during this pandemic.

2. This global pandemic has helped us as spiritual caregivers to reassess our theological points concerning our planet and cosmic community. I think in 2020-21, there began a universal re-evaluation of spirituality and grieving as well as a global effort seeking ways to adapt to and recover from this global systemic grief experience. This pandemic experience is helping us to understand and accept our interconnection, especially in mutual crisis and suffering, with the disposition to hear the cry of our patients, family, medical staff, and the lament of the earth too. As Leonardo Boff, a Franciscan theologian from Brazil, said: "such connectedness causes the interior of beings to communicate with one another."[11] Beings listening to one another's

voice and hearing the story each tells is a significant component in our spiritual care. Listening to the voice of the other mourners is not merely a metaphor in this time of COVID-19; it points toward a true and important reality. As a Mennonite pastor from Guatemala, explains: "Thus the mountain hears the voice of the wind and interaction is established between the two, the wind with the trees, the trees with the animals, the animals with the atmosphere, and the human being, holistically, with all these beings, events, and so forth." One reacts to the other and interacts in keeping the dynamic equilibrium established between them.[12]

This complexity of listening is helping us to relate with others as spiritual caregivers without imposing our feelings, beliefs, and ideas. Now, we are more aware that nothing denies the meaning of this global crisis so much as homogeneity and the imposing of a single idea, a single conviction, a single way of living together, and a single way of praying, grieving, and speaking of the transcendent. I also suspect that we are more aware that we must respect and accept spiritual and religious diversity and diversity of ideas. As Leonardo Boff states: "Together with unity as single planet Earth, a single human species, biodiversity, and multiplicity of races, cultures, and individuals."[13] This perception helps us provide spiritual care to people of different sexes, ages, races, personalities, ideologies, sexual orientations, and religious and spiritual backgrounds. This represents functioning as a spiritual care ecosystem, where we need one another, give support and affirmation, and encounter and help one another in this common global crisis. By accepting this diversity, we are learning to accept that each person's response to grief and bereavement is unique, and what is normal and what is unhealthy must be considered in the context of the patient's specific personality, relationships, and their cultural background.[14]

3. This pandemic has not only caused suffering, devastation, and sadness, but has given us an opportunity to relearn and reflect deeply on the exploration of new paradigms in spiritual care. I suspect we are relearning in multiple dimensions. For example, we have learned about the difference between social distance and spiritual care. The following poetic statements are an example of this differentiation:

> We greet each other not only with the hands but with the soul as well
> We can cry and smile, and we can even throw kisses full of good wishes, even if from afar
> We can't shake hands, but we can touch the heart
> We can look people in the eye walking with their struggles and feelings of fear, anxiety, or hope
> We can't be around each other, but we can listen in a way we've never done before
> The hugs and kisses of brotherly solidarity will come back.

We must remind ourselves that as spiritual caregivers we can help our patients, facilitating their mourning process or the process that occurs after their personal and systemic losses, which according to some therapists, involves four phases:[15]

Phase I: is the period of numbness that occurs close to the time of the loss. This phase helps the survivor to disregard the loss at least for a brief period.

Phase II: in this phase they yearn for the lost one to return and tend to deny the permanence of the loss. Uncomfortable feelings like anger play an important part in this phase.

Phase III: this is the phase of disorganization and despair. It's when it is difficult to function in the environment.

Phase IV: this is the phase of reorganized behavior, when the survivor begins to pull their life back together.

We have to recognize that there is some overlap between the various phases and we don't have any guarantee of which one will predominate. Also, we cannot handle the emotions of a loss until we first come to terms with the fact that the loss has happened and is irreversible, at least in this lifetime.[16] These are phases to help us identify where we are, but they don't rigidly determine our emotional and spiritual state.

According to J. William Worden, we have four tasks to deal with when grieving our losses.[17] I adapt each of them to our current circumstance of dealing with COVID-19. They are:

1. *To accept the reality of the loss*: The first task of the person grieving is to fully face the reality of loss. The opposite of accepting the reality of the loss is some type of denial. Some people refuse to believe that the loss is real and get stuck in the mourning process as the first task. For example, I have met people who despite having been vaccinated with the COVID vaccine are still at the

beginning, not accepting the consequences of this pandemic on their lives and losses. Some have accepted this pandemic intellectually but have not yet accepted it emotionally or given themselves time to grieve.

2. *To process the pain of grief*: COVID has been characterized by emotional and spiritual pain associated with high stress and loss of control in our daily life. Refusing to take on this second task of processing the pain of COVID could result in not feeling and denying the implications of this pandemic. Partly because of this, we have seen many people who refuse to use masks and do not follow the rules for keeping themselves and others safe from COVID. I suspect this has been a way to not accept the discomfort that this pandemic has created. The problem with this is that if the grief is not processed properly, it will manifest itself in other ways such as anger, a tendency towards rigidity, dysfunctional modes of communication, and having little creativity to resolve conflicts.

3. *To adjust to the world*: According to Worden, there are three areas of adjustment that need to be addressed. There is external adjustment, internal adjustment, and spiritual adjustment. In this current experience of COVID, we have had to adapt to a new way of living and we don't yet know the impact of this new adjustment on our present and future generations. The question is what our meaning, skills, and reflections will be after this pandemic. In this pandemic, we have been challenged to adjust ourselves, especially to losing control over what happens in the world, and to try to increase our awareness of what is happening inside us. Also, we have been exploring to see if we need to adapt

to a new spirituality or change our theology regarding the transcendent.

4. *To find an enduring connection while embarking on a new life*: I would like to call this task moving on or creating a new sense of hope in our life. In my opinion, this is the task of starting to redesign our new life. For example, after my divorce, I started to redesign my new home. I started from zero and I have had to visit different furniture stores to choose the things that would be in the different spaces of my home. I started to feel pleasure and enjoyment in my role as a nonprofessional interior designer. I felt happy decorating the home as I started to re-decorate my life, recovering my confidence and increasing my optimism in life. In this embarking, we can start taking care of ourselves physically, emotionally, and spiritually. We walk with the anticipation that hope will eventually be reborn, and we can talk about our uncomfortable feelings as a way to release them, and we can have a sense of spiritual renewal slowly beginning to occur. In embarking on a new normality, we can consider enjoying a sunrise, writing a poem, taking time to listen to music, reading a book unrelated to work, giving and receiving affirmations, and taking daily mini-vacations. If necessary, learn to laugh at yourself. Consider that life is short, and you *can* forge a good balance between your work and your personal life.

We have to remind ourselves that grieving is something that takes time, and grieving sometimes can change the foundation of our spiritual beliefs and also can create some disorientation in life. Seeing so many people die of COVID-19 and seeing so many people suffer, I have wondered what the reason is for this suffering, and it has caused tension between the perception that the transcendent is benevolent, yet on the other hand humanity is suffering, living through an unexpected pandemic with multiple losses. Sometimes this tension caused me not to see meaning in the world, and what we were living through created something of a disconnect with the transcendent.

This tension has made me find myself: born in Puerto Rico, where suffering is expected and is part of one's daily life experience, and also living the last 21 years in the United States, where sometimes suffering takes people by surprise, where there are high expectations that suffering should not be part of daily life, and where there is a strong presence of happiness. This tension reminds me of the importance of considering the cultural expressions of grief, considering class, religion, ethnicity, family traditions, norms, standards, backgrounds, variations, and restrictions. Appropriate ways to respond in one culture may be punished or rejected in another.[18] This implies that there is no one style of grief.

For example, usually Anglo-American traditions are represented by stoicism, and emotional reserve is perceived as a sign of strength.[19] It's an interesting fact that many Anglo-Americans no longer die in their own homes, but are sent to nursing homes and hospitals to die, away from their home, family, and friends. African-American traditions are influenced by their West African heritage, with beliefs in the afterlife as "going home" to the spirit world, a place of rest and happiness.[20] I learned from my students in Mexico, who see death as something natural, and view death as an inevitable and natural part of the life cycle, and even celebrate the day of the dead by making altars, placing photos, and putting out food for the deceased person. This celebration is on November 1-2. This multi-day holiday involves family and friends gathering to pray for and remember friends and family members who have died, and is a time to accept the reality of the death.[21] Another example is Shiva in the Jewish faith, a period of seven days following the burial, that is observed when the family stays home, and friends and extended family come to help them and facilitate their grief.

According to Narjess Kardan, in the Muslim tradition "When a person passes away, the family and the community get together seven days after for the respect of deceased and grieving and bereavement. And 40 days after, what is called the *arbyin*, and one year after—the one year anniversary. When Muslim families gather in these gatherings, they recite the Quran, give to charity, do good deeds on the behalf of the deceased. Muslims believe the soul is separated from the body during death. But the soul lives on and may visit loved ones on the seventh and 40 days after death, as well as one year later."[22] It comes back and visits the family, visits the home, and the soul expects a gift, it's expecting something from the family and from the loved ones. The greatest gift one can give to a deceased family member is to do a good deed on their behalf. This is a way to stay connected to the deceased. While this grieving process doesn't make the loss of a loved one easy, it helps to have the support and a memorial in their honor.

In summary, to adequately predict how a person is to grieve, we must know something about their spiritual and cultural style of grieving and the sociological factors that can impact their grief. For example, we need to understand that everyone grieves differently and we have different pathways through grief, such as those of thinking people, feeling people, and acting people.[23] This is accompanied by cultural, sociological, and personality factors that affect dealing with the losses in this pandemic.

In addition to the cultural factors, we consider sociological factors that affect our way of facing our losses and our grief process. I would like to mention two variables:

1. Socioeconomic changes related to urbanization, modernization, and technological development. This socioeconomic change can sometimes be accompanied by a lack of reflection on the meaning of the grief and losses and with a massification characterized by a lack of a sense of being in community and a lack of community support during the losses.

2. Another factor is a high inclination towards technology along with a low inclination towards personal, existential, and communitarian reflection on the sense of losses and grief. Also, with today's medical technology, we sometimes have the temptation to think in terms of immortality.

For this reason, during the pandemic, I decided to bring some questions to help my students express their feelings to increase their awareness of the impact of COVID-19 in their spiritual care practice, and to reflect on their grief process. They didn't have to answer all these questions but could select some:

1. What did you feel at the beginning of this pandemic?
2. What is your style of grief? What messages did you receive from your family regarding grief?
3. What spiritual beliefs do you have to help you deal with this exhausting and overwhelming pandemic?
4. What is your spiritual concept or theology of grief and loss?

5. What in this pandemic has influenced your spiritual belief regarding suffering?

6. Being aware of the four phases of grief, where are you?

7. Do you experience intense fear? If yes, how are you processing your fear?

8. Describe a lament, poem, or metaphor that captures this global experience of grief.

9. If a loved one died in this pandemic, who was that person, and what was your relationship with that person like?

10. Do you find something positive in this pandemic or in global and national crisis?

11. Do you have a negative view of life, yourself, the world, or the future?

12. Are you able to accept the support of others if you need it?

13. Are you blaming others or the transcendent for this global crisis?

14. Do you have social and spiritual support in this crisis?

15. Did you have to make adjustments to your spiritual beliefs during this pandemic?

16. If you are grieving, when do you expect the mourning to be finished?

17. What are the implications of this pandemic for your spiritual care practice?

In summary, the COVID-19 pandemic has made it difficult to embark on a journey of processing grief. This pandemic has been affecting us in multidimensional aspects, impacting us emotionally, physiologically, and spiritually. Also, in our spiritual care practice, there is a good opportunity to be aware of the different faces and phobias this pandemic has created and to raise our listening skills to the challenge. It calls us to a very profound spiritual practice and to take into consideration the spiritual, emotional, cultural, and sociological aspects of the grievers. Finally, it is important to be aware of the phases of the grief and the tasks needed to deal with grief and with the different implications of this pandemic. In my questions to my students, we can find opportunities for dialogue and debriefing.

Because this has been a deep time of reflection, I want to end this chapter with the poem "Turning" by Julie Cadwallader Staub:[24]

> There comes a time in every fall
> before the leaves begin to turn
> when blackbirds group and flock and gather
> choosing a tree, a branch, together
> to click and call and chorus and clamor
> announcing the season has come for travel.
>
> Then comes a time when all those birds
> without a sound or backward glance
> pour from every branch and limb
> into the air, as if on a whim
> but it's a dynamic, choreographed mass
> a swoop, a swerve, a mystery, a dance
>
> and now the tree stands breathless, amazed
> at how it was chosen, how it was changed.

---

1 Kenneth R. Mitchell, Herbert Anderson, *All Our Losses, All Our Griefs: Resources for Pastoral Care* (Louisville, KY: Westminster John Knox Press, 2001), 44.

2 Ibid., 40.

3 Allison Gilbert, "The Grief is Coming," *New York Times*, April 12, 2021.

4 Robert A. Neimeyer, *Meaning Reconstruction and the Experience of Loss* (Washington: American Psychological Association, 2007), 3.

5 Ibid.; Gilbert, "The Grief Crisis is Coming."

6 Ibid., 1

7 Adam Grant, "There's a Name for the Blah You're Feeling: It's Called Languishing," New York Times, June 17, 2021.

8 Ibid., 1.

9 Raquel Pelaez, "La Covid-19 ha dejado daños colaterales en nuestra salud mental y ha puesto de actualidad varias fobias," *XL Semanal*, May 2021.

10 Ibid., 1.

11 Leonardo Boff, *Cry of the Earth, Cry of the Poor* (New York: Maryknoll, 1997),150.

12 Personal conversation with Moises Lopez.

13 Boff., 159-161.

14 Neimeyer, *Meaning Reconstruction and the Experience of Loss. Washington D.C., American Psychological* , 25.

15 J. William Worden, *Grief Counseling and Grief Therapy: A Handbook for the Mental Health Practitioner* (New York: Springer Publishing, 2011), 37-39.

16 Ibid., 39.

17 Ibid., 39-53.

18 Therese Rando, *Grief, Dying, and Death: Clinical Interventions for Caregivers* (Champaign, IL: Research Press,1990).

19 Mary A. Fukuyama and Todd D. Sevig, *Integrating Spirituality into Multicultural Counseling* (London: Sage Publications, 2005), 117.

20 Ibid.

21 Wikipedia, "Day of the Dead,"
https://en.wikipedia.org/wiki/Day_of_the_Dead.

22 I received this information from Narjess Kardan, who is a Muslim ACPE Certified Educator student at Houston Methodist Hospital.

23 See more information of different pathways through grief in Tim P. VanDuivendyk's book, *The Unwanted Gift of Grief*, 25-28.

24 "Turning" by Julie Cadwallader Staub, from *Wing Over Wing* (Brewster, MA: Paraclete Press, 2019).

Made in United States
Orlando, FL
21 November 2023

39264374R00193